ANGELS OF DIVINE LIGHT

*The remarkable autobiography of one of today's leading
angelic healers and spiritual therapists*

Aidan Storey

TRANSWORLD IRELAND

TRANSWORLD IRELAND
an imprint of The Random House Group Limited
20 Vauxhall Bridge Road, London SW1V 2SA
www.rbooks.co.uk

First published in 2009 by Transworld Ireland,
a division of Transworld Publishers Ltd
This reissue published in 2010 by Transworld Ireland,
a division of Transworld Publishers Ltd

A CIP catalogue record for this book
is available from the British Library.

ISBN 9781848270787

The Random House Group Limited supports The Forest Stewardship
Council (FSC), the leading international forest-certification organization.
All our titles that are printed on Greenpeace-approved FSC-certified
paper carry the FSC logo. Our paper procurement policy can be
found at www.rbooks.co.uk/environment

Typeset in 12/16pt Book Antiqua by
Kestrel Data, Exeter, Devon
Printed and bound in the UK by
Clays Ltd, Bungay, Suffolk

2 4 6 8 10 9 7 5 3 1

Mixed Sources
Product group from well-managed
forests and other controlled sources
www.fsc.org Cert no. TT-COC-2139
© 1996 Forest Stewardship Council
FSC

The weak can never forgive.
Forgiveness is the attribute of the strong.

Mahatma Gandhi

Dedication

In memory of my much-loved mother, Kathleen, who was, is, and always will be my guiding light and my strength.

Thank you for being the best Mam in the world and for your beautiful gift of unconditional love. You were, and always will be, my greatest teacher and guide.

And to Patricia Scanlan, the most loving and caring friend anyone could ask for. Thank you for believing in me and for all your help with the book. It would have never happened without your loving help and direction. You are one in a million.

Acknowledgements

I give thanks to my beloved Guardian Angels, Zechariah and Hannah, and my Spirit Guide Jack, to the Holy Spirit, Jesus, Mother Mary, John the Apostle, St Bernadette, St Francis and Claire of Assisi, St Rita and all my Angels, Saints and Guides who lovingly guide and support me every day.

To my brothers and sisters who have always shown me such love and whom I love so much. Thank you for all your help and support during the writing of this book. To all my nephews and nieces whom I love, and a special word of thanks to Matthew and Janice, Paul and Martha, Tine and Peter, Jayne and John, who have been so kind to me over the past two years. I am very blessed to have you all in my life.

To my sisters-in-law, brothers-in-law and my beloved aunts, Agnes, Chrissie, Bibby, Patty, Kathleen, Alice, Rose and Tessie.

To my friends Bo Carty, Dolores O'Reilly, Bernadette McKenna, Eileen Harpur, James Clarke, Margaret Sayers, Barbara Dunne, Marcella and Kevin Rankin, Sharon Colgan, Suzanne Horgan, Sarah Halford, Fiona McClelland, Margaret Kennedy, Grainne Tyndall, Yvonne Costello, Jane Griffin,

Mary Cullen, Jayne Fitzgerald, Billy Martin, the Somers family and the Beechey family. If I have left anyone out, please forgive me.

To Susan Reddy and Rosari Poole, a very special word of thanks to you, without whose help I would have never managed to finish the book – thank you both.

To the friends who look after me, year in, year out. With bookings and workshops, Rina and Niamh, in Mrs Bees, Nuala, Matt and all the staff in Evolv, Catherine Fox in Kells, Patricia Owen and Caroline Clarke, Mairead and Anne in The Angel Shop, Ciara and Maria Marron in Angel Inspirations, Sangita in Thurles, Brid Lyons in Clay Creations, Ann and Terry in Ann's Angels, Margaret Neylon in Cavan, Elaine Downs in the United Kingdom, Maki Ikeda in Japan, Marieke de Jong in Holland and Lady Elizabeth Baring in the USA.

To Francesca Liversidge who loved and believed in the book, the biggest thank you. To my editor Brenda Kimber, thank you for your direction and your patience. You made it all so easy. To Eoin McHugh and Lauren Hadden at Transworld Ireland, Beth Humphries and all at Transworld, thanks for all the enthusiasm and support.

To Helen, Declan, Simon and all at Gill Hess Ltd for doing a great job.

To Sarah Lutyens of Lutyens & Rubinstein who very kindly advised on my contract.

To Cathy Kelly, Anita Notaro, Claudia Carroll, Yvonne Scanlan and Mairead Conlon, who read the manuscript and gave me such wonderful feedback and encouragement, thanks a million.

To Grainne Fox, my wonderful agent in the USA, thank you for your love and enthusiasm.

To Mary Bellew who borrows my bedroom in Spain every

now and then, you know it's yours whenever you need it! Love you.

To Michael McLaughlin and Patricia Deevey for their interest. It was very affirming for me, thanks so much.

To the best photographer ever, Eddie (Egbert) Scheffer, and his partner, who is one of my dearest friends, Madeline O'Conner. Also thanks to Mark and Jane of *Holistic Times*, David Mulqueen, my fitness trainer, who puts me through hell every week, Brendan Kelly of Rochestown Motors, Geraldine and Damien Grimes of Holistic Fairs Ireland, and Pat Monks, my Business Adviser.

To Alil O'Shaughnessy for all his kindness and extremely conscientious proofing, and to Lisa Gordon for her patient, good-humoured help.

To Sibby my beloved pet, thank you for your continual companionship and your unconditional love.

To all my clients, thank you so much for your very kind words and good wishes for the book. I wish you all Love, Light and Healing.

Aidan Storey

Foreword

When I came to write the Foreword to this deeply moving, healing and thought-provoking book I wondered how I could convey how blessed I was the day the author, Aidan Storey, came into my life. For blessed I truly was to be given the gift of such a dear and precious friend.

I thought of Yeats's words: 'Think where man's glory most begins and ends and say my glory was I had such friends.'

Or Coleridge's: 'Friendship is a sheltering tree.'

Or Kahlil Gibran's: 'In the sweetness of friendship let there be laughter, and sharing of pleasures.'

All beautiful, evocative sentiments but not quite accurate enough . . . and then I remembered the most perfect description of love and friendship anyone could wish for. This beautiful poem 'The Thousandth Man' by Rudyard Kipling captures Aidan's character so completely and far better than any words that I could write.

One man in a thousand, Solomon says,
Will stick more close than a brother.
And it's worth while seeking him half your days
If you find him before the other.
Nine hundred and ninety-nine depend
On what the world sees in you,
But the Thousandth Man will stand your friend
With the whole round world agin you.

'Tis neither promise nor prayer nor show
Will settle the finding for 'ee.
Nine hundred and ninety-nine of 'em go
By your looks, or your acts, or your glory.
But if he finds you and you find him
The rest of the world don't matter;
For the Thousandth Man will sink or swim
With you in any water.

You can use his purse with no more talk
Than he uses yours for his spendings,
And laugh and meet in your daily walk
As though there had been no lendings.
Nine hundred and ninety-nine of 'em call
For silver and gold in their dealings;
But the Thousandth Man he's worth 'em all,
Because you can show him your feelings.

His wrong's your wrong, and his right's your right,
In season or out of season.
Stand up and back it in all men's sight –
With that for your only reason!
Nine hundred and ninety-nine can't bide
The shame or mocking or laughter,
But the Thousandth Man will stand by your side
To the gallows-foot – and after!

Aidan and I met when I was at a very low point in my life. For ten years I'd struggled with chronic back pain after a failed operation. I feared I was going to end up in a wheelchair. I had constant spasms and sciatica and was bedridden for much of the time. Fortunately I could write my novels in bed so I didn't have to give up working, but my spirit was crushed and I was struggling to keep some sort of hope that the Divine Plan of my life was working and that all was as it should be.

In the way of synchronicity that always happens when someone comes into your life that you are meant to connect with, a woman I'd never met sent me a manuscript to read and advise her on. In the course of a phone conversation when she enquired as to how my back was, she said, 'You should go to Aidan Storey for Reiki healing.' I'd had Reiki healing from a wonderful woman called Mary Fanning, several years previously, and had really enjoyed it so I thought, yes, that would be good, and maybe there's a reason I have to meet this Aidan Storey. (When we sent off this manuscript to various editors, one of the publishers asked me how Aidan and I met, and had I expected to be 'healed'. I explained to her that no, I didn't expect to be cured and pain-free and that when I went for 'healing' it was for my spirit and to help me reconnect with the spiritual dimension in my life that I seemed in danger of losing.)

I rang Aidan and explained that I was due to have major back surgery and was worried and in bits and asked for an appointment to see him. He was fairly booked up but told me he would fit me in, in three weeks' time. I asked for directions, my heart sinking when I heard he lived in Palmerstown, knowing that it would involve a drive across the dreaded M50. (This is to be avoided at all costs when suffering severe back spasms.) There was silence on the phone and then he said to me, 'They're telling me you can't drive and that I need to go to you and you can't wait three weeks. Are you free tomorrow night and I can come and give you a healing?'

I was astonished and overwhelmed that a complete stranger would put himself out so much for me. As I got to know Aidan I realized this was par for the course for him.

We connected instantly when I opened the door to him. In his beautiful book, *Anam Ċara*, John O'Donohue writes of 'The Knowing' when two souls meet again, and that was the way with Aidan and me. We became the greatest of friends and I learned so much from him. I also learned how respectful and honouring he is of his healing gifts. I've met many people over the years that have been gifted as healers; sadly there are some in the field who forget where the 'gift' comes from; and some who work from ego. Aidan is completely the reverse: his acknowledgement of his God-given gift in all his healing sessions has never faltered despite his great success. He never puts himself forward, never makes himself out to be 'special' and never thinks he is in any way superior because he 'sees' things. He shares his gift with a quiet humility that is the hallmark of a true 'healer'.

That first night, five years ago, I said to him, 'You should write a book . . .'

'I'll leave that to you,' he said. But I persisted and persisted. Finally, last November, when he was helping me to recover from another big operation, he sat down at my kitchen table and began this book. His plan was to write a few pages so that I would stop 'nagging' him and then he could say he'd tried but he wasn't a 'writer'.

I thought I knew Aidan very well until I read his book. Even though I knew he'd been abused, nothing prepared me for the shock of reading about it. I cried for my dear friend and saluted his bravery in writing about such a devastating life experience. Nor was I prepared for the wondrous angelic revelations in this beautiful book, or the healing that flows from every page. This is a book of triumph over adversity, and of forgiveness and hope.

I know many people will be comforted as they read *Angels of Divine Light*. Anyone who has been abused will find solace in the chapter where the Angels bring him back to the scene of his abuse and erase for ever the awful words of a priest who passed a cruel and unforgivable judgement on him.

Anyone who has lost a child to death will surely find peace in the chapter where Aidan sees the powerful and loving Angel Metatron, and many more Angels, who come to be with the spirit of a little girl who is killed in a road accident.

Anyone who wants to know more about their Angels and Guides and how to connect with them will certainly find it in the pages of this book.

The questions and answers about death, relationships, the state of the planet, and many more, that come directly from the Angels in the third part of the book are thought-provoking and utterly reassuring and comforting.

An added bonus is the evocative descriptions of Aidan's childhood in James's Street, which will bring back wonderful memories to so many. I defy anyone to read his description of making his Holy Communion and not laugh.

I couldn't end this Foreword without making a mention of Kathleen, Aidan's mother, whom I had the pleasure and privilege of meeting and getting to know.

Kathleen was an amazing woman and I can see where Aidan got his courage, dignity and fantastic sense of humour. She would be so proud of him if she was here today but I know she is with him in spirit, every step he takes, and I thank her for rearing a wonderful, courageous, kind, compassionate and very loving son whom I'm deeply honoured to call a friend.

Patricia Scanlan

THE AWAKENING

Suffer the little children to come unto me

Chapter One

O Angel of God, my guardian dear
To whom God's love commits me here
Ever this day be at my side
To light and guard to rule and guide. Amen

This prayer always reminds me of my mother. It was the first prayer my Mam taught me and it is one of my earliest memories. Every night as she tucked me into bed and gave me my goodnight kiss she'd whisper in a gentle voice, 'Did you say your Guardian Angel prayer?' She would then sit or stand by my bed and recite it slowly with me, reminding me to replace the word 'day' with 'night'. Sometimes she would tell me the story of my Guardian Angel. I loved it when she did that and never tired of hearing it.

'Before you came to live with me, Aidan, you lived with Holy God way up in the sky. Because you were small, Holy God kept you safe and sound in His pocket until you were strong enough to come and live with me. Then one very warm night when we were all asleep He took you out of His pocket and left you on the back doorstep. He sent an Angel with you

3

to keep you safe until I found you early next morning. That Angel is still with you, and he's your Guardian Angel. He's your best friend and he will watch over you and keep you safe always. His name is also Aidan,' she would say with a big smile.

This made me feel so important. Imagine having an angel with the same name as you! 'Your Guardian Angel always has the same name as yourself,' Mam said. 'Mine is called Kathleen.' I loved this story because it always made me feel safe and secure before I went to sleep. And, of course, I had no reason to believe she wasn't being one hundred per cent truthful. You see, from a very young age – perhaps four or five – I could see Angels: and they were always by my side.

There were always many Angels. I don't know why I never told Mam or anyone else about these beautiful beings but I thought everyone could see them. I suppose at the age of four or five I thought that once you recited this prayer they just appeared.

I was born in 1958, and as the youngest of seven children I was a little spoiled and very well looked after by my older sisters and brothers. My father, also called Aidan, worked for Guinness driving lorries He enjoyed his job and worked hard, like many others of that era. The hours were long and often he had to stay away overnight if he was on a long run, especially coming up to Christmas when the brewery was particularly busy.

My father was a stocky man with a very straight walk and an air of authority. He was the main breadwinner in the house and he dutifully handed the housekeeping money over to my mother every Thursday night. We got sweets and chocolate that night, and our own pocket money. The amount depended on how old we were; and of course the youngest always got the least. Payday was a great day in our house!

Dad was a devout Catholic and carried out his Church duties with great faith and without question. Whatever the priest said was law and that was that. But he also believed in ghosts and the banshee and the tapping of the passing soul on the window. He told us how he saw the banshee outside his house shortly before his own father died.

She sat on the wall, a slight figure of a woman dressed in black. She sat combing her long hair, crying and wailing like a trapped cat or a lost soul. The sound could be heard for miles. He claimed he saw the banshee many times just before someone died. He also talked about the three taps on the window he'd heard on several occasions. This happened when someone close passed away and the spirit would tap on the window to say goodbye on their final journey. Every time he heard the knock on the window we got news shortly afterwards that someone had passed over. This gift has passed on to me: I always get the three taps on the window when loved ones pass over.

My father was born in 1919, and grew up in Wexford on his father's farm, the youngest boy of six. His mother was the local midwife. In his late teens he came to Dublin and went straight into Power's distillery before going to work for Guinness. He lodged for a short time with my mother's parents and that is where my Mam and Dad met, fell in love and, in the early 1940s, married.

Dad was not the easiest of men to get on with. He was the nicest and quietest of men when he had no drink in him but when he was drunk it was a different story. He never deprived the family of money through his drinking, but when he did get drunk he drank hard and turned argumentative. You certainly wouldn't dare to have a conversation with him when he was in this kind of state. So although he wasn't a bad man, and I loved him, he could be difficult to be around sometimes and I was a little nervous of him when I was a child.

Sadly, I never really got to know my father very well. He was a fairly distant figure, even with Mam, and my bond was much stronger with her. It wasn't until a couple of years before he died, when I was in my mid-twenties when he became ill, that I got to know him a little better and realized he'd had his own troubles to deal with. His childhood had been difficult, but he never wanted to discuss his past with anyone and it seemed he turned to drink to block things out. Men were not allowed to ask for help in those days, they were just expected to get on with it, and that was what he did. But he was bitter and angry as time went on and alcohol seemed to be the answer to his problems.

He was a troubled man and I'm sorry that I couldn't have the kind of relationship with him that I had with my mother. Now, though, that the Angels have given me the gift of love and compassion I know that in his own way he loved me. I'm glad he's at peace.

My mother on the other hand was very loving and always there when we needed her. She was a woman of her time. She worked in the home and cooked and cleaned from early in the morning until late at night. With so many children to care for, she never seemed to sit down and she had a kind word or a smile for everyone. And although she was a very straight-talking lady she had great warmth and a lot of love to give to people. She was highly thought of in the neighbourhood, for she would do a good turn for anybody, day or night.

My mother was born in 1915 in the Liberties, the oldest part of Dublin, and went to live in Mount Brown, just beside what is now St James's Hospital, when she was five or six. Her father also worked for Guinness and her mother was a cook. My mother was the oldest of seven children, a Wexford woman trapped inside a Dublin woman's body. She loved the country and spent most of her teens and early twenties in Wexford with relations because it was felt she was not strong and needed the clean, fresh air of the country to make her more robust. She was a tailor by trade and served her time in the local tailoring factories around Dublin.

She loved sewing and making clothes and curtains, and anything else she could run up on her machine. In fact, she made clothes for all of us when we were young – and for my cousins, and even the neighbours. Give her some material or an old dress, and in no time she would have made something for one of us. Gifted with her hands, she could do anything she set her mind to. She also took in home sewing from time to time, to make a few extra pounds. She sewed into the night and as a child I often fell asleep to the comforting rhythm of her machine as she worked away. She too was a devout Catholic and went to Mass every Sunday and any time she could during the week. She did a lot of charity work and never looked for any recognition in return.

The neighbours trusted and respected my mother for her kindness. She had a great love for the elderly and really made an effort to help anyone in need. People with problems were drawn to her and she would give them very good, sound advice, as if she was being guided in some way. I always felt she had strong healing powers and it was only as I grew older and began to develop my own that I realized she had a special healing energy about her.

Unlike my father, although she loved the Church, she was never blinded by it. She used to say, 'A good turn is far better than any praying or going to Mass.' And also unlike my father, she didn't always agree with what the priests and bishops had to say. She'd say, 'Don't mind those priests. They don't know everything. God has the last word.' This was her firm belief.

My mother gave birth to eight children: five girls and three boys. The first-born, a girl, died a few hours after birth. She was taken away from my mother a little later and then buried in the grave of the Angels in Glasnevin, a special grave for young children and babies.

Counselling was almost unheard of in those days, and Mam was sent home and advised to have another baby as soon as possible. But she never forgot her little girl and she spoke of her often. As I gained more knowledge from the Angels I was told why babies return to God so soon after birth, sometimes, or why they are miscarried. Later in the book we'll come back to this and I will pass on to you what I was told.

My brother Peadar followed a year later, in 1946, then Breda, Jim, Mary, Rosaleen, Kathleen, and myself. My mother had time for all of us – not easy when you were a mother of seven very different children. She told us she loved us all equally but felt she often had to love us in different ways because we were all different individuals, and this she did superbly. It was from her I learned about unconditional love, the ultimate goal of every soul who undertakes the human journey.

Chapter Two

Your soul is the priestess of memory,
selecting, sifting, and ultimately gathering
your vanishing days towards presence.

John O'Donohue, *Anam Cara*

We lived in Kilmainham in a terraced house on the main road between Mount Brown and Kilmainham. The area was mainly working class and most of the neighbours worked in the local hospitals, factories and, of course, Guinness's. As far as I can remember, the wives stayed at home. We never had a lock on the door, it was always on the latch, and we didn't have to take a key with us when we went out. Everyone who knew us just let themselves in. It was very common then, and it didn't matter if there was no one at home; it was safe and nobody took anything without asking.

We had very good neighbours. Mam had lived in the area all her life and knew most of the locals. Most had been her friends since childhood. Like herself they hadn't moved away when they got married. People didn't seem to go far from where they grew up in those days, they stayed close to their

9

parents. So the neighbourhood was a friendly one. Up the road about six doors to our right was the local paper mill and on the left of us was the local corner shop, Camac Stores. Beside that was a creamery.

A few sewing factories employed many of the young girls in the area. The Union, as St James's was once known, was the local hospital. It was a maternity as well as a general hospital in those days and at the time I was born it was known as St Kevin's. Many people of my mother's generation still refer to it as the Union. It and Doctor Steven's hospital were landmarks in our community.

The area also had a laundry, Dunlop's, where my mother used to leave my Dad's collars to be starched crisp. Despite the cost, seven collars were left every Saturday and collected every Tuesday. Guinness's expected all their staff to look well turned out: fresh, clean, starched collars were a must.

Guinness was the major employer in the area and the best. The conditions were excellent and to get a job in there was considered a great achievement in terms of securing your future. Working conditions in the brewery were far superior to many other places of employment. Guinness looked after its staff well, and had its own doctor, dentist and chemist. The whole family was looked after up to the time the children left school. Pensions were generous and Guinness was one of the first employers to provide a widow's pension.

I remember the streets as always busy with people walking to and from work, and bread men, milkmen, butchers and delivery boys with their boxcars, delivering their wares. The rush hour, as we know it today, didn't exist. There were few cars on the road then, but there was a hustle and bustle that had a much friendlier energy than when the area became more prosperous.

Another great asset was the St James's Band, and their

hall was only yards away from our house. Every Wednesday evening and Sunday morning you could hear them practise and even as a child I loved the sound of the music and it gave me a good, warm feeling of familiarity. On St Patrick's Day, and a couple of other special days during the year, the band would march out from the hall, returning in the evening, when the people in the street would come out to see and hear them. In their black suits with shiny buttons and with their instruments sparkling in the sun they looked so smart. They gave a great buzz to the area on those days. When we saw them we knew that summer was coming.

Our house was on the main road. We had no front garden and my Mam didn't like us playing in the front as the road was busy, but the back garden was quite big, so this wasn't a problem. In fact, the garden appeared huge to us and there was plenty of space for when friends and cousins came to us to play. In those days you could stay out all day and feel you were miles away from home.

The garden was split into sections: a little patch where my Mam had her flowers and grass, and then a wild part with bushes, trees and long grass. At the very end of the garden flowed the Camac River, a dirty, litter-filled river which would flood our garden almost every winter, and the back of the house more than once.

In our garden was a swing, but not a posh swing. This was one we made ourselves, rope going from one tree to another. It was great and we could fly much higher than on any of those shop-bought swings some of our neighbours had. The higher it went the better. An old wooden shed stood at the end of the garden. When my older brothers Peadar and Jim had kept chickens for a short time, they had lived there and when the chickens left my mother turned it into a playhouse for us, mainly for my sisters to play mammies and daddies in.

She had put her sewing skills to use again and transformed this old chicken hut, and in it we spent long summer days playing to our hearts' content. Every other day Mam would bring us down biscuits and orange squash and they tasted so good.

The garden was our adventure playground, we spent hours there and our friends loved to come to play because it was like having a little piece of the country in the heart of Dublin.

In this special place, when I was about five or six years old, the Angels came to me, but only when I was in the garden on my own.

In the early days they just stood close by and silently watched me play. I was never afraid of them. Looking back, I realize I believed what Mam told me about Angels. They were sent to watch over you, so in my mind I thought they came to keep me safe when I was alone. They were very gentle and never did anything to frighten me.

Although I enjoyed the company of others, I suppose I was a bit of a loner as a child and didn't seem to need other people around me. I guess I was a little reserved and quiet. I let my brothers and sisters do the talking for me, and was happy to play by myself. Somehow, the Angels made everything feel safe. I certainly wasn't afraid of them.

The Angels stood very tall and appeared in bright rainbow-like colours with big wings that you could almost see through. But as the years went on they became much more defined. Perhaps I'm looking back with rose-coloured glasses, but they were great days. I did feel safe and happy there without a thought of the outside world.

The house was always busy with people coming and going and with different sounds and noises coming from each room. It was a bit of a madhouse at times with my sisters playing music in one room, while in another the radio would be blasting out. And all the while, my brothers were watching sport on the television.

But if this sounds a bit cosy, the Waltons we were not! We got on most of the time, but like most big families we had our disagreements and when we did all hell would break loose.

My mother soon put a stop to it all. She was quite firm and we did as we were told without question. She never hit us, but she would 'punish' us as she put it, either by keeping us in from play, or not letting us go somewhere with our friends. And she never backed down; she meant what she said, so we didn't argue or try to get her to change her mind. We all had our jobs to do around the house and garden and we just got on with it.

My eldest brother, Peadar, when he was about nine or ten had misbehaved, so to punish him Mam told him he wasn't allowed to go to the local cinema that afternoon with his friends. Every Saturday the cinema put on children's movies and the children in the area flocked in their droves to attend. Mam was adamant he wasn't going and warned him. However, my brother had other ideas. If Mam and Dad wouldn't give him the money to go he could always get it from our granny who lived just up the road from us.

My granny adored Peadar and in her eyes he could never do any wrong. So up he went to her and without any question she handed him over the money for the movie and also money for sweets. He was delighted with himself and off he went with his friends to the Lyric, which was what our cinema was called. On her way home from Saturday shopping Mam stopped to talk to a neighbour who, in passing, mentioned she had seen Peadar go into the cinema with his friends, as happy as Larry. Mam was fuming and headed straight to the cinema.

She asked the usher on the door to take her into the

picture-house so she could take her son out, explaining to him why she was doing so. In she marched with the usher, who flashed on his torch. She searched until she found Peadar and then frogmarched him out of the cinema to his great shame and embarrassment, in front of all his friends. They went straight home and he wasn't allowed to go to the cinema again for the next two weeks and *this* time he did obey her. If Mam told you to do something, you did it without question. Mam, in her later years, often related this story to my brother and they both would have a great laugh.

My mother's days were filled with cooking, cleaning and shopping. There were no supermarkets in my younger days so we got the 'messages' in the local shops, and bread, milk and veg in Smith's at the top of the hill. Meat was always bought in the butcher's and only from Bob Carroll facing St Kevin's hospital. You got other bits and pieces in Conway's and brought the slop from your Mam's kitchen to Miss Conway's for the pig man.

This was really worth doing because when you handed in the slop you got a free bar of toffee. The other goodies came from the Camac Stores. Every shop had something the others didn't have and we always knew where to get what. On Sundays after roast beef dinner we had our dessert, ice-cream and jelly. We didn't have a fridge at that time so every Sunday just before lunch we were sent out to get the ice-cream from the Camac Stores.

It was shut on Sundays but Miss Coady the owner lived over the shop with her brother. So we'd knock on this big green door hoping she would answer and when we heard her unlocking the door we were relieved, knowing that there was a treat in store. Sometimes she was cross with us for knocking on Sundays but more often than not she was glad of the business, I'm sure. Thank God for Miss Coady living so near. Raspberry Ripple ice-cream with strawberry jelly to die for.

My favourite memories of my early days are the smell of Sunday dinner, of toast by the fire on winter nights, and the smell and feel of fresh, clean crisp white sheets. It still makes me feel warm and good inside to think of all the comforting little luxuries we were so lucky to enjoy.

Our parish church was St James's just beside the famous gates of Guinness's Brewery. Across the road stood the post office and on either side of it Guinness buildings all painted in a dark navy. On a wide street, St James's was a grey place, which never felt warm, even on the warmest of summer days. The church was a big grey cement building, not a beautifully decorated building like other churches in the city. It was built around the time of the famine and I feel it carries that sad energy. Even now I get that feeling when I drive past it.

Here we went to Mass every Sunday, Holy Day, and one Saturday a month with the school. We went to confession at least once a month. You'd never miss Mass, it was something you did on Sunday, and you never questioned it. Going to Mass was something we enjoyed. It was like a social gathering and a day out all rolled into one. Everyone did themselves up and the whole of the parish seemed to smile and chat and be on good terms with each other. When my Dad did the collection at the 12.15 Mass on Sundays, I went with him. We strolled down to the church saying hello to the neighbours and chatting away.

It was nice to be with Dad, as I didn't go many places with him. We'd go in, say our prayers, light candles and take Mass. On the way home he would send me ahead to Pauline's, the paper shop, to get the *Sunday Press* and the *News of the World* and a packet of Rolo for me and then we'd go back home to enjoy our Sunday and freedom from work and school.

Mass and religion were very important and you looked up to your priest and others in religious callings. You did what the bishops and priests said and you did it without question, and so we did our duties week in, week out, year in, year out. The whole year was worked around the church holidays. It started in January with what we called 'Little Christmas', which marked the end of the festive season and the return to school. Then came St Bridget's Day in February and the start of spring, a time when we honoured the St Bridget's Cross that we all had hanging in our homes. Shortly after that came Lent and Easter and in between were St Patrick's Day and Ascension Thursday. May, month of our Lady, and June, the Sacred Heart, were noted for the big processions. October was Rosary month, November, All Saints and All Souls, and then it was December starting with the Annunciation, then Advent, the Forty Hours, and finally Christmas Day.

During the six weeks of Lent you always gave up something as a penance. Sweets, chocolate, sugar in your tea – whatever you liked best you offered up for penance and for the forgiveness of your sins. We also went to Mass every evening at 7.30 p.m. We didn't have to, but we all went. It ended up being quite a social thing, for there we got to meet our friends. The statues and the altar were covered in a purple cloth all during Lent, which made the church feel cold and lonely.

During Lent we had a retreat where a missionary priest came and talked to us about sin and the priests' work in the Foreign Mission. The missioners seemed much friendlier than our own priests. I loved to listen to their stories about the people they helped and the work they were doing in these faraway, exotic places. I came away from these retreats wanting to be a priest on the missions; it sounded so rewarding. Films at school about the missions fired my imagination and I dreamt of working with them.

We got the *Far East* and the *Messenger* in school and when I was small Mam would sit and read me the stories about the Saints and about the work the nuns and priests were carrying out in the mission field, as I ate my dinner before the rest of the family came home. She would close the magazine and say how wonderful these people were and how she really admired them.

We didn't eat meat on Fridays in those days because it was the day the Lord died, so we had fish and chips for dinner on a Friday. I loved my Mam's home-made chips, crisp and sizzling out of the oil. Just before Easter Sunday was Palm Sunday. That week the gospel at Mass was very long and I dreaded that whole part of the Mass because we had to stand for ages. I was there with my brothers and sisters, but not with Mam. She'd gone to early Mass, at eight o'clock, to get a bit of peace! I envied the old ladies and gents who were allowed to sit during the entire reading.

That was the start of Holy Week, the week running up to Easter Sunday. We spent a lot of time in the church that week. Mam used to joke that she'd nearly meet herself coming back, we were so often in the church at the various ceremonies. Then, the services were quite different to the usual Mass and Benediction. Spy Wednesday sounded very dramatic, so called because this was when poor Judas betrayed our Lord. And on Holy Thursday there was the washing of the priest's feet. Good Friday was the most solemn day, when even the Irish broadcaster RTE played only funereal music and the pubs were closed. We had the Stations of the Cross at noon, and at 3 p.m. the Passion of Our Lord and then the Kissing of the Cross.

I felt very close to Jesus during these services and, even as a child, would connect with His pain and His great love. After the Stations when we got home we had a cup of tea and a hot cross bun. Unlike today, we only got hot cross buns on Good Friday and they always tasted so good. Once we were finished Mam would say, 'No more sweet things until Sunday. It's still Lent.' On Holy Saturday the altar was bare and there was no Mass that day.

Then came Easter Sunday when the church was beautiful again. We could see all our Saints, the cold purple cloth was gone and the altar sparkled with brass candlesticks, candles and fresh flowers. The church looked alive and to make sure *we* were alive and awake after all our praying during the past week the priest would drown us in the newly blessed Holy Water. Then after Mass it was home quickly to unwrap the much longed for Easter egg, the only day in the year you could eat chocolate with your breakfast.

Once Easter was over, we had the summer holidays to look forward to. Long warm days and no school . . . heaven. In the summer I spent four or five weeks in Wexford on my grandmother's farm. Dad took his holidays the first two weeks in July and both of us would head down to see everyone and help out a little on the farm. I would cry for a good deal of the journey down, missing my Mam and my big brothers and sisters. I told myself every year I would go with Dad when he went back to Dublin but by the time he was going home I was having a great time.

I'd stay until I was told to go home because school would be starting back soon. The rest of the family didn't come because some of them were working or had summer jobs, so Mam had to stay behind too. My grandmother lived on a modest farm, in a small country house on about sixty acres of land. My Uncle Tommy and Aunt Alice worked the farm. It was a typical farm of its time, with cows, pigs, a couple of horses and lots of chickens. Work started very early in the morning and finished late in the evening.

I loved the open space and helping my aunt and uncle. I would do small jobs for them, and then they'd tell me how great I was. High praise. My favourite job was going for the cows in the evening with Aunt Alice. She was kind to me, she always had sweets for me in her pocket and would tell me not to tell my cousins, who lived in the area and spent time up at the farm.

Alice was the gentlest of souls and had a great respect for the land and her animals. She had names for all the farm animals, even the chickens, and always knew when they were sick. She was also funny. She had two dogs and she called them both Sheila. I thought it was very strange and she gave a big laugh when I asked her why. She was a great woman for telling ghost stories. She'd have the hair standing on the back of your neck and then you would have to get her to sleep with you that night, you were so scared.

Every evening on our way to bring home the cows she would remind me it was six o'clock and we would say the Angelus, reciting it very slowly, with great faith. Then the dogs gathered the cows together and walked them back to the farm, where Alice milked them before taking them back to the field. Then we would go in and have a very large supper, usually home-made bread, cold meat, or eggs and rashers and *always* home-made jam.

Sunday was the most important day of the week. On Sunday we'd get up and do only the jobs that really needed to be done. Then we'd get washed and put on our best clothes. The day was kept very sacred and it was a very quiet, peaceful day. Even the animals seemed to be quieter. The energy of that day was very different to the rest of the week. It felt 'special'. Everything slowed down and the world felt at rest. At 11 a.m. we all headed off to second Mass in the village church of Oilgate.

It was in this very church that I first heard the word 'healer', a word that has stayed with me for the rest of my life. I was about seven or eight at the time. As I came out of church holding on to my Dad a man came up to us. He had a very friendly conversation with Dad and just before he left he turned to me, shook my hand, looked me in the eyes and winked. Then he turned back to my Dad and said, 'You have a very powerful healer here, Aidan, you'd better look after him.' They shook hands and the man left. I didn't know what he meant, nor did I question it. But it was something that stayed in my mind and I've often thought of this encounter over the years, wondering what he'd meant.

Before we knew it, August was over and we were heading back to school. I really enjoyed the summers I spent in Wexford but I looked forward to coming home and seeing all the family and they gave me a big welcome home. Once we returned to school in September everything changed again. The days got shorter and the nights longer. The next big event was Hallowe'en, when we dressed up in old clothes, smeared soot on our faces and knocked on our neighbours' doors and collected fruit and nuts. Then we all went to the bonfire, sat around and ate what we had collected before going home and playing games and telling ghost stories.

The year would start to close in and once November arrived it was time to start thinking about Christmas. The Christmas pudding was mixed around the end of November. I still recall the smell of the spices as it cooked on top of the stove and how the kitchen was wet from steam because you had to boil puddings for eight hours. Then, and only then, when you got that pudding smell could you look forward to the big day and hope you would get a wonderful Christmas present.

The Christmas tree was put up around the 18th or 19th of December and it was decorated with every colour and shape of shiny decorations we could get our hands on. Nothing like the sophisticated and expensive decorations around today! We kept our fingers crossed that the fairy lights would work. So between the smells of plum pudding and the pine tree scenting the room, Christmas was my favourite time of the year.

I loved the whole story of Jesus and how He was born. This was the only time in the year that you heard the Angels mentioned and I was always very happy to hear about them.

After Mass on Christmas morning we came home, played with our presents, had fizzy lemonade and biscuits. Sometimes we paid a visit to our aunts and uncles, or maybe they would come to our house. There were always lots of visitors and plenty of good food and everyone enjoyed the day. Then once again it was time to ring out the old year on New Year's Eve and ring in the new, and the cycle started all over again.

Chapter Three

The child is God's gift to the family. Each child is created in the special image and likeness of God for greater things – to love and to be loved.

Mother Teresa

My schooldays started when I was five. I was a happy and contented child and looked forward to joining the big outside world of my brothers and sisters. It was June, and the feast of the Sacred Heart. On my way home from Mass with my mother we journeyed home via Basin Lane Convent school, a big, grey, two-storey building with vast windows and a huge, green double front door. Tall green railings lined the front of the building.

The school was not strange to me, as I had left my youngest sister Kathleen to school many times with Mam over the past few years. We didn't enter through the main door; instead Mam led me around by the convent chapel and in through a side door, and then out through the small playground to another hall. We stood in this enormous hall, which smelt of floor wax. My Mam tidied me up and then knocked on a big mahogany door, from behind which we could hear the sound of children doing their lessons.

As the door opened it creaked a little. From behind it appeared a small figure of a woman dressed from head to toe in black, wearing rimless glasses and with pale skin and rosy cheeks. Her voice was kind and warm and she had a bright smile. As she looked at me she gently placed her hands on my head and listened to my mother as she asked if it were possible to enrol me to start school in the coming September. The nun's name was Sister Imelda, a truly wonderful person and a gentle soul. Everyone who met her loved her and it was said that the boys were lucky to have such a great nun for their first year.

When my mother was finished, Sister Imelda looked down at me and asked, 'Well, young man, what do you think? Would you like to come to school when the summer holidays are over?' Nodding my head in agreement and terrified at the same time I finally got the words out: 'Yes, please.'

She smiled and said, 'Well, we'd better put your name on the roll.' She went back into the classroom, leaving the door half open. I could see that all the boys had their heads in their arms on the desk as if they were asleep. Sister Imelda came back to us with the biggest book I had ever seen and, when she opened it, it seemed there were hundreds of names written in it. She wrote my name, address and date of birth in the roll with a pen that she dipped in dark blue ink, then dried it off with clean white blotting paper.

'There you are,' she said, 'you're a big boy now. You be good for your Mammy and I will see you in September.' She smiled at my mother and shook her hand and then placed an oval-shaped red badge of the Sacred Heart in my hand. 'Wear that and Holy God will mind you,' she told me.

I was delighted with my badge and couldn't wait to start

school. On our way home Mam did the shopping in Smith's and told me to pick out some biscuits for myself for being so good in front of the nun. As always, I pointed at the box of butter creams and said, 'I'll have those, please.'

That's all I remember until that September and my first day walking to school with my schoolbag on my back, holding my mother's hand. I was very excited and couldn't wait to get to the classroom. The hall was packed with mothers and children: it wasn't the quiet hall I remembered. Most of the children were crying and mothers were talking with each other and trying to be heard over the howling children.

Sister Imelda sat in her classroom marking the roll as the mothers dropped the children off. The noise and the crying terrified me and it suddenly dawned on me that I was going to be left here. Mam wouldn't be staying. What would I do? I had never been on my own. The tears ran down my cheeks as Mam forced my hand out of hers, kissed me and told me everything would be fine. She said she'd be outside in the hall waiting for me when school finished. My heart was racing as I saw her walk away and I really felt I would never see her again.

The room appeared to be huge. It was a big double room with four large Victorian windows on each side and a gallery at the back. Long benches lined the room and boys sat everywhere, some crying, some just waiting quietly and a few playing with other boys. At the top of the room behind the teacher's desk stood a white wooden altar with a statue of Our Lady and one of the Sacred Heart with red lights burning in front of them. Fresh flowers in enormous glass vases stood on either side of the altar. The walls were covered with pictures of nursery rhymes, and pictures of all the saints and holy people you could think of.

The picture that stood out from the rest was the one of

a beautiful Angel flying across the sky holding children's hands, bringing them safely to the other side of a valley. My mother was right again: my Angels *were* here and they would keep me safe in school. 'They never leave your side,' she told me again and again.

I can't remember what we did for the rest of that day but I do remember seeing my Mam at the gate when we came out and I can still feel the joy and happiness I felt when I hugged her and hoped I would never have to go back to school or leave her again. It came as something of a shock to go back the next day!

But, of course, everything soon settled down and school became part of my daily life. I went without much fuss and adored Sister Imelda. She was a loving teacher and I don't recall her shouting or being cross with us. The days were full of learning our numbers and the alphabet, of reciting nursery rhymes and singing songs. A couple of times a week we played with mala – a kind of Plasticine – and did colouring with our crayons.

Every day before lunch Sister Imelda taught us our prayers. We started with Our Father, then the Hail Mary and then the easy one, Glory be to the Father. She said these again and again until we knew them by heart and she would ask different boys to recite them every day. She never got annoyed if you got stuck and would recite it with you and then smile and say well done. My best ever day was the day she said she was going to teach us the Guardian Angel prayer. I was so excited because I knew it and for some reason she knew I knew this and asked me if I would like to recite it for the class.

When I finished she patted me gently on the head and told me I was a great boy and very special. 'Your Angels are with you,' she said. I took it that she could see them as they were everywhere in the room. She gave me a picture of Our Lady of Knock as a reward for saying the prayer.

The next day she told us about our Angels and about Jesus and His Mother. The room filled with Angels when she spoke of them and one stood beside every boy. No one said anything so I assumed that everybody else could see them. They had become a little more clear for me by now: they stood about six foot high and were as bright as the night stars.

Their wings attached to their back stood firm and straight. They seemed soft, like birds' feathers. I was not afraid of these beautiful Beings of Light, for they brought with them an energy of calm and safety, and I never questioned anything I saw. These were the Angels my mother and Sister Imelda spoke about so they *had* to be real. Nuns and mothers never lied.

I spent three happy years in Basin Lane School and had three extremely nice teachers. I made my First Holy Communion from here. I was then in High Babies and our teacher was Miss O'Dea, a young teacher who was new to the school, but it was Sister Imelda who prepared us for our big day. Every afternoon she taught us the prayers we needed for the First Communion day. She had no Communion wafers so instead we practised with the flat medal that hung from her rosary beads. She would say, 'Corpus Christi.' We would answer, 'Amen,' and then she would place the medal on our tongue, take it away and pass to the next boy, and so on. She also prepared us for our first confession.

I was not looking forward to that. We all walked down to the church the Friday morning before our Communion day, two in a row, hand in hand, and waited our turn to go into the confession box. It was terrible. A dark and lonely place that smelt musty. As I stood there terrified and shaking, hoping I wouldn't forget my sins, a noise came from behind the grid as the priest pulled open the little flap and muttered something. His old, grim, pasty face looked away into space, not really listening to me. I'm sure he was bored, as we all had the same sins to confess.

When I was finished he mumbled something about being 'a good boy for your Mammy and teachers', then added, 'and don't hurt God by being bold again'. He told me to say 'three Hail Marys for your penance', made the sign of the cross and closed the flap. I was in the dark again.

When we were all done the teachers took us to the centre of the church and we said our penances. We finished early at school that day and my mother took me on the bus into town to have my hair cut for my big day. In Woolworth's café we had a cream cake and lemonade.

It was then home to have a bath and an early night. I had to be strong and not tired for the next day as I was going to receive Holy God and things would never be the same again. From now on you had to be good or God would be very cross with you. If you told lies or said bad words this would hurt God and you would nail Him to the cross all over again. What a big responsibility this was for a six-year-old.

I woke up early on the morning of my First Communion feeling very excited. Everyone got up to get me ready and to see me off to the church. I wore a Glen Check grey suit with short trousers, white shirt and blue tie. Mam dressed me and told me how handsome I was and my brothers and sisters teased me and said how all the girls would run after me. When I was ready my Dad and Mam took me to the church. Dad drove, and I was allowed to sit in the front seat.

The church was full. The girls in their white dresses and veils sat on one side and the boys in their suits of different colours on the other. The mothers and fathers sat behind us. There was a feeling of happiness in the air. I sat beside my cousin and Sister Imelda. Sister Lucy, another of our nuns, came over to us and told us how lovely we were. We were all proud of ourselves.

When I received Holy Communion for the first time it felt nothing like Sister Imelda's medal, nor did it taste anything like it either. It tasted just like wafer and you had to be careful not to let it stick to the roof of your mouth. If it did you were not under *any* circumstance allowed to put your finger into your mouth. That would be a most dreadful sin and you might even be struck *dead* because only the priest could touch the Body of Christ. Only he was pure enough. All you could do was try and take it away using your tongue to peel it off the roof of your mouth and hope that in the process you didn't swallow your tongue. You could never chew the Host either: it must *never* touch your teeth.

Thank God none of these much-dreaded things happened on the day. I was safe. I hadn't committed any sin and the Body and Blood of Christ would make me strong and good.

The weekend was filled with visits to my relations in Dublin and Wexford, who all made a big fuss of me. It was an extremely special occasion in a young child's life. In every house I got sweets, biscuits and lemonade and, before I left, they pushed money into my hand to buy myself something. It was a day I remember with great joy.

After my Communion I had one more happy year in Basin Lane in first class. Then in June of that year just before we broke up for summer holidays we went into what was called the big boys' school. This school was run by the Christian Brothers. It was only across the road – but what a difference crossing the road would make in my life.

Chapter Four

Keep away from people who try to belittle your ambitions.
Small people always do that, but the really great make you
feel that you, too, can become great.

Mark Twain

These were not to be my happiest days; in fact they were days of hell but I didn't have any choice and had to go. From the first time I entered that school I was very nervous and insecure. I had a couple of very nice teachers but I was not happy. They 'streamed' the classes and I was put into the top stream, which meant I was separated from most of my friends and placed into a class with new boys. I didn't know them and had to make friends all over again.

I was always quite shy and didn't take well to change. However, as time passed and I started to make friends, which I always found difficult, things did become a little easier. I settled down to the routine of school and the following year moved into a new class – the A-grade stream. My mother and father were very proud of me! The year started, as always, with new books and getting used to a new teacher.

The master we had this year was an elderly gentleman, refined, immaculately dressed, rather dapper and with grey hair. He wore a signet ring on his left hand. During the time I was in his class I started to develop a bad pain in my right-hand side that made me very pale and left me feeling sick. This pain was never properly diagnosed, but when it happened the teacher was always very kind. He'd put his chair by the heater for me and after he'd had his break he would bring me back a mug of hot milk and pepper. He told me to drink it slowly, and when it came to going home he'd make sure one of the boys who lived near me would walk home with me.

As a very nervous child, I worried if I didn't understand something or if I couldn't do my homework. In fact, I worried so much about reading aloud in class that my mother spoke to the teacher about how troubled I was. He reassured her that she should not concern herself. He said he'd have a word with me during the day.

Words he did have with me – and a lot more besides. When I had reached the tender age of nine, this teacher, whom my mother and I trusted implicitly, and whom we thought of as a gentleman, sexually abused me regularly for a year.

It started with him asking me to stay behind, after school. He wanted to have a word with me, he said: my mother had asked him to because I was worried about my lessons. When all the other boys had left he went over to the door, locked it and put the keys in his pocket. Then, very slowly, he walked from window to window closing the Venetian blinds until the room was in twilight. He bent down and told me how special I was and how I was his pet and that I needn't worry about anything. He started to kiss me on the head, and then moved down to my face and my lips, shoving his big wet tongue into my mouth until I almost couldn't breathe. He pressed his body against me again and again, at the same time putting one hand up my trousers while having his other hand in his pocket moving it very quickly up and down. He put my hand on his privates and made me feel them.

My whole body became rigid as he pulled me in tighter and tighter to his body, all the time reassuring me that everything was OK and he only did this to very *special* boys he really liked and who were his pets. So I must never tell anyone, he insisted. As he became rougher and rougher he let out a little moan, then stopped and looked me in the eye and again told me I must never tell anyone, that this was *our* secret and if I did I wouldn't be his pet any more and then I would be very unhappy in his class.

It was the same every time he abused me.

He would leave the classroom for a few minutes when he was finished, tell me to wait, and when he came back he'd tell me to go and tap me on the head. I didn't know what he was doing then. I knew it wasn't right but how could I explain this to anybody? I didn't know what was happening. We were always told to respect our teacher and never to give back cheek and always do as we were told. So that was what I did, but from that first day of shock and horror I hated going into school even more.

I stopped going out to play when I got home and I didn't mix or even play much with my classmates. I was so afraid and nervous I had to get my mother to walk me to school every morning and hope and pray that this man would leave me alone that day. As the abuse became more regular my Angels became stronger and came to my rescue when it happened. It was happening once or twice a week and I dreaded the last bell ringing. To this day a shiver runs up and down my body when I hear the lock click on a door or the noise of venetian blinds closing. One day I prayed as he was closing the blinds, with the tears running down my face and my body shaking like a leaf, *Please, my Guardian Angel, help me,* and as I stood there, a beautiful figure of a very tall Angel came to me. He was dressed in pink and green shimmering robes, with pure white skin and piercing pale blue eyes.

'Don't worry,' he said. 'Take my hand,' and as I did I had the strangest of feelings. I felt my body moving away from where I was standing and I began to float. The Angel took me over to the door and sat me on top of a low store cupboard we called the press. I could see myself standing over at the blackboard with the teacher but could feel nothing. The Angel stood beside me and then unfolded his wings and placed them around me. I felt somehow safe and he whispered gently, 'You are safe, it will be OK.' This, I think, was the first time I heard an Angel speak, but the voice didn't seem to penetrate or even enter the space of the room. I still can't explain it, but Angels seem to speak outside of our space and energy and their voices fall softly and gently.

This was a very strange experience, which I now know to have been an out-of-body experience. I saw myself in the room and I felt myself on top of the press, but for the first time I couldn't feel what this man was doing to me. It was as if the Angel eased the pain of it all – took me away and allowed me to detach myself from the reality of what was happening. I was scared and very confused. But I could hear the Angel saying repeatedly, 'You are safe, you are not feeling anything.'

When the teacher had finished abusing me, the Angel took my hand and led me back to where I was standing. My two bodies merged and I was one again – numb with shock and unable to utter a word.

I always felt dirty and somehow guilty after the abuse and would rush out to the toilets to wash my hands, my mouth and my face before the short journey home, which seemed to take for ever. Everyone else from my class was at home by now and the lane was empty and silent. For me this was good. At least no one could see my shame – and shame is exactly what I felt. My Angels were the only ones with me, but even they were silent.

That day an Angel had spoken to me for the first time and on the way home they spoke again. Every few minutes they placed a hand on my shoulder and whispered, 'Everything will pass, Little Soul, and you will feel good again.' I did feel better when I got home and my mother gave me a big hug and I could breathe and feel safe again. And on those days I held on to my Mam for a little longer. Once I was at home I was safe and nothing could harm me. Mam suspected nothing unusual was going on at this time. I suppose she thought I was my usual anxious self, and I was never kept back in school long enough for her to be concerned about where I was.

Looking back, I see how supportive she was and if she ever asked if there was anything wrong, anything troubling me, I'd simply avoid answering her. I didn't seem to have the language to express myself; and of course, over time, I was tortured by a deep sense of shame.

Morning came quickly in those days and the dread and the fear built up again. I would hope against hope that I could leave my classroom safely when school was over and go home with the rest of my classmates. But as the year went on, the abuse continued and I became more and more of a loner – more isolated than ever. I never wanted to go out and I only felt safe when my mother or one of my family was with me.

During the next few months the Angels were with me all the time but their presence became stronger every time that classroom door was locked. They came and took me out of my body and over to the press. They instructed me to place my hands over my eyes. 'Let's have fun and let's fly and see all the beautiful things in the world.' They took me where children are safe and feel safe and they talked to me a little more, but as a child, because that is what I was. At no time did they say anything I didn't understand. They knew how upset I was, so they showed me places and took me flying high in the sky, holding me very tightly and showing me the magnificent colours of nature – of the seas, the forests, the meadows, the snow-capped mountains. They showed me these glorious places, pointing out the different colours and the beauty of, as they called it, 'God's work'. It looked just like the picture of the Angel and the children in Sister Imelda's room. They also took me to what they called 'The Gardens of the Angels', and what a beautiful place it was! In a huge flower garden the Angels gathered the essences from the flowers to take to earth, to bring healing and love, flowers of every shape and colour. It was a place of peace, full of trees, lakes and waterfalls.

A pearly white mist covered the entire garden. Their feet didn't seem to touch the grass under them as they moved with gentleness and ease from place to place, not bumping into each other. They were not singing as I'd thought they would; instead there was stillness and silence. My Angel, whom I was calling Aidan, told me this was where the Angels gathered and waited for the people on earth to call them and ask them for help and guidance. They dressed in different colours, in simple, long, flowing robes, and all were about the same height. Their hair was of different colours too and they had very pale skin with powder pink cheeks. All of them smiled and had the most beautiful bright piercing blue eyes. My Angel told me to remember this place and remember to ask them for their help. How could I forget this place?

Words or pictures could never describe just how sublime it was.

'It's time for you to go back. Everything is fine now and this will pass, Little Soul. You are very special and very strong. Don't be afraid, we will help you.' Very gently they took me back to that classroom and to my place of fear and terror and once more I rushed out of the classroom and ran home as quick as I could to feel safe and loved again.

I never told anyone about the abuse or about the Angels. It wasn't that I didn't want to, but I didn't know how to. The year finally came to an end and we moved to a new classroom and a new teacher. He was a friendly man, and a good teacher, but I didn't trust him either, so I knuckled down, worked hard, faded as much into the background as I could, and did as I was told. Doing as I was told came easy to me. I was a conscientious child, worked hard at my lessons and now felt comfortable and at ease. I started to enjoy school a little more and tried to put the whole horrible experience of the previous year out of my head.

This peace that came in my life was to be short-lived when I passed from this class into a Christian Brother's class. A small man with a reputation for being hard and very nasty, he had a red, scurvy face, black hair combed to the side, shining with Brylcreem, and cold, empty, mean brown squinty eyes that stared at you from behind black-rimmed glasses. He stank of nicotine and mothballs and his shoulders were covered in thick, white dandruff.

Believe me, there was nothing Christian about this man and he should never have been allowed to teach, or to be in a room with such young souls. His classroom was at the end of the corridor on the first floor. He didn't mix with the other teachers and instead stood at the top of the stairs looking out to the yard, smoking and then making cruel remarks about everyone that came up the stairs, except for his favourite boys; the boys who did well in class and whose parents were on the school fundraising committee.

This was a different type of abuse: not sexual abuse, but an abuse that was just as horrendous and just as soul-destroying. A mental, degrading abuse which robbed me of my spirit, the real me, and put in its place an empty, lost and fearful child, who, at the age of eleven, didn't know who he was any more and felt worthless and a complete failure. This is how this man of God taught me and most of my classmates to think of ourselves. I wasn't the only one in the class he did this to; there were others, but I was the one he did it to most often.

This Christian Brother didn't like me from day one. I'm not sure what it was about me, or if he even needed a reason; maybe he just picked on the weak boys, and on shy ones like me. I don't know and I never will but I do know he made my life hell again. His first few words to the class were that we were there to learn, and learn we would, and if we were slow and stupid, well then, we would have to work harder or we would be left behind. 'Because I don't work with stupid boys,' he sneered.

Then he used a term which I will never forget. He said there were two types of boy, the very bright boys who were intelligent – and these were the boys he preferred to have in his class; and then there were the dumbcluckers and they were the people who would never amount to anything. Everyone laughed, including myself; then, when the class settled down, he asked a few general questions and he was very pleased, he said, with the result. He went on to explain that he had all our books in his room for the coming year. He handed us out our new book list and the only one missing was the religion book. He started to talk about this book and said that as we always had a religion test at the end of September every year he didn't know what we were going to do.

I put up my hand and tried to explain to him that this had happened last year too and we'd just worked from the religion book we had from the previous year. He gave me a furious look then said, 'Now that's what I mean. Every year I get at least one and here he is . . . your dumbclucker! Sit down, you stupid, stupid boy, and don't let me hear you talk again until you can make sense.' He turned to the class, shook his head and smiled, giving them permission to laugh, and so they did. About an hour later the Brother from next door came in and he asked him the same question about the religion book and what they should do for the exam at the end of the month. 'Well, Storey?' he shouted at the top of his voice. 'Stand up.'

Turning to the Brother he said, 'Storey here will explain all about what you have to do as he knows everything.' So again I tried to explain what had happened the previous year. Halfway through he told me to shut up and sit down. Turning back to his colleague he said, 'This is my dumbclucker for this year, God help me.' Again they all laughed and the two Christian Brothers shook their heads and I felt sick and totally humiliated. I wanted to cry and run home but I couldn't. I saw my Angel very clearly in the classroom again and I knew there were going to be difficult times ahead.

Over the past year they hadn't shown themselves to me in the classroom as often. The Angel put his finger to his lips as if to tell me not to say a word.

On the way home I was on my own. I was very ashamed and didn't want to be with anybody, afraid they would jeer at me. That would make me very upset and I didn't want to let the others see that.

On that day as on many other days my Angels walked

beside me and assured me that everything would be all right and that later I would see clearly why this was happening to me. As we walked they told me that all I had to do was ask for their help and they would be there, and I was to remember that they were *always* with me. I didn't understand their words until many years later.

That was my first day back in school. It didn't get any easier as the days and weeks went by. I could do nothing right as far as this man was concerned. I opened the door the wrong way; I sat at my desk in the wrong way; I cried like a girl. And on and on it went. It got so bad that every morning when I woke up I felt so sick that I would throw up before I left the house. I was so nervous that my Mam was back to taking me to school every day. I wasn't embarrassed by this – I just didn't want to go through the pain and humiliation that each day brought.

Sometimes in class I felt sick and would ask to leave the room but after a couple of times the Brother thought I was trying to get out of doing my work and was looking for attention. He'd refuse me permission to leave and send me back to my seat. On more than one occasion I threw up all over myself. Then he would lose his temper and go crimson from his neck to the top of his head. He'd order me out of the room and send me to the staff room to get a bucket and mop. Faint with fear and anxiety, I had to clean up my vomit while he raged at me to hurry up. I was then forced to stand against a wall, my trousers and jumper stained and smelling of vomit, and, in front of the whole class, he'd ask me what kind of an animal I was. 'Go and sit over there away from everyone. You are not fit to sit with the rest of us.' Sitting on my own, weak and terrified, I wasn't even allowed to go out to the yard for my break.

I'd go home for my lunch and get cleaned up. Mam could

see how upset I was but she'd pretend not to be and would try to reassure me that everything would be fine.

'Did you ask your Angels and St Bernadette to help you? Bernadette will help you. She didn't like school either,' she'd say. 'And the nuns gave her a terrible time.' St Bernadette was someone I felt very close to. I loved the story of Mother Mary appearing to her and how people didn't believe her because she was poor and considered slow at school.

This Christian Brother was ruining my life and my mother and I lived in hope that I would get a change of teacher the following year: it would be a very important year for me – my last year in primary school, and also my Confirmation class. That June, just before we all split up for our summer holidays, he sat on his desk at the front of the room with a smirk on his cruel red face and informed us that he would continue to be our teacher for the coming year and if we thought this year was tough we'd seen nothing yet. My heart sank. Why was this happening? Why had I to spend another year with this cruel man? I was horrified.

The summer passed quickly and from the first day of the holiday I counted the days with dread and fear in my heart until that terrible Monday in September came and I had to face him yet again. Nothing had changed. Right from the start he was on my back. He said so many unpleasant and hurtful things to me I lost count. My mother went to him regularly and pleaded with him to stop and still he didn't change.

The family doctor gave my mother a note for him to say I was not well and on relaxing tablets, and to go gently with me. The doctor also gave my mother a note to take me to a counsellor in Crumlin Hospital, who recommended I be put in another class as this man was causing me great distress. The counsellor gave her a letter for the head Brother. However, when he was presented with it he persuaded

Mam not to change me as my Confirmation was only weeks away. He assured her that he would talk to my teacher and me and promised that everything would be sorted out. So Mam agreed, and really felt that it *would* all be sorted. But the promise was never kept. All that ever came of it was that I was called to the head Brother's office. He told me he couldn't understand why I was unhappy in my class, that he had checked with my teacher and he had told him I was a very good child. 'So go back to your classroom and it will be OK,' he said dismissively.

Then he pushed himself against me and tried to put his hand down the back of my pants but this time, unlike with the other teacher, I pushed him and his hand away. I think he got a fright because he stood back, his face white, and told me to get back to my class quickly. I wasn't going to let anyone push up against me in that way ever again. My hopes were dashed once more. Nothing changed: I went back into that man's class and prepared for my Confirmation.

Even then he couldn't give me a break. We had to learn our catechism off by heart – about a hundred questions, and if you failed to answer the question the bishop asked you, well then, he wouldn't confirm you. Again and again the Brother said to me, 'Do you understand, Storey? Stupid people like you won't get to be confirmed if you don't answer the bishop's question.'

The day of the dreaded Confirmation came. I had to get up early in the morning for 7 a.m. Mass and Communion. I was wishing the day away and the more I thought about the questions and tested myself, the more I forgot them. After breakfast I went to my room to dress myself and I felt really sick. I looked up at the Sacred Heart picture and begged for Jesus's help and then I called on my Angel, whom I still called Aidan. The room became brighter and he appeared in front of me. He placed his hands on me and said, 'Little Soul, what is it you want?'

I told him how worried I was and how I couldn't remember the answers to the questions. He smiled and said, 'Don't worry, I will look after you. Just you wait and see what we do for you. Enjoy your day and be happy.' This was the first time they promised me anything specific, but, being me, I still didn't stop worrying. All I could do was wait and see. So I went up to the school and into my classroom.

All the boys were there, most of us in our wine school blazers, grey trousers, white shirts and the wine school cap. We had to form a straight line in the yard and walk down to the church in pairs. When we reached the church we were put into our seats, the boys on the right side and girls on the left. I was about six or seven rows from the front. Great, I thought, if I don't answer the question everyone will see me being marched out of the church. I was terrified but kept thinking: my Guardian Angel said it would be OK. The music started and the bishop made his way down the aisle as we all stood and sang the entrance hymn. In those days once the bishop entered the church, the doors were closed and locked until the service was over. My legs shook. Before I knew it he was at the first row and had started asking the questions. Row by row he went and as far as I could see everyone had answered the question they were asked. But then again, all the bright pupils were seated in the front rows.

Now the bishop was at the row of boys in front of me. I started to shake. I think if he had asked me my name I wouldn't have known it. Everything was becoming a blur. I closed my eyes as he asked the last boy on the row his question. Oh God! Four more boys and then it was my turn. How was I going to explain to everyone that I wasn't able to answer the question? Then as he stood in the aisle the bishop said something to the priest assisting him and the priest nodded his head and smiled. With that, the priest indicated to our row to move forward a seat. The bishop skipped our row and moved on to the next. I was so pleased the Angel had done this for me! How great was that?

When the bishop had finished asking questions he went back to his chair and two by two we went up to be confirmed. We knelt in front of him, he asked what name we were taking – mine being Peter – and then he gave us a little slap on the cheek and we were now soldiers of God. When he had finished confirming us all he gave us a talk, saying that the Holy Spirit had descended on us all today and made us stronger in our faith and, like all the saints and martyrs, we would now have to be willing to die for our faith. We also took a pledge not to drink alcohol until we were over twenty-one.

The church doors were opened, the bishop left and we all went home. The day was then spent visiting aunts and uncles and being made a fuss of. Just as they had on my First Communion day, they all gave me money to buy myself something. We had dinner in one house, tea in another, and finally supper. It was a great day and in the end I really enjoyed myself. That night, the Angels stood at my bedside and smiled and I went to sleep happy.

The next day we went into school for long enough to have our picture taken and we didn't have to take a schoolbag or books with us. It was a happy day and we all brought the Brother in a packet of cigarettes to say thank you to him. Twenty Gold Bond, I will never forget the brand.

It was the first time this man was ever nice to me. He took the packet of cigarettes from me, smiled and said, 'Thanks. Did you have a good day?' I was happy. Maybe he wasn't that bad after all. But how wrong could I be? The following week he was back to himself. Even when he was giving out the Confirmation photos he remarked in front of the whole class, 'Just look at the cut of you with your hat all crooked and to the Kildare side.'

For the next few months I put up with the same insults week after week. I wasn't going to the CBS secondary school: I had had enough of the Brothers so I didn't do the entrance exam, much to his annoyance. I had decided, with my parents' consent, to go to the local Vocational School in Inchicore.

By the last two months of my stay in that school I was counting the days but the Brother decided to give us a summer test. He loved giving tests. As we were about to finish our maths test I tapped the boy in front of me to ask him for my rubber, which he had borrowed earlier, as I needed to correct something. When the exam was over, the boy sitting beside me asked the boys behind me did they see what I had done? The two behind me said yes, 'he was copying.' I couldn't believe it when my so-called friend whom I had known for years went up to the Brother and told him I had been copying from the boy in front of me. I didn't know what to do.

He looked at me with his eyes popping, his face as red as a tomato and the blood vessels in his neck about to burst. He shouted at the top of his voice.

'Storey, come up here, you cheat!' He stood me in front of the class and told me that I was stupid, a cheat, and a good-for-nothing fool. I stood there and I started to cry. 'Look at you!' he shouted. 'Crying and shivering like all cowards when caught doing no good. Look at the state of you.' Then he spoke words I will never forget. He asked, 'What are you, a man or a mouse?' He waited a few seconds for me to answer but I couldn't; all I could do was cry. His next words were to haunt me for twenty years: 'You are nothing,' he said. 'Do you hear me? *Nothing*. And do you know what, Storey? You will never amount to *anything*. Get back to your desk, you good-for-nothing waster.'

That was my last day in the school. When I got home and told my mother she said I should stop worrying, that I wasn't going back and she would deal with it from here. The next day she went to the school, went to his room and when he came to the door to speak to her he told my mother he didn't want me back in his class. To his shock, my mother said she had no intention of ever letting me near him again; that he wasn't fit to wear the collar of God and that some day he would have to pay for what he had done to an innocent child. He told her that she could get into trouble with the school authorities if she were to keep me at home for the next six weeks. At this, she looked him in the eye and said, 'Well then, my dear man, you will have a lot of explaining to do. My son may be nothing to you but he is the world to me and I love him. I have seen you take every piece of his childhood from him, but enough is enough. No more from today.'

Many years later my mother was at a fundraising event in the parish and this Brother happened to be there. On the way out, the woman she was with turned to say hello to him and my mother stood with her. When they were finished speaking Mam introduced herself to him. 'I'm Mrs Storey, do you remember me?'

'No,' he said.

'Well, well,' said my mother, 'you should. I had to knock on your door often enough. I'm Aidan Storey's mother, do you not remember him? He remembers you.'

'Oh, yes,' he replied. 'I do now. How is he doing?'

Do you know what she said to this tormentor of children? My lovely mother said, 'He is doing very well, no thanks to you, and despite all you put him through. I hope God can find it in his heart to forgive you when your time comes.' Then she went on, 'You know what people say about the Christian Brothers: give them your boy and they will give you back a man. I gave you my boy and you gave me back a broken boy and do you know what? Despite all you put him through he is more of a man than you ever will be.'

She was so proud that night when she got home as she sat and told me what she had done.

Chapter Five

*The teacher who is indeed wise does not bid you to enter
the house of his wisdom but rather leads you to the
threshold of your mind.*

Kahlil Gibran

Life started to improve again when I left primary school. I
spent that summer in Dublin. I didn't go to Wexford because
I wanted to be around the family and my home, feeling safe
and taking it easy. I'd go out with my sister Breda to the shops
or the cinema, and I felt loved and supported by the family.
They knew what a very hard time I'd had at school.

I also got a dog. Her name was Trixie, a crossbreed black,
curly dog who stole my heart from the moment she arrived
in the house.

They say that pets come into your life when you most need
them, and boy did I need her. She showered me with love
and protection from the moment she entered my life. That
summer, Trixie filled my days. She went everywhere with me
and loved going for walks and playing in the garden. She
took my mind off the past years and stopped me worrying

about starting my new school in September. I took her for walks every day and this also gave me time alone with the Angels.

The Angels were still gentle with me and walked by my side just talking about general things, like how I was doing. Every now and then they would reassure me that everything would be fine in the new school and that I would do very well. I really wanted to believe this. It was at this time that I asked them about other people's Angels, explaining that I could see Angels around people often, but not all the time, and that when I was younger I saw them everywhere. They explained I could still do this but because I'd been so upset in school for the past few years I had blocked it out and wasn't able to concentrate but in time I would see them again. Then, one day in St Stephen's Green near the city centre, after walking the dog, I had just sat down to enjoy the sun and to rest before I started my journey home.

It was a lovely late August day and although the park was busy I had managed to find a quiet spot to let the dog off her lead. Now I sat looking at the people, who seemed almost far away. There was a strange but very comforting silence and peace hung over my space. Then the Angels made themselves visible to me. They were laughing and sat on either side of me. My Angel spoke and again the sound of his voice didn't seem to enter the space I was in; the gentle sound just flowed into my hearing. 'Would you like to see the Angels at work?' he asked.

'Yes, please,' I said, not knowing what he meant. But I felt safe and by this time Trixie had come and sat beside me. I am sure she could see them. The Angels told me to look across the park where lots of people were, some sitting, some lying down, some walking. Then I was instructed to close my eyes and open them again. When I looked back at the people there was a sea of Angels with them. They wore differently coloured robes and were standing by the people they were assigned to. Everyone had at least two Angels and they all looked happy. 'What are they doing?' I asked.

'They are protecting them and helping them just as we do you.'

'That's good. That one over there,' I said, pointing at a middle-aged woman sitting on a park bench. 'What is the Angel doing with her?' I asked.

'This poor woman is feeling a little sick. She has a bad head-ache and her Angels are healing her by placing their hands on her head.'

'Really? So that's what you do to heal someone, is it?' I said, remembering the word 'healer' that the man had used about me in Wexford when I was a young child.

'Well, it's not quite that simple. We will show you how it's done another day,' they said, and smiled at each other. Over by the pond a number of Angels walked or stood at the edge, almost in the water.

'What are they doing in the water?' I asked.

'You see the children playing? They are keeping them safe and protecting them from falling into the pond,' they explained. It looked as if the Angels were playing with the children as they ran in and out and all around the children sometimes helping them to catch a ball or cushion their fall and making them gentle so they wouldn't hurt themselves. Their robes flowed like a silk rainbow in the summer breeze. They walked very close to the old people and it was as if they held their arms and gently guided them along their way.

'This is what we do. We help people and we make it safe for them. We show you this so you won't worry about anything and to let you know we are here for you. Ask us for anything and we will give it to you, as long as it is for the higher good.'

I wasn't quite sure what was meant by 'higher good', but said, 'I just want to be happy in school next month and to like my teachers.'

'We promise you this will happen and we also want you to enjoy yourself and have fun again. We love you very much and we are your friends.'

I made my way home and a great feeling of peace came over me that day. I didn't fear the start of school after that. I started school in Inchicore a couple of weeks later and loved it. The teachers were people who really cared about you and helped if you didn't understand something. I was astonished. This was the way school should be. So, very slowly, I began to trust teachers again.

Shortly after I started, my mother was called to the school as they were concerned about the number of days I had missed the previous year in primary. When Mam told the Career Guidance Teacher my story she was assured that nothing like the bullying by that Christian Brother would ever happen in this school and that he would inform all my teachers of what had happened to me. From that day on, to the day of my Leaving Certificate, the teachers were wonderful to me, and school was good again, although I never really had the confidence I would have liked. This is something I have struggled with all my life.

My time in senior school is one I look back on and feel good about, and I can genuinely thank my wonderful teachers for this. I was still having visits from my Angels and I started to relax with them quite a lot. They spoke to me about the importance of having fun and not letting the past hold me back. They shimmered in their elegant pale robes. So every day over the years these amazing Beings of Light would come visit me and help me with anything that was worrying me.

Then, one day in school, when I was about fourteen, my classmates started talking about ghosts, spirits and the devil, and what they did, and the stories about haunted houses and how spirits could overtake you and make you do things that were evil. Then I heard myself asking the question out loud. 'What about your Guardian Angels? Don't they keep you safe from all that evil stuff?'

My friends all looked at me and laughed. 'You are joking, aren't you? Nobody believes in that, you eejit.' I laughed back at them as if to say: only joking.

This played on my mind for the rest of the day and evening. The next day was Saturday and after breakfast I went down to the end of our garden beside the river and called on my Angels to come. Within seconds they were standing in front of me. A white mist engulfed us and they looked more serene than ever that morning. The angel I called Aidan spoke to me. 'Good morning, Little Soul, you are worried and a bit nervous today. Look – your energy is flat. Tell me, what can I do for you?'

I turned to them. 'You are Angels, is that right?'

'Yes, we are.'

'Can everyone see you, or is it just me?'

'Oh, my blessed child, everyone can see us but most choose not to.'

'Why can I? Why me?'

'Because you ask us for our help and you always knew of our existence.'

'What do you do and where do you come from?'

'We come from the same place you come from. God. The same God that made you, made us. He made us to help and look after you in life. We are your friends.'

'So I don't need to be afraid of you?'

'Never. We are here to protect you.'

'Why can I see you and what do you want from me?' I queried.

'You see because you believe, and you have never questioned. And you are here to help others to see and work with us. The people have forgotten about us and don't work with us any more.'

'So what do you want me to do?'

'You will tell people about us and our great power and how we can help them and make their lives easier. You too will help people and healing will come through you.'

I panicked. I didn't understand this and was sure I wouldn't be able to do it. And there it was again, that word: *healing*.

'I can't do this. Nobody will listen to me. No, no,' I protested.

They looked at me and smiled and then my Angel spoke very gently.

'Not now. But in time you will do this work and we will teach you more.' They enfolded me; their wings surrounded me in a group-like hug, before they left.

That weekend, loneliness engulfed me and I didn't know what was going on. Was this all in my head? Were they really there? But then, I thought, they are there to help me. Weren't they always around? Didn't my mother and Sister Imelda speak about them? Aren't they always mentioned in Mass? On and on I argued with myself.

I didn't know what to think. My head was bursting so I decided to ask a couple of people I really trusted. First I would ask my Mam. So as she worked her way around the kitchen I started with my questions. 'Mam, you know your Guardian Angel? Well, is he with you all the time?'

'Oh he is,' she said firmly. 'Even when you sleep, he never leaves your side.'

Good, I thought. At least they are there and Mam believes in them. Now for the big one. 'Do you talk to yours, Mam?'

'Oh I do, son. I'm always talking to her. She always helps and keeps me out of danger,' Mam assured me.

'That's great,' I said. 'Do you ever see your Angel and sit and talk with her?'

'Oh no, son, nobody sees them. They are only spirits and you can't see spirits, you just know they are there.'

'Right,' I said. 'You don't see them. They are spirits . . . but can some people see them?'

'Well, some very holy people and some Saints have seen them, but not everyone. But don't be worrying about that, Aidan love. You don't need to see them. You just need to know that they are there.'

I decided to leave it at that. Angel, spirit or ghost – which one was it? I fretted.

I then asked a good friend whose opinion I respected, on my way home from school one day. 'Do you believe in Angels?' I was hoping against hope his answer would be yes.

'No way!' he said emphatically. 'That's all mad stuff. Superstition. Someone hanging around you with wings and keeping you from danger?' he scoffed. 'Yeah, well, where are they when someone is murdered or killed in a car crash? No, it's a load of crap,' he said confidently.

'OK,' I persisted. 'What about ghosts?'

'Yeah, I *definitely* believe in ghosts. Everyone knows someone who has seen them, so they are there and most of them are evil.'

I was shocked. 'What do you mean, evil?' I demanded.

'They do terrible things on earth and their spirit lives

on for ever and they get no rest. This is their punishment. Sometimes they even pretend to be good spirits and say they will help you and then that's it, they take your soul and you are left wandering the earth for ever,' he declared.

I had heard enough from him and decided not to ask any more. He was frightening the life out of me! So I would give it one more try, I decided. I would run it by another friend and see what she had to say. She was in the Legion of Mary with me and I only met her on Wednesday nights. We were chatting away and I asked her about ghosts or spirits and if she believed in them.

'Yes, I most certainly do. Without question,' she said. 'They are people who died before their time and their spirit roams the earth until their time is up and then God calls them to rest.'

'Right,' I said. 'So they are not evil and they wouldn't do you any harm?' I asked anxiously, longing for reassurance.

'Well, I am not sure about that. I wouldn't want to be in a room on my own with one,' she said and she laughed.

'OK then, what do you think about Angels? Do we all have one?' I persisted.

'I don't think so,' she said, much to my dismay. 'We were told this as children so we wouldn't be afraid. Sure we don't need them. God will protect you,' she added, with a great air of authority.

It was all very strange. People my own age didn't seem to believe in them, and as for seeing them . . . well, the Angels had said not everyone does see them.

My friends didn't believe they even existed. The guys in school thought I was an idiot. Even Mam didn't believe you could see them. According to her only very holy people could see them, and that certainly wasn't me.

Maybe they were ghosts, I worried. Oh God, have I been

talking to ghosts or is it all in my mind? I was plagued with doubts and fears.

That night as I walked home after saying goodbye to my friend and I was alone, the nerves got the better of me and I begged the Angels, or whatever they were, to please not come to me that night. When I got home I went to bed and I was so afraid that I slept with my head under the blankets for most of the night. Was I mad? What was going on? From that day on I was terrified of them and didn't want to be on my own.

A few days later, and it was a cold, wet day. I had come home from school and the house was empty, which was very unusual as Mam was always there. I had sat down in the kitchen to do some homework, when the Angels stood in front of me and my heart started to race. They looked more radiant than ever and their energy was soft and calm.

'Hello, Little Soul, why are you so nervous and why does your heart beat so fast? Are you not happy to see us?' they asked gently.

What was wrong with me? I never was afraid of them and they always gave me such peace, but now I was so afraid I just wanted them to go and I found it difficult to speak.

'Yes, I am. No, I'm not. Oh, leave me alone. You scare me,' I heard myself say.

'Why are you afraid of us? We will not harm you, we are here to protect and mind you. Have we ever harmed you or hurt you, little one?'

'No, but I don't want you to be around me any more. Please stop coming to me. I'm not sure who you are and none of my friends believe you exist,' I tried to explain.

'But you believe, don't you? That's why you see us. We have told you this many times. It is what makes you different and special.'

'Well, I don't want to be different or special. I just want to be left alone and not be frightened. I want to be like everyone else.' I heard myself say these words but at the same time I felt I was being harsh and ungrateful – as if I was letting down a friend. They looked at me with their pale blue eyes and I could see love and understanding shine from them as one of them began to speak.

'We will give you what you want, Little Soul, and we will stop coming and stop being visible to you. But remember, we will never leave your side. We can't. As we explained before, we are with you for ever. If you ever need us just ask and we will come. Don't be afraid and remember there is no evil, only love. I know now that we will work together again and I know you will talk about us often in the future. You will believe again. As we have told you time and time again, ask us for what you want and we will help you. So today, Little Soul, we will give you what you want. We will leave your sight but not your side. Don't be afraid. Go and search for what it is you need to learn and be joyous in your life.'

Then with a bow and a warm smile they faded away slowly in the white mist and the room became still and silent. I felt cold and alone, something I hadn't felt in a long, long time. I sat at the table, confused. These Angels were my friends and had helped me and I felt safe with them – but on the other hand maybe they were ghosts and that wouldn't be a good thing, I reasoned.

From that day on I believed they were ghosts and didn't call on them again. I was completely spooked by them and didn't like being on my own any more. I even slept with my Rosary beads in my hands every night, just in case they were evil and made an appearance.

I pretty much got on with my life. The years passed and I finished school. I had enjoyed my five years there. I had been lucky enough to have had helpful teachers and good classmates. In all honesty, I was sad to leave the safety of the classroom and my friends. It was scary having to face the real world of employment and responsibility. It was the late 1970s when unemployment was high and if you weren't successful in obtaining a position in a bank or the civil service there wasn't much else open to you unless you emigrated.

Very few families had escaped losing a child to foreign lands during these years. A heavy, dark, depressed energy hung over Ireland. I hadn't really thought about what I wanted to do but one thing I did know was that I didn't want to leave Ireland, so after leaving school I spent my time cleaning floors and working in a restaurant.

After a year of this I decided to do a business course in a commercial college in Dublin. It was a pretty basic course where you learned computer skills and general accountancy. It lasted a year and I obtained a diploma on completion. I enjoyed what it had to offer and my fellow students were interesting and easy to get on with. The social life was great too. Like all students, we didn't study enough and often drank too much but we did have fun. A couple of months after completing the course, and after many interviews, I was offered my first position: in a small engineering company and with a salary to match. It was a miracle that I got this position and I was happy that I didn't have to leave Ireland.

It was a good place to work but even then I knew it wasn't what I should be doing. But what that was, I really didn't know. From time to time I prayed to my Guardian Angel and asked for him to watch over me and guide me, but always with caution, as I still didn't want to see anything. I was in my late teens at this time and didn't want to go to pubs or nightclubs, for they always left me feeling disconnected, tired and drained for days.

I grew fearful and anxious and didn't know what was

wrong with me. I became isolated from people and only wanted to be at home. My world was small, but safe. To the outside world I am sure I looked like everyone else my age, but inside I was a lonely, sad individual who was very afraid of change and terrified at the thought of having a relationship. So I turned to God and the Church for help and guidance. I threw myself into it fully. No taking it easy for me!

Every evening on my way home from work, I went to Mass. I started reading the Bible and said the Rosary every night before I went to sleep. The Church became a sanctuary – a good place for me at that time. I read, and I asked questions even though I believed everything the Church taught. And, like most people now and in past generations, I focused on sin and on God's punishment, not on the love and compassion of God.

Now that I had placed myself yet again in a place of control, and was very much controlled by everything I read or was taught by the Church, my mind became a hell to me yet again. So for a short time everything I did, or even thought, I questioned. My past came back to haunt me. The hatred I had for the Christian Brother and the guilt I found in myself because I couldn't forgive him tormented me. That made me even worse than him in the eyes of God, as I saw it then. Then the memories of the sexual abuse plagued me. I tried hard over this period to put it out of my mind and tried to convince myself that it never happened: it was all in my mind. No, it wasn't abuse and, if it was, well then I had allowed it to happen so that made me just as bad as that vile teacher and how could I tell anyone about it?

I felt so dirty and unworthy of God's love. I went to confession time and time again but couldn't bring myself to say the words. I was now in my mid-twenties and still carried the pain, the guilt and the shame. I continued going to church and looking for answers but just couldn't find peace, and finally, in my late twenties, I fell into a deep depression and couldn't cope any more. Everything had become too much: the past, my work, fear of going out and the conviction that I had sinned. By this time I had moved to another company and was having difficulty there with a manager I'd had a very good relationship with for a long time but who had, for some reason, turned against me and become very controlling and a bit of a bully.

I went to a doctor, who treated me with kindness and care. He put me on a course of antidepressants and explained how in three months' time he would reduce the dose and within six months I would no longer need them. Then he asked if I would like to go to talk with someone as he felt it would do me good. This person would help me to piece everything together and work with me on my fears. I agreed and he gave me the name of a psychotherapist who, he said, did counselling. He gave me her phone number and told me to do it right away. When I got home I rang her and she gave me an appointment for seven o'clock the next evening.

Her name was Mary and she lived in Rathfarnham. I was very nervous about going to her and didn't tell anybody, as I felt people might think me mad if I had to go to a shrink. Little did I know how much this woman would change my life or that she was to start me on a new path of under-standing.

THE JOURNEY

Love keeps no record of wrongs.
Love does not delight in evil but rejoices with the truth.

1 Corinthians 13: 4–7

Chapter Six

The seeds of beauty, goodness and truth lie within us.
Though often unacknowledged, they are the seeds from
which we grow to be strong beautiful people.

Sister Stan

It was 6 a.m. the next day and I was wide awake and had been for the last few hours. My sleep pattern was all out of order and I lay in bed exhausted, empty, and feeling sick. How was I going to get the energy to go and see Mary tonight? Maybe I'd cancel. I didn't have the interest and that was my problem. I had lost all interest in myself and everything around me.

I was in great darkness, a darkness that didn't let go of me and controlled everything I did or thought and there was no getting away from it. It followed me every waking minute. I felt as if I had a great big ball of knotted wool in my head, which I couldn't unwind, and it made it difficult for me to concentrate and make decisions. I was lonely, in despair, feeling totally worthless and hopeless. The crying I just couldn't control. Who cares? I'm the invisible man with the invisible illness, I thought gloomily.

Suicidal thoughts rampaged through my mind every day. Sometimes in the darkness of that world, like many others in the same boat, I'd find a reason to live or maybe discover that I didn't have the courage to kill myself. Going to bed didn't do anything for me. It was just the end of another miserable day and the start of a long, sleepless night of everything turning over and over in my head non-stop. Life seemed an even bigger problem in the stillness of the dark nights.

In that inky silence of despair you can hear your heart beat and feel it pounding and all the time you're twisting and turning and screaming at your head to stop, please stop. It's in that darkness that you realize there is no bright tomorrow, just one endless dark, agonizing day to follow the dark, agonizing night. When daylight does come, you are back in that black hole and it all starts over again – the heavy chest pain, the panic, the loneliness, the sadness and the darkness. And you plead for help. I didn't call on the Angels – at this time I doubted absolutely everything, even their very existence. They'd surely just been part of my imagination, I thought.

So many souls have endured this dark night of the soul but back then I felt I was the only one to go through such pain and misery. Where was that little boy who once had love in his heart, joy in his soul and the spirit to laugh and have fun? Then it hit me, it had been snatched away from me a long time ago. Those words that still haunted me: *'You are nothing. Do you hear me? Nothing. And do you know what, Storey? You will never amount to anything, you good-for-nothing waster.'*

How could that obnoxious Brother be so right?

The doctor had given me a month off work and this was my third day at home. I finally dragged myself out of bed and down to the kitchen, where my Mam made me tea and toast and did her best to cheer me up. She tried everything to get me up and about – even asking me to take her to places she didn't want to go! But I simply didn't have the energy. I could barely get myself into the sitting room to lie on the couch. I'd watch all sorts of rubbish on daytime TV, but couldn't even follow the silly afternoon soaps.

I was still debating whether or not to go to the counsellor. What excuse could I come up with? Being tired was not enough; I was always tired lately. Well, I couldn't drive, I was too sick and the antidepressants had made me even more drowsy and tired. That was it, I decided. I couldn't go. Great. I had the excuse I needed so I dozed off and went into a deep sleep.

I woke up with a fuzzy head and to the sound of my Mam's voice asking me the one question I didn't want to hear. 'Don't you have an appointment tonight with someone? It's time to get up.'

I heard myself saying, 'No, I'm not going.' I was in a very pleasant sleep and was annoyed that my mother had woken me up. She knew I wasn't sleeping at nights; how could she? I thought indignantly.

'What?' she said. 'You're not going?' Her voice was razor sharp and I knew that she wasn't letting me get away with this. I sat up, not really awake, and told her I just couldn't go. I wouldn't be able to drive, because the tablets were making me drowsy. But even that didn't stop her!

'Look, you'll never get better lying on that sofa. Get yourself into that bathroom and get ready, then come and have your dinner and you can order a taxi to take you,' she said in that voice you didn't argue with.

Oh why had I told her? I must remember to keep my mouth shut in future, I thought furiously. But I had a bath and got dressed. I looked a lot better but still felt shit and really didn't want to go anywhere. I had my dinner and called a taxi. I was so nervous, not only about meeting Mary, but also about going out in a taxi and then having to get one back home. My stomach was churning and my heart was palpitating as I heard the taxi driver ring the doorbell.

There was no going back. I was in the taxi heading for Rathfarnham. It was a lovely September evening with a clear sky and a warm breeze. All the way over I was thinking, what was going on? Me going to a shrink! How had I ended up in such a position? What would it be like? Would I have to lie on a couch and would she be asking me questions and taking notes? What would she ask me and what was I willing to tell her?

I had decided that I wasn't going to divulge too much about myself and that I would just listen. At last I arrived, and the taxi ride hadn't been too daunting. I was outside an ordinary semi-detached house with a neat, tidy front garden. I rang the bell, my knees knocking and my hands sweaty. Soon the door opened and a tall, heavily built lady in her late forties or early fifties stood there. She had dark brown permed hair and wore a navy twinset and skirt. I don't know what I was expecting but not what met me. 'Hello,' I said, 'I'm Aidan,' offering her my sticky hand, which she took and shook lightly.

'Welcome,' she said. 'Come in, come on,' as she waved her hands just a little impatiently.

So far I don't like her, I thought glumly as she opened the door to what looked like her sitting room. A tastefully decorated room with a large fireplace and couches on either side of it, and some little bits and pieces on tables around the room.

'Wait here, I'm not quite ready yet,' she instructed me briskly. Not liking this at all, I decided I would get tonight over with but wouldn't be making a return visit. About ten minutes later she came back into the room and started to light white candles, then she burned some incense with a horrible smell.

'Right,' she said in a rather grand accent. 'Let's get started. I'll tell you about me and then you can tell me about yourself. I'm a psychotherapist and also a holistic therapist and I work from a very spiritual place. To get you right we will have to work on the mind, body and the spirit. It won't be easy but the more honest you are, the better and easier it will be for you and for me. You will need four to six sessions and then we can assess how well you're doing. Is that OK with you?'

'Yes, that's fine with me,' I said.

She turned, looked straight into my eyes and smiled. Suddenly all my misgivings and doubts disappeared and I knew then it was going to be great.

'You are going to love this, Aidan. On the holistic side we will do Reiki, Hands-on Healing, and massage. On the spiritual side we will do the Cutting of the Ties. We will connect with Spirit, but we'll have to do the head stuff too, which will involve you talking me through what it is you feel is going wrong in your life. The work will be hard but we will only do whatever it is we need to do. No pressure,' she said. 'I don't ever want you to be worried about coming to see me. Look on me as your best friend: everything we discuss is between you and me and that's where it stays. Do you understand that?'

'Yes,' I said, feeling more at ease with her now.

'I'm a mix between your best friend and your worst nightmare but we will get on, and honestly, I am not as hard as I look.' She gave a big laugh and then gave me a warm hug. 'You thought I was a right bitch when you came in at first. I could see it in your eyes. We won't do too much tonight so let's get to know each other a bit better. How are you feeling,

Aidan? You look very afraid and your eyes are a little wild,' she said in a caring voice.

'I'm very sad,' I heard myself say, 'and I just can't seem to take myself out of this darkness.'

'Why are you sad?' she asked.

'I'm really not sure. I went to bed one night feeling OK and then woke up the next morning with this great, heavy darkness and I was in a deep black hole. And no matter what I did I just couldn't dig myself out of it.'

'Right, we have to see what we can do with that first.' She turned to me and asked if I'd ever had Hands-on Healing, and would I like to try it?

I told her I'd heard it mentioned and would love to try it. I was too embarrassed to tell her that years ago my father was told I was a healer but I didn't know what it was then, and still didn't.

'Let's go to the healing room upstairs,' she said.

I followed her as we went into a room with a high bed with white covers and pillows. The room was warm and calming; there were candles glowing and low music playing. I felt strangely at ease. For the first time in a long time I had not a hint of anxiety or tension so I decided to trust this woman, and to place myself in her care.

'Get up on that bed and make yourself comfortable,' Mary instructed me.

I did as I was told, looking forward to this so-called 'healing'. In fact, it was something I was longing to experience.

Mary said she thought this would be the best way to start my treatment and that she could balance my energy by working on the negative energy that had gathered around me. In time, healing would lift my energy and help the depression to pass. She explained that it would take more than one session but over the coming weeks we would mix and match treatments.

What had I let myself in for, and what was she talking about? I wondered a little apprehensively. I wasn't quite sure if she was mad or if *I* had actually lost the plot.

Then she told me to close my eyes and to relax and enjoy. She said that this was my special time and I would feel the very special healing power of God and His Angels.

That word – 'Angels' – stayed with me for a moment. I'd not thought about them and now, suddenly, Mary was reintroducing them into my life. It felt good – comforting – to have them back.

I closed my eyes and felt Mary's gentle hands on my body; first she touched my head, and then shoulders, stomach, hips and all the way down the legs to the feet. It was strange but extremely relaxing. Her hands were warm and comforting and I could feel a soft and gentle energy bring peace and calm to my body – especially to my head, when she worked on it. It didn't frighten me and it didn't feel weird. The treatment felt familiar and somehow very sacred. It was as if I could feel God and, stranger still, the old presence of my Angels. Not only that, but I could smell their very special scent, that delicate, mild scent of sweet pea on a warm summer's evening.

I lay there, relaxed and feeling a little more at peace. I prayed she wouldn't stop. I had not known peace like this for a long time and my head felt empty and light. I also prayed to my Angels and asked them for their help. Then someone stroked my right cheek very, very gently with the back of their hand. That touch that said all is well. That soft reassuring touch a mother gives a child when she is awaking them from a nightmare. That touch that makes you feel safe and loved.

It must be over, I thought, but I was not sure. I opened my eyes slowly, not really wanting it to be over, but Mary was nowhere near my face. She was at my feet; her eyes were closed and she looked very serene. I closed my eyes and lay there for another fifteen minutes or so feeling relaxed and a little confused. Then in a quiet voice I heard Mary telling me to open my eyes and to gently bring myself back to the present. As I sat up, she sat on the side of the bed and spoke to me in a caring way.

'Well, how was that for you?' she asked.

'It was great! I was scared at first but then it felt as if I'd done it all before. It felt good but very relaxing. I haven't felt that way in months,' I said, but I didn't tell her about the caress I'd felt on my cheek.

'Excellent. That's what I needed to hear and I picked up lots of things too. Your energy is very low and all your chakras are out of line and balance. You have very recent issues you need to deal with. You also have a few deep-seated problems, and we'll have to tackle those. All in all, Aidan, you're in pretty poor shape. That's the bad news. The good news is we can fix you, but it involves a lot of hard work,' she said in a rather upbeat voice. 'So tell me, can you take on this challenge?'

'I hope so, but how hard will it be?' I asked warily.

'It's nothing you can't handle and just think how much better you'll feel and how light your mind will be once you let go of that energy.'

'OK, I'll do it. I've nothing to lose,' I agreed.

'Wonderful – so I'll see you next week, same time, same place. We've done enough for tonight,' she said kindly.

I got home about 9 p.m., went straight to bed and slept much better than I had for a long time. But when I woke up early the next morning everything felt the same. Still, I did have *hope* and I liked Mary and felt she could help me. The feeling I had during that healing I couldn't get out of my mind.

What was she doing? How did she do it? It had felt so good;

I would love to work the way she did. And that feeling of the Angels around me. Was it really them or was I just imagining it? Why now, when I hadn't thought about them since before I left school and I was now in my late twenties? I began to feel optimistic: maybe they would come back and take away this terrible feeling. But then something inside me said, *'Stop! You are over-reacting. They don't exist. It was all in your mind. They were never really there.'*

I sank back into my bed and thought, yes, I *am* mad! That was all right when you were younger and believed every-thing you were told.

I fell asleep again and woke up a couple of hours later. While I was having my breakfast Mam came in and she looked surprised.

'Don't you look very well today! How did it go last night?'

'It was good,' I said, 'but it will take a few more sessions before I feel any better. I like the lady.'

'That's great; let's hope she can get you through this.'

I was glad Mam looked so pleased. She'd been worried sick because I was eating only bread and jam washed down with mugs of tea. It was all I wanted – comforting nursery food, I suppose. And I had lots of disturbed nights and felt tired all the time.

Little happened that week, although every now and then I got that feeling of the Angel hug. By the time Wednesday evening came around, I was quite happy to be going to see Mary again.

This time she gave me a big hug and, as she did, she said, 'What a beautiful healing hug you have, Aidan: you should hug more often.' Once in her room, she asked me how I was after last week. I told her I felt a little improved and that my Mam thought I was looking better. Mary was delighted.

'Once you have hope you can do it.' She smiled. She asked me about work and what was causing me problems. I explained that they had started someone new in the job and then given him the easier half of my workload. Then they'd promoted him and he was now my manager. The work they'd left me with was getting on top of me and I just couldn't cope.

Mary listened, every now and then asking the type of questions I imagined counsellors usually asked, like, 'How did that make you feel?' 'Did you respond to that?' and 'What were you feeling as you said that?'

About half an hour into the session we went up to the room for a healing and I lay on the bed. Before I knew it I was relaxed and she began laying on her hands. Her energy was even warmer this week, almost hot but so comforting I felt safe. I had the sensation of a gentle breeze flowing up and down my body inside and outside. A picture came to me of green air flowing into the soles of my feet, then passing up my body, out the top of my head and then covering the outside of my body. It was strange. I hadn't seen colour the last time.

While all this was happening I felt as if I had a group of people working on me. It didn't frighten me and I could have stayed there for ever. Again it felt sacred and familiar; the darkness that had invaded my life had gone and I felt at peace. This is what Heaven must feel like, I thought. Then someone touched my cheek again very gently with the back of their hand, the reassuring touch that said *All is well.*

My Angels were back. I could feel them and that was fine. It was like being in the presence of God. They were there and I just knew it.

Now I heard Mary gently calling me back. When she asked me about the healing I told her about the colour and about the feeling I'd had of many people around me. She explained that the green light was the healing energy light the Angels of

Healing brought and the many people I felt around me were the Angels and Guides bringing me healing. She wasn't a bit surprised. I lay there with my mouth open, for I'd never heard anyone speak so openly about Angels before.

How astonishing, I thought. Maybe I was not imagining things. And who were these Guides she was referring to? I decided I wouldn't say anything yet. She started to talk about my healing, and about the sacral chakra. She explained that it was where you held on to emotional issues and where your creativity was stored or, in my case, 'blocked'. 'We need to work on your anger and hurt,' she said. 'You have kept it bottled up for years and by doing this you are allowing people to control you.

'We'll start work on this next week. It won't be that hard, Aidan. Your Angels pointed out the problem very quickly,' she said as if this was perfectly normal.

'My Angels told you this?' I was taken aback.

'Yes,' she answered as she searched for her diary, not giving my question a second thought. I was shocked. I didn't know what to say. Was I hearing her right?

'Right, for next week I want you to do a little homework for me,' Mary ordered. 'Write out your strong points and your weak points.' She glanced at me and said, 'You look pale – are you OK?'

'I'm not sure,' I said shakily. 'Did you say my Angels told you what was wrong with me?'

'That's right,' Mary said, matter-of-factly. 'You know something, Aidan, we all have them. You are surrounded by them and they can help make your life better, so go and *ask* for their help. That's all they ever asked of you so don't be afraid. Now go home, but first let me see those beautiful eyes of yours shine and give me one more of those hugs.'

I had so much to ask but where would I start? At the door,

71

just before I left she said, 'I know you have a lot of questions, but I'll answer them next time. You did a lot tonight. Talk with your Angels.' Then it was as if she had read my mind. 'Look, you're not going to see them yet. You're not ready. They told me to let you know.' She laughed and said, 'They love you so much. You are blessed.'

On the way home my mind was all over the place. My Angels hadn't been around for a long time and I needed to find some answers to the many questions I now had.

How did Mary know I was afraid to see them? Could she see them around me and were they the same Angels I saw as a young child? What was going on? Did this mean other people could see them?

I must have looked very tired and a bit wild, for Mam looked at me and asked if it had been a hard night. 'It was,' I said, 'and I need to go to bed. I'm not sure what's going on. I'm a little muddled.'

When she brought me up some tea and toast she found me in tears. With the mixture of excitement, fear and anti-depressants I was exhausted. I just wanted to close my eyes and give my head some rest. I fell into an uneasy half-sleep.

My mind kept travelling to my past, dwelling not so much on my hurts as on the time with my Angels. I saw myself with them in the garden and on my walks with my dog, Trixie. I could feel them and see them in my sleep and they were unchanged, with their pale skin and the piercing blue eyes that looked at me with such love. It felt so good to see them. Then just as I was about to take their hand a group of people appeared and pointed at me and laughed a cold and jeering laugh.

In my nightmare the laughter and jeering became louder and louder and when I looked to the Angels they faded further away until they vanished and I awoke in the darkness and silence of my bedroom, my heart thumping and wishing the morning light would come.

I could handle it in the daylight, I thought. And I was right; in the morning everything did seem a little better. I got up earlier than usual, had breakfast and decided to go for a walk to get some fresh air and to see if I could make any sense of it all. This in itself was a big step as I hadn't been out on my own for weeks. As I opened the door I said my *Oh, Angel of God* prayer and, as I walked up the road towards the Phoenix Park, I heard myself talk with my Angels.

I talked to them and asked them to help me enjoy my walk and not to have a panic attack before I got home. They walked with me that day and I felt safe again. The darkness that had engulfed my life seemed to lift a little. As I walked I asked them to help me come out of this awful place I found myself in. I got home safe and even looked forward to going out again the next day.

That week went very slowly and the dreams continued much in the same pattern. I was dying to see Mary and wondered if she had any more messages for me. I asked for the Angels' help with other things that week – getting up earlier, reading, and doing things around the house – and they did help me. I was beginning to take more of an interest in what was going on at home and felt a little happier.

This time I decided to drive to Mary's. Then I wouldn't have to leave in the middle of a conversation when the taxi came. It was the first time I'd driven on my own for ages so I asked the Angels to help me get to and from my destination in good time and safely. It was amazing: 6.15 and usually the cars were bumper to bumper in the city rush hour but that night the roads were clear, there was very little traffic, and all the lights were green. The Angels were working for me again.

When I got into the hall of Mary's house she looked at me. 'Give me one of your hugs. I'm waiting all week for it,' she said.

I thought she wasn't going to let me go. 'You should bottle that hug. So many people need a hug like that. You need to start hugging yourself,' she said with a smile. 'It can be done, let me show you.' With that she gently took my two arms, crossed them in the front and then brought my hands around to the back of my shoulders. 'Embrace yourself tightly and say "Aidan Storey, I love you,"' she instructed me. I did this but didn't feel comfortable. She stood back and looked me up and down. 'You're looking much better. Your eyes are so very clear. Your soul is happy again.'

It was good to hear these words. We went into the sitting room and talked again about my work and how I was still not ready to go back. Again Mary asked why and how I would feel. She agreed that I still wasn't ready but soon I would be, she promised, and I would go back with more confidence. In time I would realize what was going on. Then it was healing time. 'We won't go to the healing room tonight because you have something to ask me,' she said with a smile. Now was the moment for me to ask the questions that had been bubbling inside since my last visit.

I asked her if she really believed in Angels and could she see them? She looked at me kindly and told me she had always believed in them and couldn't remember a time when she didn't see them. 'I can't imagine life without them.'

'Are you afraid of them?' I asked.

'No. Why would I be? They are here to help and guide us through life and they are another of God's great gifts to us. Are you afraid of them?' she asked me.

'Yes . . . I don't know . . . I'm not sure. I would very much like not to be afraid,' I said.

'Tell me about your Angels,' Mary said. So I told her how I could see them when I was a child and how they would talk with me and help me. She asked me to describe them.

'They are beautiful. Their beauty is not of this world. They shimmer in their robes of different colours. They stand about six feet tall and have piercing, pale blue eyes, large wings, which stand very firm and tall and they enfold you in them from time to time when you are worried or alone. When they move they glide and their feet never seem to touch the ground. When an Angel speaks their voice comes from somewhere outside our space and it is so soft and trusting.' My heart lifted again and I felt them gather around me as I spoke.

'You've described them well. They also show themselves to me in many shapes and colours. Some people see them as winged, others without wings, some see them in colour – and colour is very important when you begin to see them, but they say to leave that for now and it will be explained to you later. So if you can describe them so well, and they are so beautiful, then why are you afraid of them?' she probed.

I told her the story about asking my friends and how I found they didn't believe in Angels but did believe in ghosts and evil spirits. She looked at me and laughed. 'But you don't believe in that any more, do you?'

'Not really but I am still a little unsure and afraid of the Angels. Still, this week I've started asking them for help again in small ways and they are helping. I do feel better. I really do want to believe,' I assured her.

'There's no reason why you shouldn't believe in them, Aidan. They believe so much in *you*. They have gathered around you over the past week. They promise they'll start showing themselves to you very slowly again, but only when you're ready. Do you understand?'

'Yes, I do,' I said, relieved to be able to talk to someone who didn't think I was mad. 'Can you see my Angels or just your own?'

'Yes, I can see yours too and they are still as you describe them,' she said.

'What are yours like, Mary?' I asked.

'They're much the same as yours.' She looked me straight in the eye and asked: 'Right then: do you want to see them and do you want them back in your life?'

I took a deep breath. I knew my answer would change my life. 'Yes,' I said finally, 'but please ask them to take it easy and tell them I did feel them this week and it was good.'

'That's great. They are *so* happy and they said, "Welcome back."' To this day I can see Mary's face, her eyes wide open, looking straight into my eyes as she asked me, 'Does "Little Soul" mean anything to you?' The hair stood up on the back of my neck.

'Yes,' I said, 'it does.' The tears poured down my cheeks. I'd pushed all the bad things to the back of my mind and those words were the words that had made me feel safe. I needed to hear them this night just as much as I did when I was a child. They were among the last words the Angels spoke to me that day in the kitchen when I asked them to leave me alone.

'Good,' Mary said gently. 'They knew you would believe when you heard these words. Let's finish for this session and we'll meet again next week. In the mean time you keep working with your Angels. It's very important and don't be afraid,' she urged.

For the next four or five weeks when I saw Mary we talked and she gave me Hands-on Healing. We talked about work and about my time in school. I didn't mention the sexual abuse. I'd long since blotted that out of my memory – or at least, that's what I tried very hard to do. But I did tell her about the horrendous bullying I'd endured at the hands of the Christian Brother teacher; I said it was he who had taken my confidence away, and that I'd carried with me deep and painful memories all these years.

Mary was extremely kind. 'This man made you believe you were worthless and as a result you allow people to control and bully you,' she said. 'People see something in you they don't understand and when they don't understand they start to mistreat you because they feel threatened and insecure. This is about their insecurities, not yours,' she said firmly. 'Bullies will torment anyone around them, and then target the quiet one, or the one who is good at their job, or the one who has more friends in work than they do. Often it is people who have been bullied as a child who then become bullies themselves. Don't allow the victimization to continue,' she counselled. 'You were a victim long enough. Stand up for yourself and believe in *you*! You're doing a great job and let everyone at work know you are. And don't be afraid to answer your manager back. Ask him to explain what it is he's looking for. Play him at his own game.'

This was the sound advice Mary gave me. By now I had been off work for six weeks and was just about ready to face going back. Mary agreed to see me the week after I started back, to see how things were. 'Remember your Angels and work with them and they will make the starting easier,' were her parting words.

The Sunday night before I started back I sat up in my bed and asked the Angels to help me the next day and to stand with me in the coming weeks. The following morning, feeling nervous but determined, I arrived in work to find that nothing had changed. My desk was almost as I left it, just more untidy with mail for me everywhere. All the staff welcomed me back, and most of the management too. It was good to see everyone.

When the bully came in muttering something under his breath I finally decided, this was it! I would take no more nonsense from him. Very politely, I asked if he could repeat what he'd said because it made no sense to me. It felt good to challenge him, and this was a turning-point for me. I wouldn't let him get away with anything any more. He looked shocked at my attitude: he was used to shouting at people and getting his own way. I was exhilarated. Quite suddenly, I had stopped being a victim. It was a moment of victory.

It wasn't always this easy, but in time we reached a better understanding of each other and his bullying eventually stopped when he realized that I was no longer willing to put up with it. And although I didn't get any extra help with my workload, I stopped putting myself under so much pressure and things began to feel a lot easier.

When I went to see Mary I was very happy. She laughed when I told her about my manager and was surprised that I had started standing up to him so soon. Then I heard myself saying, 'But why would I be afraid? My Angels were everywhere with me that day, and have been with me ever since.'

'Our beloved friends are smiling so brightly at your words,' Mary said, delighted. 'They want you to understand that you have work to do in this company and when it's complete you will move on to other work you agreed to before coming to earth.'

'The Angels told you this?' I questioned, intrigued.

'Yes, they did,' she assured me. 'I need to do a small piece of healing on you before you go.' In the healing room I lay on the bed. Mary placed her hand on the middle of my chest and then said words I will never forget. 'You have tightness here in the middle of your chest and you have had it for years. Sometimes you think you're having a heart attack.'

How did she know this? I wondered. It was as if she could feel it too. 'Yes, I do have pain there,' I agreed. 'It often pulls me down and the pain winds me.'

'This is your centre of love and healing and you are not using it. You carry unconditional love and people are very drawn to your energy.'

'Not that I've noticed,' I said drily.

'Aidan, you were told a long time ago that you are a healer but all these years you've ignored your gift. People with problems, your friends, people at work, your family, and even at times strangers, come to you, and they pour their hearts out. You listen to them and they trust you. This is healing in itself. They go away feeling much better. Many times you gave them good advice and you didn't know where it came from. This comes through your Angels from God.'

Once again I was shocked by Mary's remarks. Was there nothing she didn't know about me? 'Tonight God will take this pain away and that will help you to work with this gift of unconditional love and open up many doors for you in the future,' she said briskly. She pressed her hands into my chest a little harder and I could feel my chest loosen and then relax. I opened my eyes. The whole room was filled with a wonderful cool white light and I felt the pain and tightness that had lain on my chest for years lift and go, and I was totally calm and at peace.

Later, Mary told me everything would work out for me in the future. She said I still had some healing to do, but that it would happen in time. 'The Angels will always help you and will send someone to help you with your healing. You've done enough clearing for the moment; start finding out who you are again. Start asking questions. Do some reading on healing and begin to work with your Angels. Tomorrow, someone will remark on how well you are looking and then you will start believing in yourself and this wonderful healing gift you have.' She was completely confident in what she was saying and I longed to believe her.

'So you do believe I can do healings?'

'Oh yes! You're very powerful. Don't be afraid of your gift. So, Aidan, let's call it a day,' she said. 'You don't have to come to see me any more. Go and do what you need to do. My work with you is finished.'

My heart sank as I thanked her for everything. 'You've made my life so much better, Mary,' I said with heartfelt gratitude.

'No, it was a great mix of God, the Angels, you and me. And life will become easier and better for you. I love you very much, Aidan, and I'm so pleased to see your amazing eyes shine so bright again and know your soul is alive,' she said warmly. I told her I loved her too and would never forget her.

'Give me one of your healing hugs,' she said. As we hugged tightly and for a little longer than usual I knew deep down I would never see Mary again. 'Remember to hug everyone, Aidan, your hug is very important. So many people will feel much better after one,' she reminded me. At the front door she looked me straight in the eyes as she had done so often. 'Don't be afraid and remember you are *very* special,' she told me. When I reached my car I turned to say goodbye, but her door was already closed and the lights turned off.

On my way home I reflected on what had happened over the past few months, how much better I felt and how much more strongly I believed in and respected myself. I felt I had come a long way in a short space of time.

Next day just as I was leaving work I bumped into a colleague and in a loud voice she said, 'Well, Aidan, I must say I've never seen you look so well in all the years I've known you. Can I have two of whatever you're on?' she teased.

'Thank you. I needed to hear that,' I said, marvelling at the accuracy of Mary's prediction. I headed home feeling happy and believing that everything Mary told me must be true. A new chapter in my life was beginning. The word *special* kept going around my head. I felt an eager anticipation to find out what being 'special' meant and was sure that the Angels would guide me on my new journey.

Chapter Seven

Happiness is good for the body but sorrow strengthens the spirit.

Unknown source

Over the next few months things really started to settle down for me at home and in work. The once dark and miserable days began to brighten and I was feeling a lot better in myself. I started to enjoy my work again now that I'd made a conscious decision not to allow anyone to step on my toes, and I questioned anything I didn't feel happy about. When the guy that was employed over me left, I was offered the position and took it. For the first time in ages I was confident and very happy; I gained respect from senior management and life felt good.

I was working with my Angels again and asking for their help and guidance. I had started to read up more on them, but back then the few books about Angels that were published were limited in content. What I did read made a lot of sense to me. Although I was talking to my Angels, praying to them and asking questions, I still didn't see them. It wasn't until much later that I realized that this was because I'd been through a serious depression. They felt I wasn't spiritually ready, and didn't want to alarm me.

I was very comfortable to have my Angels around me. All I had to do was ask them for help and thank them at the end of every day. The books also made me feel more at peace with myself. Knowing that many people believed in them and many had seen them was reassuring. Maybe I wasn't mad after all.

It was in the late 1980s that sexual abuse stories had started to appear in the newspapers and on television. The stories had shocked the country and like everyone I was very upset. The difference was that the upset ran deep within me. These stories triggered the painful memories I had been trying to suppress and I was hurt and angry all over again.

This anger wasn't only for the children I was reading about: it was also about me. Deep inside I was screaming. The sexual abuse was something I didn't want to admit to. I was afraid to think about it, afraid to dredge up the horrific feelings of pain and shame again. But there it was – in their stories, and that word again . . . *special*.

Eventually it all fell into place. I was reading about myself in most of these reports and I was only one of the thousands who had gone through this nightmare – and still were going through it. But what could I do? Should I tell someone, and if I did, would anyone believe me? Would people question why I'd kept it a secret for so long? After all, I was now in my mid-thirties. Did I really put it out of my head for all those years? Perhaps I could do it again: let sleeping dogs lie, I thought. He didn't rape me. I was over-reacting. Let it go.

The more I tried, the more difficult it became to blot it out of my mind. I remembered every detail. The noise, the smells, the fear. My hands would start to sweat and my heart would race. My whole body was shaking. I needed to get rid of these feelings. I'd run into the shower and wash my body over and over again. Even after all these years, I still felt unclean – just as I had as a small boy.

And the questions remained unanswered: *Where do I go from here? Who will help me? Should I tell the family or my friends?*

Then one evening on a walk, I ended up in the centre of town, in a church, waiting for confession. I was looking for answers and for some direction, and I thought maybe God would give me what I was looking for here in this church. Who better could you ask? Surely a priest could advise me on where to go or what to do. When my turn came I went into the confession box, knelt and waited for the priest to pull open the grid. When he did, a middle-aged priest with very little hair and a chubby face appeared.

I began as you do, 'Bless me, Father', and so on, then looked at him and decided I would tell him about what had happened and ask what should I do. In a shaky voice I heard myself say, 'Father, I was abused in school by a teacher when I was eight or nine.'

'Abused!' he said, squinting. 'What do you mean?'

'Sexually abused,' I said.

'Sexually? Yes, I see. So can you tell me about this so-called sexual abuse, then?'

I was taken aback by his lack of compassion and concern but I gave him the whole story and he listened with what I felt was great unease. When I was finished he didn't look at me. Instead he kept his eyes focused ahead of him and said, 'You must examine your conscience and ask what part did you play in this and why you left it so long to ask for God's forgiveness.'

I was deeply shocked and said, 'I didn't play any part, Father, do you understand? I'm looking for help. I was a child and yes, it happened long ago. I need God's help and yours at this moment.' I was almost pleading.

'You knew at the time that it was wrong but you continued to allow it to take place and you never thought of telling an adult about this? So did you not allow it to happen, then? Go, young man, and examine your conscience.' He shook his head in disgust and still didn't turn to look at me. He gave me absolution and my penance, shut the grid and left me in darkness. I was shocked. I couldn't believe it. It had taken me almost thirty years to speak to anyone about this or even to admit to myself that it had happened, and here I was, in a dark, musty box in the house of God, all alone.

I had moved beyond anger. Numbness filled my body and mind and it took me all my energy to get on my feet and push the door open. This numbness then seemed to explode and my entire body was filled with hatred. I spoke not a word as I made my way to the centre of the church to sit and reflect. From deep down inside my silence and in the quiet of the church I felt the need to scream and shout and roar. How *dare* this man say what he just had? With each step I took, the rage inside me expanded to proportions that words cannot even begin to describe.

I sat in the church and looked at my crucifix. Jesus, this Jesus I loved and who I knew loved me, where was He? I couldn't get my head around any of this. Until now, I had known at some level that I, the child, had no blame for that vile act. Now, though, this priest had planted a seed of doubt in my head, even though I was now in my thirties.

I remember quite clearly that my arms and legs began to go numb, and that there was a deep ringing sound in my ears that echoed those words *What part did you play?* Over and over it tormented me as I sat unable to move for what seemed an hour, wondering if I was in some way to blame.

The church was beginning to empty and candles flickered in the dusky light. I looked at Jesus and said to Him, 'I am tired, Jesus, just tired, and I don't understand what You or God want from me and at this moment I am *so* angry with You both. I came here looking for help – please don't break me again. Send me help and guidance because I can't do it any more. I am tired of the battles.'

Then as I was leaving I turned and said, 'You know what? I'm not sure I can or want to do this any more. I always try to do what is good and what is fair but this is not what I get back. Give me a break, God. For once, give me a break! As for you Angels saying, "All you have to do is ask and we will give it to you . . ." Yeah, right! I'm fed up with you lot too. I'm tired of being on your side and getting nothing back. And you know what? I'm not sure about any of your airy-fairy stuff any more. I'm exhausted and disgusted. Oh, and by the way, I will never be back to confession again.'

That night I went home numb and deflated and went to bed. As I lay in bed, my mind was buzzing. As the night wore on, I had second thoughts about the Angels. I remembered how they had helped me in the past and how they'd often come to my rescue and made things easier for me. So I asked my Angels to help me that night, to bring me understanding and to help me find my God – the God of love and compassion. I was grateful that this episode hadn't happened a few years ago when I was in the depths of my depression. I think that would have really pushed me over the edge.

I finally drifted off to sleep. Later that night I awoke. The room was filled with a radiant white light. Within this brilliant white were orbs of different colours, mainly purple, green and gold. I tried to reach out to them, but could feel nothing. All I know is that the room felt safe and I was protected. I wasn't afraid, so I asked, 'Who is there? Who are you and what do you want?'

From out of the silence a voice came. 'It is us, Little Soul; we are here to help you. Do you want us to enter your space?'

My heart lifted.

'Yes, please. Please let me see you,' I said eagerly. They floated over to my bed looking and sounding the same as when I'd seen them all those years ago. The look of love and peace in their bright blue eyes said it all. 'I am so very glad to see you again. Will you stay?' I said like a big child.

'We never left you. We helped you as much as you asked us and we even helped with some small things that you were too stubborn to ask for. We have never left your side and we never will,' they assured me.

'Thank you,' I said. 'I could really do with your help, for I need to understand about the vile things that happened to me. I am totally mixed up.'

'That's why we are here. We heard your call earlier and we don't want you to give up on us. We will help you understand. We love you and we will protect you.'

'I badly need help,' I reiterated.

'Get some sleep and we will talk soon. Sleep well.' With that the room went dark and I drifted off to sleep.

The next morning I woke up very early and had a great peace within me, a peace I hadn't felt for a long time. I lay and wondered if I had really seen the Angels the previous night, or had I just dreamt of them? Then I thought about the priest and what he had said, and felt my heart sink.

No, I told myself, no, it wasn't my fault – how could it be? I was only a child and didn't know what was happening. I hadn't told anyone because at the time I didn't like or even understand what was happening. I also feared that people wouldn't believe me, and so in time I had blocked it out of my mind and buried it so deep that even *I* didn't believe it had happened.

Even now as an adult I felt shame and fear. I was no longer angry, but I did feel the need to tell someone. The problem was, with the reaction I got from the priest, I wasn't sure if I should ever mention it to anyone again. The question '*Did* I have anything to do with it?' went around and around in my head all day.

By that evening I'd decided not to let it get to me. I had let it all go before and I could do so again. I now realized what the whole *special* thing was all about: that it was all about my Angels, so I would just get on with my life.

I vividly recall how I went off to my bedroom to do some reading and a little meditation but as hard as I tried I just couldn't let it go. I had arranged to go to Lourdes with my mother in a couple of weeks, and hoped I would find the answer there. But the way I was feeling now, I didn't want to go to Lourdes or anywhere else. I heard myself screaming silently, *Help me, please help me!* Suddenly, a still energy fell around the room and I felt a presence next to me. I looked around and saw my Angels standing there. They folded their soft, gentle wings around me and I knew I was safe. 'What is it that is upsetting you so much, my precious soul?' my Guardian Angel asked.

'I'm tired of not understanding why I always have something to worry about. Just when things start to go right in my life something from my past comes and upsets me again,' I replied.

'Well, let's have a look at what it is that's upsetting you so,' they said.

So I told them about confession, and what the priest had said. 'Do you really think you had a part to play in that, Aidan?' my Angel replied with great kindness.

'I don't know any more. I am so mixed up.'

'You, my dear soul, are not mixed up, but you are afraid. You are afraid to revisit that time because you think you will have to feel the pain and all the dreadful things that go with those experiences – that you will have to tell this to your family and friends and then explain your innocence.'

'You're right,' I agreed. 'I don't want to feel the pain and I don't want to tell anyone. I don't want their pity or the shame, but how can I stop blaming myself?' I asked in desperation.

'I know it is hard on you, but I am going to take you back to that time and place just for a few moments. You will be safe, I am beside you. Now close your eyes and feel yourself going back, travelling back in time to that classroom . . . and when you look to the top of the room you see yourself and the teacher. Tell me what you see,' my Angel said.

'The room is dark, the blinds are closed. He's standing over me, one hand on me, the other in his pocket.' My voice was low and shaky and I felt very apprehensive.

'Don't be fearful. Now what are you doing? Look at the little boy.'

I looked at this little boy. The boy is me, a very young child, and he has no concept of what is happening.

'What do you see?' the Angel asked.

'An innocent child,' I answered.

'Yes, exactly, an innocent child. Is he asking the man to do this to him?'

'No, not at all. He just wants to leave and he is very upset,' I said. 'I really want to give him a big hug. He's so afraid and so alone.'

'Now could this be your fault in any way?' my Angel asked.

'I know it's not, but it's that seed of doubt that people sow, do you understand?' I really wanted this sorted out.

Then they put this question to me: 'If you saw your niece or nephew of eight or nine standing at the top of that classroom being abused by that teacher would you blame them? Would you think they had any part to play in it and would you think them dirty?'

'No, no, no!' I exclaimed. 'I would want to protect and love them more and do everything in my power to help them. They are only children and they don't understand.'

'So why are you so hard on yourself and why can't you see that it's the same for you?' they probed.

'You've shown me how to look at this in a completely different way and I'll work on this. Thank you. But I will never understand why God would let this happen.' I was still confused about this aspect of it.

'Are children not the purest and most special gift God gives to mankind?' they asked.

'Yes, they are pure souls who bring great light into this sometimes dark world.'

'And do you think for a moment that God doesn't feel the pain of abuse? He is very sad when He sees man's inhumanity to man. It hurts Him also. Does God not dwell within us? Well, if so, then why should you think He wouldn't feel this pain? Remember always that God dwells within each and every one of us. You went through a lot in your young life and you will understand why all this happened to you very soon, and you will help others with all your knowledge. Don't be afraid: it will all fall into place in Divine Timing,' I was told.

It was the first time I heard the words 'Divine Timing', but they were to become my favoured and sometimes my most challenging words. The Angels were back; and from that day to this I have seen and talked to them every day. They are a huge part of my daily life and I do all my healing work through them.

Later I learned that every person carries the energies of good and bad, of light and dark, of love and hate and of the abused and the abuser. We all carry these energies and are all capable of using or abusing these powers. The only thing that sets man apart is free will and how people choose to use or misuse their power. Abuse is ego driven and again is mainly due, not to God, but to the free will of man, and to a lack of God in the abuser's life. People who abuse have closed hearts and shut themselves out from God's love and light and in doing so they inflict pain and suffering on the innocent. It is all about choice and free will.

Time passed. In the early 1990s I began to question lots of things about what I believed and what I was told to believe in by the Church and so I started my journey to find *my* God. It was shortly after this episode that I went on that pilgrimage with my mother to Lourdes, where Our Lady appeared to St Bernadette. Lourdes holds many happy memories for me and to this day it is one of my spiritual homes.

Once you leave the madness of the commercial world at the gates and walk down by the river and into the Grotto area, the energy and healing in this holy and serene place words cannot describe. The true energy of Mother Mary awaits you here, an energy of love, of nurturing, of hope and belief. Here, in what can be an extremely busy place, I always feel loved. Lourdes was my first trip abroad. I went there with my mother at the age of twenty-two and I have travelled to this place of healing every second or third year since. It would later be the last holiday Mam and I shared. Here in her beloved Lourdes she was to take ill and die six months later.

On my trips to Lourdes I take a walk down to the Grotto around 11 p.m. when most people are heading back to their hotels. I love it at that time. You can sit very near the Grotto and feel safe in the arms of Mother Mary. There in silence

I lose myself in prayer and meditation. The coolness and stillness of the night air, the gentle sound of the flowing river behind me, the smell of the hot candle wax and the flicker and brightness of the hundreds of candles burning away for people around the world make it a very sacred place, a portal to a spiritual dimension.

It had been one of those long, hot days in Lourdes, a day when I just didn't get a moment to myself. Everywhere I went someone from my group appeared. I had decided not to go to the torchlit procession and instead went to my room and read for a while.

Around eleven, I got very uneasy and couldn't rest so I decided to head down to the Grotto. I hadn't made my night visit and felt it would help me to relax. The Grotto was quiet; the night air was still warm so I sat a little further back than usual, closed my eyes and began to breathe in and out very slowly before starting my Rosary. The Rosary, recited, as it should be, very slowly, allowing you to focus upon the Mysteries, is a powerful meditation. I felt myself drift slightly and I began my prayer. Everything was still and I could feel my body and mind relax for the first time that day.

Suddenly, out of nowhere a sharp, cold breeze blew around me and brought me back to the moment and, as I came to, I noticed the figure of a very tall man sitting on the bench beside me. He was dressed in priest's clothing, a long, black heavy cloak down to his ankles, and was holding Rosary beads. He was looking away from me. I didn't pay him much attention; I looked away and returned to my meditation. With that he moved closer to me and in broken English said something I couldn't understand. When I looked at him, I saw a distinguished man with whitish grey wavy hair, a long narrow nose, bright eyes, thin lips and a kind and warm smile.

Gentleness and a great feeling of friendliness radiated from him. Underneath his black cloak he wore a blue cassock or robe, which was very unusual, but then again in Lourdes you always saw unusual clerical habits.

'Sorry, I didn't catch what you said,' I replied.

'You pray with a great heart; you are very close to the Blessed Mother,' he said.

'Thank you. I love to pray here at this time: it's easy to concentrate and meditate when it's quiet,' I replied, not really knowing what to say.

'Yes, the Blessed Mother hears your prayers. You carry a powerful healing energy which you must bring to the people,' he said in his unusual English. 'You haven't had it easy up to this point. You had a hard road and you still judge yourself. You are hard on yourself. This is why you can't see what you really need to see. Cast your burdens and your worries to the winds and set your soul free. Stop dwelling on the past and look to the present.

'The present is where your work lies, not in the shadows and pain of yesteryear. The God you search for is in your heart and in your knowing. Bring this God energy into your life and use it in your work. Jesus is your friend and He walks with you.' The man said this with fire in his voice.

'I am sorry – I don't understand what you mean,' I said, stunned.

'Your healing gift, that wondrous light that shines from you. You have been told about this by others,' he replied with a smile.

'What could I bring to anyone? I've lived a quiet life,' I replied, a little unnerved, to say the least. 'I don't have the education or the confidence to advise people. As for God's work, I am not worthy, ' I explained earnestly.

'Ah yes! God's work is not of paper and certificates. No, it comes from the heart and from love. You, my dear friend, are like the wise old souls. You sit, you listen, you observe and you learn. You don't interrupt, you stay silent and you only say what needs to be said. This comes only with wisdom and knowing, and this you have in abundance. This is your education. Your love is your healing: this you also have in abundance. As for worthiness, the very fact that you feel so unworthy is the very energy that makes you worthy.' With those words he lifted his hands to the heavens and his Rosary sparkled in the candlelight.

'What do you mean?' I asked, feeling nervous and wishing this conversation had never started.

'You need to listen more to what people are saying to you. They tell you time and time again how relaxed they feel when they're with you. They tell you that you look at things differently from most people, how much better they feel once they have talked with you and how you always have the right words to help or ease the situation. Very soon you will have people knocking on your door waiting to see you. Remember this,' he said with gentleness.

'OK,' I said, as words failed me.

'They don't have to tell you very much, do they?' he said.

'I still don't understand.' I was now feeling very uneasy.

'You can see Angels around people. Sometimes you don't understand what's going on but you see them. You can also see pain in people and you can see what they have been through. Your Angels give you messages for these people. Please don't be afraid of this. If you work with your Angels they will make things much clearer for you and for the people you will deal with. Don't be afraid: many people see them.' He looked at me and smiled.

'Yes, this I am now beginning to realize and I *do* want to know more about my Angels,' I said, feeling more at ease.

'Your Angels give you help, protection and direction. You must always ask them for their help. You have free will so you can choose whether to work with them or not. They won't hand you everything on a gold plate. If there is something you need to learn or experience in this life, well then, my friend, all they can do is give you direction and support. They will always do their best to make it easy for you. So you see if they were just to do everything for you you would never learn about life, would you?' he asked.

'No, I suppose I wouldn't,' was my answer; I was still not too sure what he was talking about.

'In each lifetime we learn new lessons and these lessons make us stronger and wiser,' he said. Then he stood up, and I saw the rich blue under-gown beneath his cloak. He crossed his arms across his chest, bowed slightly and said slowly, 'May the good God of light and love travel with you.'

After a couple of seconds or so he continued. 'May that very light that burns within your heart shine out to all who are in need of love, understanding and healing.'

'What a graceful blessing. Thank you so much and may God also bless you,' I said.

The man turned to walk away, then turned back and looked at me and said, 'In the morning go to the Sacred Baths and wash away your past and know that you are not to blame. Work with your beloved Angels and all your answers will be found. The waters will set you free and give you great peace.' He walked away, up the steps just behind the Grotto, a long steep climb for a man of his age. After a couple of minutes I looked away, blessed myself, and then headed for the same steps, hoping I would catch up with this great man, but when I reached them he was nowhere to be seen and when I got to the top there was still no sign of him.

I reflected on what he had said about God's work and how

he had drawn my attention to the times when I had helped my family, friends and workmates. These are those moments when you do small acts of kindness without realizing you are doing anything at all. It's listening to people's worries and troubles or being there at the right time. Helping them to see things from the other person's point of view, giving them that shoulder to cry on. It is when you don't judge someone for something they did or said. All these small things mean an awful lot to people when they think no one else is listening or caring about them. It's talking to that old person sitting opposite you in a coffee shop or bus stop. I was told these are great acts of healing and of love and yet many people, including myself, don't realize this is what we are doing. Everyone can do healing by just doing a simple act of kindness.

The streets were empty, all the shops were closed and there was no one on the street except for me and my Angels whom I called on for protection as I walked back to my hotel in the early hours of the morning. 'Who was that priest I was speaking to at the Grotto?' I asked my Guardian Angel.

'Ah, he was a very wise soul and you must listen to him, he came to help you tonight,' my Angel said.

The next morning after breakfast I went down to the Sacred Baths and the miracle water of Lourdes. Unusually, this day there was no queue and I went straight into the waiting area, stripped to my underpants and waited my turn to be called into the bathing area. A cold damp blue cloth was tied around my waist and I walked into a concrete bath of ice-cold water. I had done this on every visit to Lourdes but this time it was different. As the two men placed their hands on my shoulder and waist to submerge me in the water I felt no fear and when I came up from the cold water I felt free and much lighter.

I dressed myself without drying and I felt different. My body might have been wet but it felt clean and good and my head felt sharp and clear. I felt refreshed, reborn, and when I walked outside the sun was shining and everything was new and fresh. And as I prayed and gave thanks, my Angels gathered around me; I knew I was going to work with them and listen to them as never before. I couldn't wait for my journey to begin and to put all my questions to them.

Chapter Eight

But of that day and hour knoweth no man,
No, not the angels of heaven,
But my Father only.

(Jesus, in Matthew 24: 36)

I always said my journey of understanding and awakening started during that visit to Lourdes. However, my Angels assured me that it had started long before then, but that Lourdes marked the start of the *spiritual* soul journey I was now beginning. Life felt fresh and good again and I was better able to control the emotions and the pain caused by the abuse I'd suffered. I began to realize this was now in the past – a past that I had no control over. I needed to stop reliving it, to get beyond this barrier.

I now had hope and felt strongly that I had a far better future ahead of me. I didn't have to be a victim of my past. It was time to get on with my life and I was happy to be alive. Work was going well once more, but something in the back of my head constantly told me that I needed to be doing something different. But in those days the kind of spiritual path I wanted to follow wasn't too common in Ireland. I also lacked the confidence to make the change and was probably avoiding making the final commitment for fear of failing. Change wasn't something that sat well with me – but I just knew there was a missing link in my life and my work. I also knew I needed to find out what it was if I was ever to feel fulfilled and happy.

I began to have longer, deeper conversations with my Angels. They were certainly around a lot more often and I was no longer afraid of them. They were around everyone I saw. I realized fully at this time that not only could very few people see them, not many believed in them either! Yet these great Guardians of Love and Light stood beside everyone, protecting and helping – even those who didn't believe. At least two, and sometimes three, shimmering silhouettes of illumination stood behind and slightly to the side of each person.

These Beings of Light didn't take up any space, nor did they block the way or cause any difficulty when people moved around. This display of magnificent colour and gracefulness was a sight to behold and I began to realize for the first time in my life just how honoured I was to be given this blessed gift.

I now needed to work with them and to ask them for their help and guidance. To do this I needed to learn more about them, and to know what they expected from me. So over a period of several months, every night, before I went to bed or when I had the house to myself, I'd call on my Angels and ask them about themselves.

I wanted to ask them so much and decided I would start with some basic questions. I'd ask them to confirm for me anything I had read in books about them or anything I'd heard. Was I a 'Doubting Thomas'? I sometimes wondered.

I was still a bit negative even though I had come a long way. But the Angels were always patient and answered whatever questions I put to them. Our conversations would go something like this. 'Can I ask you some questions about Angels?' I'd say.

'You certainly can, my Little Soul. Anything you want to know about us I will tell you,' my Guardian Angel would answer.

'What are Angels?' I asked.

'We are messengers from God and Beings of positive energy and love, light and healing.'

'Why did God create Angels? What is your work?' I said.

'We bring His message to mankind. We bring answers to prayer. We help in times of danger. We care for you during your lifetime and at your time of death. We praise, worship and rejoice in God and His work. We are your link between Heaven and earth.'

'Is my Guardian Angel more powerful than other Angels?' I asked.

'Ah, powerful, that's not a word we use. All angels are equal and we all have our own work to carry out. So our work is equally important. Your Guardian Angels work very hard on your behalf and will always try to guide you and make your life easier,' he said, looking very pleased with himself.

'You say Guardian Angels: do we have more than one? I know I have more than one Angel around me at times,' I replied.

'Yes, you do, you have at least two. Some people may have more but always two,' he said, knowing what I was about to ask. He put his hand up to stop me speaking.

'One Guardian Angel has been with you in every lifetime and a new one comes to you every time your soul is reborn, to help and guide you. I am the one who has walked with you in every lifetime.' This Angel always came when I called: he was dressed in a beautiful soft pink robe, while the other dressed in either pale green or blue robes.

'So,' I said, 'what are your names, what shall I call you?' I was longing to hear some very biblical names.

'We don't have names. We don't possess any worldly titles. It is you humans who lovingly give us names. This makes you comfortable and it makes it easier for you to call on us. We love the earthly energy and the meaning these names carry,' he said with a big smile.

'Right, I'll call you Zechariah. I feel that's a strong name and it suits you because you were always very strong when you came to me in my early days. You also made me strong and helped me cope better,' I said to my pink-robed Angel. I gave a small bow and waited for his reply.

'I shall accept this beautiful name. Do you know the meaning of this name?' he asked.

'No, I don't, but I always loved the name,' I said, feeling more than a little foolish.

'It means "God has remembered". Isn't that glorious?' he said, very happy.

'I am so pleased with the meaning now I know why I picked it for you. God remembered me and sent you to help me.' Shivers ran down my spine at that moment. Turning to my other Angel I asked, 'What name should I give you? Your energy is gentle and feminine – I will call you Hannah. Is that OK?' I asked.

'Yes, I am very pleased. This name means "Graceful". Thank you,' she said.

'That is also beautiful. I picked these because they are among my favourite names and I felt they would suit you both and they do,' I said.

'Yes, beloved soul, they are very beautiful,' Zechariah replied.

'There are hundreds of Angels so do I work with both of you only, or can I ask others for help?' I asked, slightly confused.

Hannah spoke. 'There are billions of Angels eagerly awaiting your call for help. So don't be afraid. Work with them and with us, we can all help.'

'So when I speak with you is there anything else I should be doing?' I asked, to make sure I wasn't being disrespectful to them.

'When you communicate with us we ask that you simply speak to us as you would to your family, friends and loved ones.'

'Do you help us without us asking for your help?' I asked.

'This is always a hard one to answer. Generally you must call on us for help and guidance. Because you are Beings of free will it's up to you to ask for this help. If we were to interfere we might prevent you from learning a valuable lesson in life. But if you are in extreme danger and it is not your time to pass over and it's the will of God, then we are allowed to intervene.' He smiled and nodded. 'Your Guardian Angel never leaves your side and walks with you during your entire life. We will help you in times of danger and comfort you in times of illness and mourning. We are that strength and support that comes from within during these hard times. These are the times we assist without asking because these are the times you are often so lost you don't remember to ask. Remember also that when you call on God and ask for His help God will send us to assist you and any other Angels you may need at that time. God and the Angels love you without question.'

'What about the other Angels? How do I work with them?

How do I call on them when they don't have names?' I was totally confused at this stage.

'Names! You place so much importance on names and titles on earth. It's simple: all you do is call on the energy of the Angels you need to help in the situation. So if it's to do with work you call on the Angels of Career to help and guide you through the issue. If you need laughter and fun in your life you call on the Angels of Joy, and if it's relationships, you call on the Angels of Romance, and so it is,' he replied.

'Oh thank God, that sounds very simple,' I said, relieved.

'Yes, always keep it simple. Please keep it so simple that even a child can look and understand. Everything has become so difficult and hard to understand. Church and religions have made God so complicated. People have given up because they can't feel God's love. Religion often talks of the judgmental God and not of the loving God. This is the God you must find, and you will only find this God in simplicity and love,' Zechariah said.

'Where will I find this God? This is the God I have been looking for. This is the God Jesus speaks of but I haven't found this God yet. Where is He?' I replied.

'This God lives in every one of us. God lives in our heart and soul. God is love. When we live in love we live in the energy and presence of God. God's love is unconditional and does not judge. When you open yourself to God's Divine energy and allow it to flow through you, you are doing God's work of giving healing and love to others,' he explained.

'What part do Angels play in the healing?' I asked.

'God is the power of all healing and we Angels assist in bringing this Divine healing into the world through you. Angels use their healing energy to touch you on a deeper spiritual level. A healing can be a hug, a smile, a kind word or an act of kindness; it's when you open your heart to others with empathy, love, forgiveness and understanding without judgement,' my Angel said.

'Do Angels know everything?' I asked.

'Like humans, Angels are created by God; this means that like humans we don't know everything, nor can we answer everything. Angels are also subject to the Divine will. This is what we mean when we speak of Divine Timing. It's God that decides, not us. Only God holds all the answers,' they replied.

This was the way these conversations would go from day to day. I remember thinking how very accurate and appropriate the names were for my two Angels. These were names I had loved from a very early age and to this day I don't know where I heard them and why they were always there in my head. It also made a lot of sense to me that they didn't have names apart from the ones I gave them. I never called out their names when I needed them to help me. I remember calling for God and His Angels to come to help me. I do remember my Mam telling me my Guardian Angel had the same name as me but somehow I stopped using it a long time ago; and yet these names – Zechariah and Hannah – seemed to fit my two beautiful Angels perfectly.

I had nobody to talk to about these fascinating conversations. Going out to public places, like restaurants, bars or nightclubs, had become a nightmare. These places drained me of energy and I sometimes felt hemmed in and on the verge of a panic attack. My body would become heavy, I'd experience shortness of breath and extreme tiredness. The venues felt overcrowded with a mishmash of people, flashing lights, loud music – and, of course, Angels. And although part of me really wanted to stay and have fun, I found I could only stay for an hour or so before I felt compelled to fight my way through the crowded dance floor and to the exit. Once out in the street, I could breathe again. I'd wave down a taxi and get home as fast as possible. It took me two or three days to recover; I also suffered from severe migraines and vomiting, which didn't help.

At first, even though I was never a big drinker I put these episodes down to food or alcohol. So I stopped taking alcohol and was careful about what I ate when I did go out. But it made no difference, and I started to find excuses not to go. Little did I know then that it had nothing to do with the places, or with alcohol or food: I needed to learn how to protect my energy. I had so much to learn and longed to meet another like-minded person with similar beliefs and experiences.

I was never short of company during these times. I had a few very close friends, James, Bernadette and Christopher, and lots of acquaintances. It was just that I never felt comfortable going out to bars or clubs. It wasn't my scene. My friends never questioned this and never got cross with me when I didn't go.

I was very depressed at this time but didn't realize it then. What I did enjoy was travel and seeing new places. With James or Bernadette, I visited many parts of Europe, America and Asia. We always had a great time but, unlike most people of my age, I didn't spend these holidays drinking, dancing and doing drugs. My idea of a holiday was much more laid back: relaxing by a pool, reading, and eating in good restaurants in the evening.

Much as I had loved these holidays, at that time in my life I'd become a bit of a loner. It was around then I asked my Angels what was going on and where I was going from here. I explained I was feeling lost and needed their help and direction.

'My beloved child, open your heart wide to God's Divine

love, and become the shining light that God and His Angels believe you truly are. Follow your heart and say yes. Look deeper and find the real you,' Zechariah replied.

'I will – but you will have to help me find all these things you say I have. I will do whatever you want of me but I need direction. I need people around me that are just like me, people I can talk to and learn from. Will you send me this help?' I almost pleaded.

'This you can have. We will put people and opportunities on your path always. All you ever have to do is ask,' he said.

'Thank you,' I said. 'I need people and I need guidance too.'

Zechariah placed his gentle hands on my head; they felt cool and very light. Then, placing his hands on my shoulders, he embraced me and whispered: 'Everything will be good for you from here on. You will shine bright in your work now and you will find happiness. Go and find the real Aidan.' And with that he was gone, and a great sense of peace and fulfilment filled my body.

I was happy at this particular time in my life, if a little lonely, and the reason I was alone was because I needed to find myself – the Aidan I'd lost a long time ago. I had forgotten my true essence and I can truly say that now for the first time in my life I began to see things for myself, and do things for myself. I allowed myself time to sit and be still, or walk and think things through – and it felt invigorating. I could look at my life and say, 'Yes, Aidan, you *are* a good person.'

I was content to talk with my Angels and they had started sending the help I asked for. It was around this time a new girl started in work. Her name was Pauline and she and I had to share an office. She was only in her late twenties and I was in my early to mid-thirties but I soon discovered that she was highly evolved spiritually, and we got on well from the start.

Looking back, I know that Pauline had a major impact on my life. She believed in Angels and Spirit Guides and we shared many conversations and could talk for hours on a lot of absorbing subjects. It was so refreshing to have someone in my life who understood where I was coming from. We had much to teach each other. Pauline introduced me to her friends, who also believed as I did and had been on their journey for a long time. I began to socialize with them and had a lot of fun. Being on the spiritual path certainly did not mean that life had to be dull and dreary, devoid of fun and laughter. In those days when people spoke of you as being 'spiritual' they automatically thought you were 'holy' and 'religious', and I was far from being like this. Life was for living and for having fun. My whole world was beginning to open up in ways I'd never imagined as I progressed along this new and fascinating journey.

Chapter Nine

If one asks for success and prepares for failure, he will get the situation he has prepared for.

Florence Scovel Shinn

In the mid-1990s, spiritual and holistic work was just taking off in Ireland. But you had to be careful what you said to people, as many still believed you were dabbling in some kind of witchcraft, or even worse, black magic. Having a like-minded person around me every day at work made everything a lot easier.

At first we were very careful what we said to each other regarding our beliefs. It was as if we were circling around each other, testing each other out. But finally we opened up. It was a bright spring February morning; I'd had a strange dream the night before. It was to do with how a certain manager was going to ask Pauline to take on some of my work. It bothered me, because I got on very well with this manager. During tea break I related my dream to Pauline. We laughed and agreed it had to be anyone except this man, as it was clear that he trusted and respected me. We sat there trying to analyse the dream, coming up with all sorts of weird and wonderful things and laughing our heads off.

Pauline said she would ask her friend, who interpreted dreams, what she thought it meant. Back in the office we continued to talk about dreams and how certain subjects in dreams meant different things. It was at this point that I knew instinctively that Pauline's outlook on life was very similar to mine especially in relation to the spiritual path. About an hour later the door opened and the manager in my dream walked in. He went over to Pauline, sat by her desk and handed her a sheet of paper with an invitation to attend a meeting in Holland regarding logistics. She went white in the face. The invite should have gone to me, as I had been doing this work for the past ten years. She asked him to leave it with her. When he left the office we looked at each other, astonished that my dream had been so accurate.

I could feel that old pain of rejection coming back. I didn't want to go back to that place again: I'd thought I'd put it behind me. Pauline was just as upset as I was. She had been put in a terrible position and didn't know what to do. I wanted to clear my head, so after lunch I went out for a walk. I really needed time alone to talk with my Angels. As I walked, I called on them. I asked them what was going on with this manager and why was I being overlooked in work once again?

'This is not about the manager or how you carry out your work, Aidan,' Zechariah said.

'Well, what is it about then?' I asked.

'My Little Soul, it is about you standing up for yourself and not allowing people to take advantage of you,' he replied.

'But the damage is already done, I feel hurt and let down. I should be the one to go to Holland. Why is this happening just when I thought work was going well and I was happy there?' I protested. I could feel anger build up inside me.

'This is so true, my dear child, but why do you say it to me? Remember what we taught you. Everything in life is a lesson and you don't ask: *why* is it happening again? you ask: *what* do I need to learn in this situation? Once you learn the lesson it will never repeat itself,' Zechariah explained patiently, and smiled.

'So I should go back and confront him?' I asked.

'Yes, go back and claim what is rightfully yours. We will be by your side as always and if you can't find the words we will give you the words to say. Be strong. Your lesson here is to not allow old patterns to repeat themselves,' he said with great authority in his voice.

'My dream was telling me about this, wasn't it?' I asked.

'Yes, indeed it was, but as time goes on you will be able to understand your dreams much better,' Hannah, my other Angel, explained lovingly.

I was a little late getting back to work and Pauline was at her desk. I told her I was going to see the manager and confront him about the whole thing. She was relieved, and very happy to leave it to me to sort out. She asked me, was I psychic? She just couldn't get over how sharp my dream was. Another new word for me: *psychic*.

I wasn't sure, I told her, but things in my dreams often came true. Then she asked me about my feelings. Could I tell things about people without them saying anything? she wanted to know.

'Yes, I can often do this but I've never really sat down and tried to analyse anybody,' I replied. Then she wanted to know if people ever came to me for advice and could I see things they needed to look at or let go of? And tell them things about themselves that no one else knew about? 'Yes, it happens often,' I told her, wondering why she thought it was so unusual.

'Well then, you *are* bloody psychic,' she said.

I needed to find out more about this so she offered to introduce me to her friend, who was also clairvoyant. She felt we would get on like a house on fire. It was after 2.30 so I called on my Angels to walk with me and put the right words in my mouth as I went down to the manager's office. There, as he sat behind his desk, I could see his Angels standing behind him, tall and powerful, shimmering in yellow silk robes. He greeted me warmly, as he always did. 'Can I have a word with you, Hugh?' I asked.

'Yes, of course. Is there something wrong?' he enquired.

'Well, I was hoping you could tell *me* that. Can you please explain why you asked Pauline to attend the meeting at Head Office in Holland when I'm the one who does that work? I have to say I'm very disappointed with the way you've handled this, Hugh,' I said, almost gasping for breath.

My manager looked at me, upset and taken aback. 'I didn't think for a moment that you would want to go,' he said. 'It's a series of very boring meetings. Two days of listening to people going on about figures. They wanted someone from each country to attend. If you want to go, Aidan, by all means go. I'd be very happy to have you there. I'm really sorry if I offended you and it has nothing to do with your work. I just presumed you wouldn't want to attend.' He struggled to find the words.

'Don't worry too much about it. I was a bit put out and thought I must have done something wrong. However, I would like to attend,' I said, relieved that it had all been a storm in a teacup.

'Yes, go ahead, it's yours. I'll talk with Pauline later. Again, I'm very sorry, Aidan. I meant nothing by it,' he apologized.

We shook hands and I left the office. My Angels looked at me and told me how happy they were with me and how strong I was and that it was another lesson I had learned. It would show people that I could, and would, stand up for myself.

When I told Pauline what had happened, in some strange way it sealed our friendship. We arranged to meet up with her friend, Rebecca. I was thankful that Pauline had come into my life and was looking forward to meeting both of them on Saturday night. What is it they say about waiting for a bus? You wait for an hour and then four or five come together. Well, that was happening to me now: I was being introduced to people who had beliefs and experiences very similar to mine.

An old friend, Gerry, had returned from Australia after a not so happy ten years. He phoned me that week because he wanted to meet up on the Saturday but of course I had already made plans with Pauline. I was dying to meet up with him, though. We had worked part time together in the evenings, in a restaurant in the city centre, for a couple of years making holiday money, as we called it. We often met up and went out together. He'd do anything for a laugh and drank far too much. Like myself, Gerry had major childhood trauma in his early life and we understood each other. If we didn't feel like doing something we never had to explain the reason why to each other, we just knew.

He had met and fallen in love with his soulmate, as he put it, while on a three-week holiday in Australia. He returned home full of the joys of spring and immediately applied for his visa, sold his house, left his job and returned to Australia all within six months. Nothing would convince him he was doing the wrong thing. We spent endless nights talking about what he was doing and all the time my instinct was telling me he was making a terrible mistake. I had said this to him but he wouldn't listen. I had asked my Angels and his to help him see that it was a big mistake and I begged them to stop him or at least to protect him from being hurt. But my Angels told me they couldn't interfere and that this was an essential lesson for Gerry and it was something he had to do.

Being a friend, I had to tell him what I could see and that he was going to be hurt. When the money ran out, so would this so-called soulmate. I warned him to be careful as I could see that his newfound partner had some kind of addiction problem and Gerry would get caught up in that lifestyle and it would cause him a lot of grief and pain.

Gerry, being Gerry, laughed and told me I was off my head. They had spent three weeks together and were in constant contact by phone. He could see nothing of what I was talking about. My Angels told me to leave it and let him decide himself and so I did. Shortly afterwards he left for Oz happy, and, as he put it, 'in love'. Now, ten years later, he was home. We were to meet up on the following Sunday afternoon in town for something to eat. So I had two enjoyable social engagements to look forward to: it was great to be socializing again after my years of depression.

Saturday night arrived and Pauline, Rebecca and I met up in a small bar in Parliament Street. I was the first to arrive and I found a quiet place beside a wall. I always had to sit by a wall in those days, as it helped protect my energy and made me feel more safe, more secure.

I ordered a drink while I was waiting for the girls. The bar had a calm energy and the Angels were very much present. Soon Pauline and Rebecca arrived. Rebecca had the most amazing eyes that pierced you. You just knew that she could see inside your soul. She had a smile that would brighten the darkest of days and she came with a band of Angels all around her. Pauline introduced us, and when she gave me a big hug I felt as if I had known her for ever. The first thing

Rebecca said was, 'Thank God you're sitting by the wall: you must be like me – you pick up everyone's energy if you're in the centre. It's best if you protect yourself. We don't want to be drained tomorrow.'

She had a powerful presence; she wasn't that tall but I felt I was with someone about six feet tall. Her energy and warmth embraced people and they felt safe in her company. I am usually very shy when I meet someone for the first time and have to get to know them a little before I open up, but not with Rebecca. I knew I could tell her anything. She wasn't intrusive by any means but she was direct. After finding out about each other, where we came from, what we worked at, all the usual stuff, she floored me.

'You're very psychic, aren't you?' she demanded.

'Well, people say I am, but I'm not sure. I suppose I have told people certain things which came true but nothing major.' I shrugged.

'Nothing major to you, but to the people you helped it made a very great difference,' she said firmly.

'Rebecca is great at giving readings. She was always very accurate, she would knock your socks off,' Pauline said with great admiration.

'*Was* great? Does that mean you don't do it any more?' I asked.

'I never did it for a living, I only ever did it for friends, but it got too much and I stopped doing it,' Rebecca said.

'Can you do a reading for me some time?' I asked excitedly. I was longing to see what she would say about me.

'We'll see. Maybe at a later stage. I don't really like doing them now. They can have a very negative effect on me at times. Leave it with me,' she said, to my disappointment.

The bar was becoming crowded and as usual I started to get uneasy. I knew I would have to leave very soon and I really didn't want to. We had just begun a conversation about religion and we were all on the same wavelength and getting on extremely well. Then Rebecca looked at me and her eyes opened wide. 'You need to leave, don't you? You're starting to pick up heavy energy. Your aura is dropping,' she said knowledgeably.

'I don't know about my aura but my head is very light.' I was astonished.

'Let's leave now. You're coming back to my place and we can talk some more,' Rebecca said, grabbing her bag with one hand and my arm with the other.

We hailed a taxi and went back to her place, a perfect little house on the north side of the city, about twenty minutes from the city centre. The house felt warm and safe and smelt of sandalwood. There was a diffuse mixture of candlelight and dimmed sidelights, and soft music playing in the background. She made tea and then sat down and talked. She told me that my energy was very sensitive and because of this I could absorb other energies, especially if I was around negative people, or people in pain. She told me I needed to protect myself when I went out, especially if I was going into crowded places. She then showed me how to protect myself.

'It's no big deal,' she said matter-of-factly. 'Just call on Michael the Archangel and the Holy Spirit and ask them to shield you from negative energies. In your mind's eye cover yourself in their light. Blue for St Michael and white for the Holy Spirit.'

'That seems easy enough,' I said, impressed.

'You poor man, you must be worn out most of the time if you're picking up everyone's energy. And are you "seeing" most of the time too?'

'What do you mean?' I asked. I wanted to make sure we were talking about the same thing.

'You're seeing Angels and Spirits all the time. I saw your eyes dancing about when we were in the bar. You can't continue like this, Aidan, you'll burn yourself out. Tell them to give you a break.'

'And how do you do that when they're always there? That's why I never want to go out. I feel suffocated. Can you tell me what to do?' It was amazing: she seemed to understand my experiences so well.

'Well, I think you know what it is you need to do. Just ask them to go away and give you a rest – then call them back when you need them. You have to work with them on your terms or you'll go mad. They don't have a sense of time and their energy doesn't tire like ours,' Rebecca explained.

'I did tell them to go away before and they left me for a long time. I don't want that to happen again,' I protested. I knew I couldn't live without them now.

'Yes, but they came back when you asked them to, didn't they?'

'They did and they've been with me ever since.'

'So what are you afraid of? Call them when you need to see them and ask them to leave when you need space. If not, you'll burn out. Your Guardian Angel is always by your side, you know, and all you have to do is ask them to come and go when needs be,' she insisted.

We talked well into the night about Angels and how Rebecca worked with them to help her through her daily life. She could see Angels and communicate with them, just as I could. Pauline didn't see them but she could sense them and worked with them as I did.

'You don't have to see, you just have to know they are present,' Pauline asserted with confidence and I was impressed with her deep belief in their goodness.

We all agreed to meet again in Rebecca's house, the

following Saturday. Rebecca said she would show me how to protect myself and then we'd head off to town and see if it made a difference.

The evening had flown by. It had been one of the best evenings I'd had, and I felt that at last I had friends who understood me. On my way home I thanked my beloved Angels for sending these great people to me. They were pleased I was happy and assured me there would be many more like-minded people coming my way and that now was the time for me to come into my own energy and light. From now on everything would start to become easier.

Chapter Ten

We do not need to grieve for the dead. Why should we grieve for them? They are now in a place where there is no more shadow, darkness, loneliness, isolation, or pain. They are home.

John O'Donohue, *Anam Ċara*

The next morning I was feeling very light and my energy seemed unusually up after such a late night. It was still early and I didn't have to meet Gerry until around five that evening. I took Mam to Mass and then went for a walk in the Phoenix Park, Dublin's biggest area of parkland, where deer roam freely. The day was fresh with blue skies and white clouds but a sharp breeze. A good day for a walk.

The daffodils swayed back and forth in the cold breeze, bursts of golden sunlight in the grass. It was good to see the park coming to life again and the daffodils reminded me that Mother Earth's winter rest was over and that colour and renewal were returning to our lives. A great joy filled my heart as it does to this day when I look upon the beauty and simplicity of nature. My two Guardian Angels stood with me.

'This time of the year reflects the Jesus Healing Energy. The spring flowers and the budding trees reflect the risen Jesus, the living Jesus, His renewed love and strength. All that is born and reborn carries His healing energy. Just like Jesus, Mother Earth dies and comes back to life to delight, nurture and feed our bodies,' Zechariah said.

'So this is why so many people feel so much better in springtime?' I said.

'Exactly, it's the most powerful healing time of the year. At the time of growth and renewal you should make your wishes and create the life you want,' he said.

I made my way home and reflected on the Angels' beautiful message. Soon I was off out again, heading into town. It had been over ten years since I'd seen Gerry and we hadn't kept in touch that much. In fact, it was only recently that we reconnected. We met outside Fans Restaurant in Dame Street. There he was, I could see him a mile away, with jet-black hair and his big smile. 'How are you, mate?' he said in his best put-on Aussie accent and then gave me a big bear hug. He looked well but tired. He had lost a lot of weight but although his eyes were tired his energy was good. We went in and ate and we talked for hours.

He told me how he had been to hell and back but said that now he was in a good place and he was happy at last and had great peace. He laughed as he talked about the 'soulmate' and how right I'd been about everything I had told him, even including the addiction. Yes, his then partner had spent all his money and was mixed up in drugs and drink, and had dragged Gerry into the same scene. Gerry stayed in the relationship for about four years, until he was picked up off the street one night, having overdosed on drugs and drink. He had nowhere to live and no money. By his own account he didn't even know who he was. But by some miracle he survived and went into rehab and after a long and sometimes painful time he found himself again.

But now life was good and he was home for three months to see if he could settle in Ireland again. He was looking at me strangely and I knew he wanted to ask me something. Behind him stood the most splendid Angels, five or six of them dressed in pure white, and another two non-winged Spirits: one male not very defined but glowing in a rich gold light, the other female, also glowing but in a bright silver light.

'You want to ask me something, don't you?' I said to him.

'How did you know? You're weird, do you know that?' And he laughed.

'You know me. I still get these feelings, but I'm much more comfortable with them now.'

'Good. Can you tell me what you see for me in the future? I'm stuck and don't know what to do about going back to Australia. Can you throw any light on it? You were so accurate before I went to Oz, I should have listened to you. Would you tell me what you see now?' He looked at me like a lost child.

I became nervous, but I was also excited. This was the first time someone had specifically asked me to help them, and the first time someone had acknowledged that I was capable of doing this work. It was strange; the restaurant suddenly grew quite peaceful. We had a secluded corner where no one could see us.

'OK,' I said, 'let's have a look.' I called in my Angels and asked for their help. Gerry sat opposite me, his eyes wide open, and soon he began to confirm all I was saying. I talked about his past and told him he must learn from it and not dwell in that dark place. I was quite surprised to see that he was well advanced on his spiritual journey, that he believed in Angels and had great love for Jesus and Mother Mary, who, he informed me, stood beside him. Like many of us on this spiritual journey through life, he had found his God during the saddest of times, but he was walking a much kinder path now, and I was relieved that everything was looking good for him.

'But what about the future? Is it Australia or Ireland? What are they telling you, or what can you see? Come on, do what you do best and tell me what to do!' He laughed, but he really did want an answer, and some direction.

I looked and looked at his aura but couldn't see anything. What was it all about? I became anxious and didn't know what to say. Maybe I wasn't any good at this after all. Perhaps I had just been lucky up until now, or maybe it had been only guesswork. All I could see was a plane trip and then this awful feeling of sadness engulfed me. I asked my Angels for more help. Somehow, I couldn't get past this sadness and it worried me.

'Tell him to follow his heart and that someone else will make the decision for him,' Hannah said.

'Well, well, come on. You're getting slow in your old age,' Gerry teased.

'Ah, I don't know. I think you're right. I can't see what you are to do. Follow your heart, the decision will be made for you is what my Angels say,' I told him.

'That's good – maybe I'll get an offer I can't refuse and that will help me decide. These Angels are always coming up with surprises,' he said, throwing his head back and rolling his eyes.

'So you know all about Angels, do you?' I asked him.

'Without my Angels and Guides I would never have got through the last four or five years. They're very powerful, aren't they?'

'They sure are. They have given me back my life again too.

Tell me about your Guides. I see two different kinds of Beings with you. One in gold light and the other in silver light. The energy that comes from them is powerful.'

'Oh my God, you can see! Amazing! Well, silver light is usually associated with Mother Mary and gold with Jesus. It's great that you can see them and confirm they're there. Most times I can sense them but not always. Jesus and His Beloved Mother gave me a second chance. You'll probably think I was mad or it was the drugs and the booze wearing off but for weeks I could see them and feel them as they both, one after the other, held me in their arms and told me I would get better. They cradled me and sang gently in my ear until I was well and then I couldn't see them any more. But I know they watch over me,' he said quietly and I could see in his eyes the pain of the memory of that difficult time.

'You don't think I *am* mad, do you? You're so lucky to see them. See – I always said you were weird,' Gerry said, half laughing, half crying.

'Yes, that's me, weird, and I know how lucky I am. Can you tell me more about Guides?'

'Yes. In a few words Guides or Spirit Guides have lived human lives and have learned all of life's lessons. They're sent to us in spirit to help us with their knowledge and wisdom. Just as the Angels do,' Gerry explained.

'I'd really like to know more about them because I'm beginning to see much more clearly and I need to find out much more,' I told him.

'You should keep your eyes open for courses and workshops; they're usually great fun and you get to meet interesting people and learn a lot at them. I do them all the time in Australia,' he said with great joy in his voice.

'Where would I look for these workshops?' I asked, thinking: *this is not bloody Australia, this is Ireland!*

'I notice over here it's the health shops that seem to advertise them,' he observed as he signalled for the bill.

We agreed to call it a day and said we'd revisit the Australia/ Ireland issue at a later date. He still had about six weeks left before he needed to make up his mind and in the meantime he agreed to leave it with God and the Angels, knowing they would sort it out. He was excited because he was going to Greece soon for a week, to an old friend who now lived in Crete. We left the restaurant around ten and promised to do it again when he got back from Greece. A great sadness came over me as I left Gerry that night. I couldn't understand why as we'd had a wonderful evening, as we always did, and we'd laughed a lot. However, he had planted a new seed in my head and I was going to go to the health shop and see what courses if any might be coming up soon.

As I sat in my bedroom that night I gave thanks for all I had learned that weekend and for all the people I had shared it with. The Jesus energy was certainly very much part of my learning this weekend. It had come up a couple of times over the course of the day and I was hoping to learn much more in the coming weeks. What an honour it would be to work with and understand that special and sacred energy. That night I welcomed Jesus into my life and asked that He guide and direct me to do what I believed I was born to do. As I fell asleep I was covered in a beautiful Gold warm light, which felt firm but gentle and very safe.

It was work as usual the next day and Pauline and I had a chat about how much we'd enjoyed Saturday night. I talked about Rebecca and said how impressive I'd found her. Then I told Pauline about meeting Gerry.

The week went as every other week went, with the usual highs and lows, and thankfully there was nothing soul-destroying going on. I remember looking forward to going into town to check out the local health stores and I was looking forward to meeting up again with Rebecca, who would show me how to better protect my energy.

On that Saturday, just before I left for town, Gerry called. He was about to leave for Greece and he wanted to say good-bye and thank me for my help. In town I had a look around a few of the health stores and yes, they had leaflets with every kind of workshop known to man. I took some home with me to browse through.

That evening I took a taxi over to Rebecca's and she greeted me with a big hug and a smile. Her house was so relaxing and she made me feel very much at home. She made tea and then asked me about my week and how I was feeling. She looked all around me, her eyes dancing in the candlelight.

'Your energy is far better now than it was last week. You seem much more relaxed,' she remarked.

'Yes, I feel more at peace. I think it's since I talked with you and Pauline. You make this all very normal,' I said.

'Normal? What the hell is normal and who in the hell would ever want to be *normal*! That's boring.' She sighed loudly.

We were to meet Pauline in the same bar as before so Rebecca decided we'd better protect ourselves for the evening. She told me to stand in the middle of the room and close my eyes.

She then instructed me to call in my Angels and Guides and ask them to stand with me and guide me. Then she told me to visualize a bubble of bright white light and when I saw it to step inside it and seal and close it. This is the light of God's love, she explained.

Then she asked me to visualize a bubble of bright blue light within the white bubble and, when I saw it, to step into it and seal it too. This was the light of Archangel Michael the protector.

'You are now sealed in the most powerful light and energy which nothing can penetrate or enter. You are safe and protected,' she said, repeating it three times.

We then headed into town. This time the bar was much busier, and I didn't get to sit by the wall. I couldn't protect my energy and started to panic. Pauline came over with another girl, Maria, a quietly spoken young woman who helped me to feel at ease. We all talked for a while and stood around, but I felt my breath was about to go.

Rebecca looked at me. 'It's OK,' she said. 'Just ask them to make themselves invisible. Go on, tell your Angels to do this for you.' I took a deep breath and asked that they become invisible. I couldn't believe it: they just faded away and I could breathe again.

'Are you sure they'll come back?' I asked anxiously.

'I'm more than sure. I *know* they will come back. OK, just ask them to come back and then ask them to leave again,' she instructed me.

I did as she said and was astonished by what I was seeing. They came, and then they went when I asked them to leave. It was great. I was in control and it felt wonderful!

'Thanks, Rebecca. I can't believe it was that simple,' I said.

'Yes, it's that simple. Ask them for what you want – isn't that what they tell us? Simplicity is what it's all about, Aidan. Like you, honey, I had to do it the hard way first. Remember also, if it is only your own Angels and Guides you want to see, that's all you call in. Also, if in the course of the day certain Angels appear to you and it's not a good time for you to deal with them, ask them to go away. You can deal with them later when you're not so busy. In time you will know what you need and what you don't need to see. They are very loving

Beings and all they want to do is help you. So never be afraid to call on them. They will communicate with you only when you initiate the communication,' Rebecca said and smiled.

Surprisingly, I didn't feel suffocated or feel the need to leave the bar early. I felt calm and I was enjoying myself. Rebecca, however, did keep a check on me and I felt safe in her company. I also felt the presence of my own Angels much more strongly. I could sense them with me. There was still a part of me really wanting to call them back to check they were still there. Before closing time we went back to Rebecca's. I was still feeling calm and an overwhelming sense of peace came from within me. I smiled, thinking how different this was to the panic I had become so used to feeling. Rebecca knew I was dying to check that my Angels were still with me.

'Go on, call them in before you burst.' She was laughing and rolling her eyes to heaven.

I asked them to show themselves to me, first just my own, and there in front of me my beloved Guardian Angels appeared in bright light, smiling. I was *so* relieved. Then I called on Rebecca's and Pauline's and they became visible to me. It was as if I was seeing them for the first time. My heart was filled with joy. This would make life much easier. Now I was more in control. I was thankful to Rebecca for explaining this to me.

Over the course of the next few months she was to explain and confirm many things for me. I was grateful to my Angels for sending me these two very special friends. When I got home that night I gave thanks for the blessed day and the wonderful new lessons I had learned. Then I asked Zechariah why he hadn't explained to me about seeing and not seeing as Rebecca had. Did he not know that this would have made things a lot easier for me?

'My dear child, we have always said to ask for what you want and we will give it to you if it be God's will. Your lesson here was about asking and accepting help from friends in the human world. This is something you are not very good at doing. Asking for help is a sign of strength and power. Not asking for help is a sign of weakness and stubbornness,' he whispered.

'I shall remember this for the future,' I replied. So, not asking for help was a sign of weakness. How interesting, I thought, determined to ask for help in future, from anyone I might need it from.

From then on things got easier and, I suppose, I was more relaxed. I had also found a course I wanted to do. It was called 'Connecting with your Angels and Spirit Guides', and was being run in Navan, so that wasn't too far to travel. I booked my place on the course, my first course, and didn't tell anyone I was taking it. I wanted to go and experience it for myself. It was a one-day workshop on the last Saturday in April. Over the next few weeks I read a lot of books on Angels and had long conversations with my Angels but also with Pauline and Rebecca. It was good to air my ideas and talk freely about my beloved Angels.

Almost four weeks had passed since Gerry had gone away and I thought he must be back by now even though I hadn't heard from him. Or perhaps he'd decided to stay in Greece for good. I had intended to make the call for the past week or so, but for some reason had only felt OK about it that night. I dialled the number, expecting to hear his put-on Aussie voice telling me how cool and great Greece was and how I needed to get my butt out there.

As I finished dialling his number I knew something was not right. A very sad girl answered the phone. 'Hello,' she said. 'I'm Maeve, Gerry's sister. How can I help you?'

'Can I speak to Gerry, please? Did he come home from Greece yet?' I said.

She went silent, a broken-hearted silent.

'What's wrong? Please tell me. He is one of my best friends,' I said, feeling very apprehensive.

'Well, you see, Gerry went to Greece a few weeks ago and on his first night there he was hit by a motorbike and sent twenty feet up in the air and was killed instantly. We only found his phone book a few days ago and today I was to call all his friends and let them know,' his sister said, fighting back tears.

'So can you tell me where I can visit his grave? I would love to pay him a visit,' I said, stunned.

'It's strange you should ring today and ask that. Our parents travelled out to Australia two days ago and they're scattering his ashes on Bondi Beach. It was his favourite place. He found a kind of inner peace and love there,' Maeve said tearfully.

Words failed me. How could this beautiful soul who suffered so much be taken from us? How could this guy who made me, and so many more, laugh heartily not be with us? I was sad, really sad. Something inside me had just died and I was in shock.

As I walked in the park that afternoon it hit me that was why I couldn't see where he was going in the future and why there was so much sadness around his trip.

'Was this what I was picking up on? Did I see his death coming?' I asked my Angels.

'Yes, my dear child, that is what you picked up. But you won't see many of these, you will be glad to hear. You will also be very glad to know Gerry went straight to the Light and felt no pain in death, for he crossed with the greatest of ease. He was tired and had wanted to come Home for a long time. He said you were right about someone else making the choice for him to go back to Australia. It was his parents' choice in the end and he loves it there, lying in the sun. He told me to pass on this message: "Remain weird and remember your weirdness is your greatness," and that he loves you and always will.' My Angel laughed and said, 'You will understand.'

Gerry was probably one of the best friends I ever had and it was a great gift to have had this friendship. To this day Gerry walks with me and helps in my work. My first workshop was coming soon and I had decided to do this in Gerry's honour. Only a week to go before the workshop and I was really looking forward to it.

Chapter Eleven

All men by nature desire knowledge.

Aristotle

At last I was on my way to my first ever workshop and I was keyed up and surprisingly not at all nervous – I couldn't wait to see what was going to happen. It was a beautiful April morning and the sun was shining. I had given myself plenty of time to get there as it was Saturday and I wasn't sure about parking. Everything was going to plan. I arrived in Navan about half an hour early and found a parking place without any trouble near the holistic centre where the workshop was being held.

It certainly wasn't what I expected. It had an old shop front with an office on the ground floor and the centre was on the first floor. The door was locked but I heard music coming from upstairs so I knew someone was there. I knocked a few times but got no answer so went for a coffee in a small coffee shop I had noticed just up the road.

The coffee shop was tiny with about three tables and it was crowded. I spotted an empty chair and headed for it. After a few minutes a couple got up and left and I found myself sitting with a young girl. She was in her early twenties, with short fair hair and big wide eyes. She was very pretty. I had never seen anyone with so many Angels around them. We started to talk and it happened that she was also attending the same workshop. Her name was Anne. Her Angels shimmered in clear light around her, protecting her. It was almost as if they held her slightly off the chair she was sitting on.

Like myself it was her first time to do a course like this and she was very nervous. We finished our coffee and made our way back to the centre. I noticed even when walking her Angels held her on both sides and carried her a little, as if physically supporting her.

The upstairs room was nothing like I expected. I'd imagined a bright room with large windows and white walls, with a fresh, clean and airy feel to it. Oh boy, was I wrong!

What hit me was a small, dark room with a tiny window. It was full of smoke, loud American-Indian music, and a damp smell, and walls that hadn't seen paint in a least a decade. The lady giving the course, Barbara, was a jolly woman in her mid-fifties. She was very slim, with long jet-black hair, and dressed in what looked to me like old sixties, flowing hippie clothes in warm, autumn colours. She wore a lot of crushed velvet, which made her look quite exotic. She made us most welcome and told us not to be nervous. There were about ten people on the course, all around my age, in their late thirties/ early forties except for Anne. I was the only man present.

Barbara introduced herself, though most of the people there knew her. She burned more sage and cleansed us all one by one, to clear away the negative energy surrounding us, moving the smoke up the front of our bodies and down the back, humming and rolling her eyes as she did so. It all felt a bit strange. When the cleansing ritual was over she invited us to sit on the floor and make a circle around her. Then we were told to close our eyes, listen and relax to the sound of the beating drum while she shared with us the ancient Indian sacred healing chant.

For the next thirty minutes or so she chanted and banged on a drum, and to be honest it made no impact on me at all. I had to open my eyes before she was finished as I felt very uncomfortable and, looking around the room, I wondered what the hell had I let myself in for. There was Barbara sitting in the middle of us banging away on an old drum, repeating and repeating the same thing over and over again, swinging her head around and rolling her eyes and most of the people were doing the same thing. What was I doing here? How was this helping my spiritual journey? I just hoped it would get better. I called on my Angels and they stood in front of me shaking their heads with their fingers to their lips as if to say sshhh. I could see they were laughing.

When she had finished we remained in the circle and she asked us to exchange what we had experienced during the meditation. Well, they all had the most wonderful time and they had either travelled back to a past life as an American Indian, or had had a visit from an Indian medicine man; they were all on a high and very excited. My gaze caught Anne's and we shook our heads slightly and nodded as if to say, *I got nothing. Did you?*

This being my first class I told a white lie because I didn't want to admit I had experienced nothing, gone nowhere and been visited by no one, so I just said I felt comfortable and relaxed but hadn't seen anything and Anne more or less said the same thing. We eyed each other again and smiled. The group was very friendly and all agreed this was because it was our first time and we were probably apprehensive. Barbara was also extremely helpful and told us both to ask questions at any point and if we felt uncomfortable at doing anything, to tell her.

She then gave a talk on Angels, where they came from and how we should work with them and how we should call on them to help and improve our lives. I really enjoyed this. She talked a lot about Archangel Michael and how powerful he was at protecting you and how he could help you let go of the past and help you cut the ties that keep you there.

The powerful ritual of Cutting of the Ties made a huge impact on me. This is where someone can ask St Michael to cut the cords of negativity that bind them to a person, or to something, perhaps an addiction such as bad relationships, drugs, alcohol, food or gambling. This cutting, Barbara explained, couldn't be done in a workshop setting. You would have to come to her for a private session, as it could be a very emotional and upsetting experience. Everyone who had been to her for such a session agreed, confirming how powerful it was, and how good they felt afterwards. The morning went quickly and after lunch we were told we would meet our Guardian Angel and our Spirit Guide – and Barbara would even give us their names.

Anne and I went back down to the coffee shop for lunch and agreed that it wasn't exactly what we'd thought it was going to be. What the heck, we decided, curious to see what the afternoon would bring. Like myself, Anne was very much into her Angels: she believed in them and asked them constantly for help and support and they never failed her. 'Do you know, Aidan, I was so nervous this morning that I asked my Angels to carry me here. Would you believe that?' she asked. I just smiled and nodded in agreement, thinking not only did I believe it, I *saw* them carry her. I said no more as we didn't have enough time and I felt I didn't know her well enough to be so personal. When we got back Barbara asked us all to sit on the floor again and hold hands, crisscrossing our arms so as to link our energies to create a circle of sisterhood and brotherhood and to allow our energies to flow into each other as she beat her drum again and went off into her chanting and eye-rolling.

I wasn't having any of this! My energy was flowing nowhere and I didn't want anyone else's energy flowing into mine. I called on my Angels and asked them to protect me from this energy flow. It was amazing. They put something like an electric current of light all around me, making me feel safe and very protected, and I could sense the energy pass by me like a quick-flowing stream. I opened my eyes and saw my Angels standing there smiling and nodding their head in agreement with me. I was so glad I had learned from Rebecca how to protect my energy field.

When Barbara called us back from our meditation and we had disconnected our energies she told us she had met all our Spirit Guides and one by one she gave us their names and told us how they would help us in our life. I couldn't wait for her to get to me. So far each of the others had an American Indian for their Guide and they all felt very connected to their Guide. I did tune in but I could only see Angels around everyone. My Guide, I was told, was also Indian: his name was Muraco, or White Moon. He stood tall and brave and would help me achieve what it was I needed to in the business world.

I didn't know enough about Guides to have any sense of him around me and the message was very general. Nor, if I am being honest, have I ever seen or felt this great Spirit around me.

We had a short break and I got talking to a very nice lady whose daughter was going through a bad time; she was depressed and had split up from her husband about four weeks earlier. But she was still very much in love with him and didn't know what was going to happen. Then my Angel whispered in my ear, 'Tell her it is going to be all right, they will be back together. They have a baby on the way. Go on, tell her – she needs to know.'

I took a deep breath and told the lady what my Angel had told me. She looked at me with that look that says, *God love your innocence, but are you not listening to me?*

'It's not possible. He's with someone else,' she murmured. With that Barbara called us all back and we did yet another meditation, this time to meet our Guardian Angel, and it was a relaxing and a safe journey she took us on. I could see, feel and sense everything. When we came to meet our Angels I met Zechariah and Hannah. Barbara instructed the Angels to stand by our side for ever, then brought us gently back. She told us that during the meditation she could see our Guardian Angels standing beside us and we were all safe and well protected. Then she gave us names, which she'd received from them. When she came to me she stopped, looked at me and said, 'You know who your Angel is, you know his name. He is very powerful. You must continue to ask for his help.' She smiled and gave me a big hug. 'What beautiful warm energy you have, Aidan. There's healing in that hug.' I had been told that before, I thought, surprised to hear it again.

The day had ended and we all gave each other a hug and wished each other well. The lady I spoke to at tea break was the last person I said farewell to. She thanked me for the chat and my kind words.

Anne and I walked part of the way back to our cars. We both agreed that although it was an interesting day, it was a little strange in parts and it wasn't exactly what we were look-ing for. We were both looking for something more Angelic, more understandable; but realistically, this was only our first workshop and we had nothing to compare it with.

We hugged and exchanged phone numbers and promised to keep in touch. Yet again, it was great to have met another like-minded person to talk with and run things by. I reflected on the day and the workshop. What had I learned? I'd learned more about the Cutting of the Ties. Perhaps I had been meant to attend the workshop just for that, as I had learned nothing new about my Angels and nothing at all about my Spirit Guide. I just didn't feel any connection with the Guide Barbara had told me about. What was wrong with me? Was I resisting? I put this to Zechariah.

'No, my dear one, you are not resisting, this is not the energy you need to connect with yet. You are tired and we will talk about this later but know that *everything* is in place and you need not worry.'

I was so glad to be home. I made myself a cup of tea and then went into the sitting room and flung myself on the settee. As my head hit the cushion I drifted away into a beautiful deep sleep. I woke up about 10 p.m. but still felt tired so I decided to go to bed, which was unlike me as two or three hours' sleep a night was normal for me. I got into bed and felt myself fall into a most peaceful and restful sleep.

At about 3 a.m. I suddenly sat up in bed.

My two Guardian Angels were standing beside me and the room was covered in mist. They radiated their energy, which was strong, and I knew something was about to happen. They assured me everything was all right but I wasn't afraid. I had complete trust in them and I was keen to know what was happening. They took my hands in theirs and I felt their warmth and protection, then they asked me to close my eyes and told me they were taking me on a short journey and not to open my eyes until they said so.

My whole body tingled with excitement. As I sat in my bed I rose out of my physical body and I felt light and free and at total peace. I could feel myself float and it felt good. After a few minutes I was told to open my eyes and I was speechless. They had taken me to a glorious meadow of lush green grass and yellow daisies. A forest, which stood at the foot of a mountain, looked almost barren compared to the meadow. The air was fresh with a warm gentle breeze, which carried that familiar scent of the Angels, of sweet pea on a summer's evening. It felt good but I still didn't know why we were there.

'Do you not recognize this peaceful place? This is your sacred place, your place of healing and your place of perfect peace, your holy place, your God space,' they said.

'This is mine?' I asked

'Yes, Little Soul, this is your place, your sacred place. No one but you, your Angels, your Guides and your God can enter this space. Here in this quiet space of stillness and silence you will move beyond the limitations of your physical body and reconnect with the healing energy of the Divine Master. Fill your heart and soul with this pure love and pure light and in accepting this your light will naturally shine stronger and brighter.' Zechariah bowed gently and smiled.

'I will accept this beautiful gift,' I said.

'So, my dear child, you can visit this place at any time. All you need do is close your eyes and call on us and we will take you beyond the physical to this place of perfect peace. In times to come this is the place you will travel to during your healings,' Zechariah said.

I didn't reply. I couldn't believe how beautiful everything was. It was all so bright, clean, fresh and invigorating.

'Let's go back. You have had a long, busy day. We shall return again,' he said.

I took their hands and within moments I felt myself connect back into my earth body and I was safe in bed. My Angels stood at my bedside as I fell back into a deep sleep.

The next morning I woke early. I felt as if someone had sucked the life out of me. My whole body ached. I was exhausted and my head felt heavy. I looked around my room and everything was still as it always was. Did I just have a beautiful dream or had I had the most wonderful experience of my life? I did my usual ritual upon awakening.

Every morning I look to the morning sky and give thanks for the gift of another new day and the light that it brings. I give thanks also for the protection it covered me with during the dark, restful night. Then I invite in the light of the Holy Spirit, all my Angels, Saints and the Beings of Love, Light and Healing. I ask to be protected and guided along my true path of learning and understanding.

That morning I couldn't wait to talk to my Angels. They came and explained that I had indeed travelled to my sacred place during the night and I would travel there very often over my lifetime. Tonight they would take me there again to meet my Spirit Guide, they said: it wasn't Muraco but someone who had stood with me since the day I was born. Hannah explained that Spirit Guides, unlike Angels, have taken human form and have lived many lifetimes on earth. They have learned all of life's lessons and in doing so have become the perfect soul. They choose to be our Guides and, like the Angels, are there to help and guide us along life's path. They are the wise old soul that dwells within each and every one of us. They are the voice that tells us right from wrong.

I was like a little child waiting for Santa. The day was dragging and the tiredness was not getting any better. I tried to sleep but couldn't. I felt restless and agitated. I had arranged to meet Pauline and Rebecca that evening for coffee and a chat so I forced myself to go. I was glad to see them again and I wanted to tell them I had been to a workshop. They were delighted I had made the decision to do it alone. Rebecca felt it was best to do that kind of thing with strangers so you could express yourself and be free to say anything without wondering what a friend might think. Otherwise, it is not worth doing them. You might restrict yourself if you knew a friend or acquaintance was there. Pauline said I should have asked her about Spirit Guides. She was reading a book about them and said she'd let me read it in a day or so. Rebecca thought it was spooky but interesting that we were becoming aware of them at the same time.

I said nothing about my sacred place yet. I felt I should wait until I knew what was going on myself. We decided to go home around eight o'clock. When at last I went to bed that night I gave my Angels thanks for my wonderful day and for all the help they had given me. I asked for their protection during the night hours and that I be kept safe under the darkness of the night sky. I lay in bed that night, exhilarated by the prospect of being taken by my Angels to meet my Spirit Guide.

Chapter Twelve

Hatred does not cease by hatred,
But only by love, this is the eternal rule.

Buddha

Hard as I tried, I just couldn't keep myself awake. I could feel myself drifting slowly into a deep sleep. Suddenly I awoke. My heart was pounding and the room was again covered in mist. My Angels stood on either side of me. They didn't say a word, they just took my hands in theirs. I closed my eyes and again I could feel myself leave my physical body and that floating feeling returned. Within minutes I was transported back to my sacred place. It was just as it had been the night before: bright, beautiful and fresh.

A short distance away what looked like a yellow bus was parked under a tree by a crystal-clear lake.

Zechariah instructed me to walk over to the bus and assured me everything was perfect and I was safe. Although I was walking I couldn't feel my feet under me. It felt strange but I knew I was safe, and I sensed that I was about to embark on an unusual journey to somewhere special. I wasn't at all fearful, just excited.

As I got nearer the bus I saw that the passenger door was open and there seemed to be someone sitting on the lower step. I looked around at my Angels but they just indicated very gently to move on.

The bus looked similar to the old yellow school buses you'd see in the American movies. It was surreal. This couldn't possibly be my Guide, I thought. As I approached I could make out the figure of an old man with white curly hair dressed in a light blue suit. He had his back to me and at that moment he stood up and turned around. Here stood the most beautiful old black man, small in height – only about five foot two – and stocky in build. He smiled a big wide smile to reveal a set of perfect white teeth, and his warm, chocolate-brown eyes glittered like diamonds.

He gave me the biggest hug I had ever had, then gently pushed me away, still holding my shoulders. He looked me up and down and smiled. 'At last you came. You took your time, Little Soul,' he said in a soft voice.

'You are my Spirit Guide, aren't you?' I heard myself asking.

'You're good. Yes, I am. You're surprised, I can tell.'

That was an understatement! I was more than surprised. He was nothing like I'd expected he'd be. I guess I was expecting someone more Angelic, Saint-like, or even a Native American Indian. A Being with an energy like my Angels. But what did I get? I got an old man dressed in a blue suit and a check shirt. His energy was more solid than the Angels', more grounded, and when he spoke his voice sounded just like ours; it didn't come from outside our energy field. Half of me was thinking, *Are they having me on?* while the other half was quite relieved he was so normal and I could feel his love and wisdom all around me.

141

'Do you have a name?' I asked

'Yes, you can call me Jack. That's easy, isn't it?' He laughed.

'That's very easy, I'll remember that.' I smiled back.

'Come and sit by my side and I will tell you a bit about myself as I already know everything there is to know about you,' he suggested, giving me a wink and placing his hand on my shoulder.

We sat down on the grass and Jack told me he'd had many past lives. Too many to talk of, and a mix of the good and not so good. He had chosen to become a Spirit Guide and I was the first soul he was to guide. He was looking forward to working with me and explained that, like the Angels, he could only guide me; he couldn't do the work for me because that would deny me very valuable lessons. He would help me if I listened to him and followed his advice.

He also explained all about the bus and his appearance. In his last life he had been an African-American living in the southern states of America. He had always wanted to drive the yellow school bus, but his sight was bad and he never fulfilled his dream. So he had taken on this persona and told me he would be taking me on a journey in the coming weeks.

This journey would help me clear old ways of thinking and old habits, so that I could move on with greater confidence, he explained; and I was not to worry or be afraid – as it would all become much clearer to me as time passed. The bus was to take me to the top of Sacred Mountain and from there I would see things more clearly and from a different perspective. Just then my Angels took my hands and Jack gave me a most loving and warm hug and reminded me that he would be by my side too and all I had to do was call him and he would be on hand for me.

My journey with Jack was to start in a couple of days. They

felt I needed to rest because travelling between the two energy fields would make me tired at first. I would adjust in time as I had to, because I would be doing this quite a lot in the future, I was told. Before I knew it I was back in my bed and in a deep sleep within seconds. I woke the next morning and the very same tiredness and exhaustion as before seemed to take control of me. Nothing would lift me.

My Angels assured me it would not always be this hard but moving between the two energy fields would always leave some tiredness. I did hope so, because I couldn't live with this exhaustion.

For the next couple of days I felt different. Although tired, I was also very relaxed but not fully here. I didn't feel connected to anything or anybody. I had that faraway feeling; people spoke to me but I couldn't make out what they were saying, nor did I need to. A smile and a nod of my head seemed to satisfy everyone.

Gradually, over the next three days my energy came back to its normal level. I had struggled to go to work but it was a special kind of tiredness and in fact I felt quite well and very grounded. Jack's presence was always very much around me at this time – earthy and solid. I felt I could almost touch it. His energy was that proud energy a father carries for his children. My much-loved Angels brought a much lighter, softer energy. But both energies carry the same God energy of unconditional love and protection.

It was four nights before I returned to my sacred place and this time Jack came and took me. We started our journey up Sacred Mountain right away. I looked up and saw that the mountain was covered in a soft white mist but the summit was clear. We boarded the yellow bus. It was old but clean and bright and had seats halfway down on both sides. At the back on the right stood a small metal filing cabinet and on the left a comfortable light green armchair and side table. Jack took me to the chair and I sat down.

He pointed to the filing cabinet. 'In this filing cabinet there are many files, some that need work, some that don't. These files carry the story of your life so far. I want you to start reading them from the beginning and when you're finished reading each file call me and we will work through it and see what it is you need to do and if you need to heal, or if there is something you need to let go of or something more you need to learn. This time we are going to work on releasing the pain and the hurt of the past. In your files there are things that will make you laugh and things that will make you cry and things you need to experience in life. Don't be afraid – you have already done most of this work. Little Soul, your Angels and I are here to protect and guide you during this.' He looked straight into my eyes and his dark brown eyes sparkled with great love. I knew I was perfectly safe.

From the cabinet he handed me the first file: it was a dusty blue file with '1958 to 1965' written on it in the most beautiful gold handwriting. I went back to the chair and couldn't wait to read what was inside.

Jack was now behind the driving wheel of the bus and we were already moving. I looked out the window but the mist was thick and had already blocked my view. I opened my folder and began to read. It was light and funny in places. It made me feel good and I was really enjoying reading it all; except for a short stay in hospital, everything felt safe. I had not lifted my head to look out the window since I'd begun reading but by the time I had finished the mist had lifted and it was clear, bright and fresh outside. The landscape was surprisingly dry after such a heavy mist. I sat back in the chair, stretched and told Jack I was finished. He stopped the bus and came down to me, a smile on his face.

'Well, how was that? Did you find any part of it difficult?' he asked.

'No, I found great comfort and peace reading it. The only place I felt sadness was when I was in hospital and I missed my Mam and Dad and family. I can still feel the fear I felt then, but mostly I was not sad or lonely,' I said.

'Fantastic! So what did you learn in that period of your life?' he probed.

'I learned a lot in those years. It was a happy time. It was safe. I loved my Mam, Dad, sisters and brothers and they loved me. In one word, it was "LOVE".' I felt warm and good inside.

'Love – how beautiful. A fine lesson to learn so young, and what a great memory to carry of your very early years. This was your foundation. This is what has shaped the rest of your life. Nothing can destroy love. Love is the pure energy of our Divine Master. So I want you to leave here now knowing love, knowing that you are loved and feeling love as you did back then: pure unconditional love.'

With that he took my hand and we stepped off the bus. He said we would meet here in a couple of nights to continue my journey. Within seconds I was back in my bed and fast asleep. Over the next couple of days my energy was low, as before, and so it was for a long time to come whenever I made this journey.

So began this great journey of learning, accepting, letting go and forgiveness. Over the course of the next five to six weeks every second or third night I went to Sacred Mountain. Everything was always the same.

The journey started with another file. The next period was '1966 to 1970'. These were the horrible years, the years of pain and shame, I thought as I read and reread this file. When I had finished I told Jack. He stopped the bus but the mist was still with us and the energy felt a little grey.

'It didn't go so well today, did it, Little Soul? I can feel it in my energy. We need to work together on this. You thought it was gone,' he said in the most loving voice.

'I still feel hatred in my heart for these two people. I don't think about them much now but when I do I just feel hate and I can't move past that,' I confessed, feeling hurt and angry.

'That's fine, we can work on it. First you will have to forgive yourself. This you still haven't done. Then we will work on forgiving your abusers. You *can* do this and your Angels and I will guide and protect you during this forgiveness ceremony. We won't be doing this tonight. I want you to read on another couple of decades before we do any work. It will be easier then because you will see more clearly what has happened and what it is you need to learn. Please don't be afraid: we will never let you feel any of the pain of the past again and when you return home nothing of what you read tonight will upset you. What do you feel you learned during that time?' Jack asked.

'To trust only a few and to guard your heart and soul because people can rob you of these glorious gifts. They are your essence and when people steal and break these they rob the real you,' I replied.

We left it at that and I was returned to my bed. The next few days were filled with reflection on what I had read as I waited to be taken back to continue the journey. Around this time I received a call from the woman I'd met at the workshop whose daughter was very depressed. She phoned to tell me her daughter and her husband were back together. He had left the other woman and begged her to take him back. Not only that, but they were expecting a baby early next year. She had called to apologize for doubting my message. I was so pleased she had rung; knowing everything was fixed up gave me great encouragement to listen to the messages the Angels gave me for others.

Soon I was back on my journey. The bus was still parked where we had left it a couple of nights ago and the mist had become heavy. The file I received this time was '1971 to 1985', my teenage years and up to my mid-twenties. This file would take two sittings so I was told to take my time and relax. It wasn't the worst time of my life. It was an up-and-down period.

Although I'd been happy in senior school and had made friends and was getting out and about with them, it was also around this time I turned away from the spiritual world and asked my Angels to leave. I'd started to have bouts of depression and looked to religion – and the man-made rules and rituals that it used – for answers. In a way, I turned back into myself, and I eventually almost stopped going out.

Even then, I'd allowed friends to use me and I became very good at controlling my own feelings and pretending everything was OK. It was my transition from broken boy to happy teenager to depressed man. Jack and I didn't talk again until I had finished reading the file completely.

'Good,' he said. 'Not as hard this time?'

'No, not so hard but exhausting. It was a time of great pretence when I put up a huge façade. A time when I did what I felt people wanted me to do. I craved approval then from everyone for all that I did or said.'

'Yes, it's those in-between years, the years of great growth and huge energy change in the human body, both outside and within. Your soul awakens, develops and questions everything during these years. Your soul moves from its childlike soul, which is the soul that doesn't question but just accepts, into the young soul, which is a searching soul and doesn't always accept what it feels. It's the time of the restless, often troubled soul,' Jack explained.

'I can now relate to that. It's how I would have felt,' I agreed.

'What did you learn during that period?' Jack asked again.

'*APPROVAL* – I was asking for other people's opinion and not trusting my own voice,' I replied.

'You are good, do you know that? You're doing very well,' he praised me.

'But where is all this leading to?' I asked.

Jack assured me it was all coming together and I just needed to have patience and not to rush things or worry about anything. For the past three or four weeks I'd been travelling between the two energy fields and at last was beginning to adjust. I was no longer heavy-headed or half as exhausted and I slept well the nights I didn't travel. In those early days Jack use to joke that one day I'd make a great airline pilot.

The next time we met the mist was beginning to clear and I saw that we were more than halfway up the mountain. Jack took me to the edge and told me to look out into the distance. Here I saw people in great numbers lining up waiting. To the right someone on stage was performing to an audience and to the left what appeared to be a classroom, and again people listening with great interest. I sensed that many of them carried a grey, depressed, heavy energy and they looked very worried and tired. I couldn't understand why he was showing me this, and why now? Why were these people in my sacred space? Was that not just for me? I queried, puzzled.

'My dear soul child, these people are not in your space. No one can enter that space. Do you not see how far away they are? They are outside your space but they are trying to reach you. They are waiting for you to come. They need your help and your energy. The stage and the class settings are also part of your future and what you agreed to do,' Jack said.

'What do I have to offer these people? I would truly love to help people, but how?' I asked, completely baffled.

'Well, believe it or not, it will happen soon and you will welcome it. People are already being put in your path. Keep your heart and your eyes open. Let's go and do some more work,' he said as he beamed his sunshine smile and gave me a comforting hug.

The next file was also very full and the golden date was '1986 to 1996'. It would bring me very near to the present day, which was now late summer 1997.

This was a period of contrasts for although it would prove to be one of the blackest periods of my life, when I walked through this world like a lost soul, bullied at work and with low self-esteem, I also experienced periods of great happiness because it was when I truly found my Angels and my God. I also experienced a peace that I hadn't had for a long time. The file was large and I had to come back a third time before I finished it and was able to talk about it with Jack.

'This one was very mixed,' he said kindly. 'I saw pain and sadness in your eyes at times, but I also saw those Angel blue eyes of yours sparkle and smile. You have come a long way and you have already experienced many of the lessons you came to learn. Be proud and know that all is well with you. What lessons did you learn during this period? You travelled from your young soul to your adult soul. The adult soul is the soul of self-discovery; it is the soul that finds answers,' my loving Guide explained

'Yes, it was a real rollercoaster of emotions; it has been great to look over my life and look at it now with no fear and no pain and I thank you for giving me this opportunity,' I said with heartfelt gratitude.

'So can you tell me what pattern you saw recurring in each chapter of your life?' he asked.

'Yes, it's clear to me now. I have allowed other people and situations to control my life,' I answered and reached out and gave him a hug.

'Ah, my soul child, you can't keep anything from me. Your hug is flat and your eyes tell me a different story. You are not happy within yourself. You are uneasy. You have to say what it is that is not yet settled in you. Please say it and then we can fix it for ever.'

It was true. He knew me inside out.

'It's forgiveness,' I said. 'I feel I can't heal because I can't bring myself to forgive those two teachers. As hard as I try, I just can't! They destroyed my life and they robbed me of everything,' I raged, the anger surging up in me.

'Good. You can now start to heal. You have admitted how you feel. But always remember, in forgiving you are not setting them free, you are setting *yourself* free. Staying in a state of unforgiveness is keeping *you* in the darkness of the past, in their darkness and under their control. The real you, Aidan, wants to live in the present. That's where your energy is needed and where you will find happiness. Don't allow bitterness and negativity to destroy your life. You need to be out there spreading your energy, your love and healing amongst the many people who are waiting for you,' he said.

By this time my two Angels had joined us. How could they take away this hatred I was feeling and how could they expect me to go out and do healings? Did they not understand the guilt and shame I felt for allowing this to happen? I hated myself and I felt unworthy to help anyone or to even attempt to do the work I felt called to do. Yes, I was blaming myself and I was still angry with those two abusers. I knew I had to move past this stage but I was blocked. My blocks were resentment and anxiety. My resentment was my hatred for those two men and my anxiety was my fear of moving on. Being the victim had become the norm for me. I realized how badly I needed help from both my Angels and Jack.

'First you will have to forgive yourself and admit your innocence. Remember that time I took you back in time? Remember what you said to me?' Zechariah said.

'Yes,' I said. 'I could see it happening.'

'Again admit your innocence and replace your fear with courage and then move into that inner peace of love, which is God, the energy of unconditional love,' Zechariah encouraged, and smiled.

Then it was time to deal with my abusers. I knew I had to do it or be trapped for the rest of my life in that dark energy. My forgiveness would set me free, it would cut the chains they had placed on me many years ago. These were the chains of guilt, shame and darkness. I saw them in my mind's eye – the abusers who had tortured me and caused me so much pain. I faced them, confronted them, and now, no longer fearful or angry, I forgave them. I asked that they go in love, light and forgiveness. I asked that they, like me, be set free from burden.

To end this 'ceremony', my Guardian Angels and Jack called on the energy of Archangel Michael to cut the ties that kept me bound to these two men. Michael stood tall and strong in a flame of blue-white light. He covered me with his light and I felt a sharp pull in my heart and an enormous outpouring of energy. His mighty wings enfolded me and he held me in his warm protective energy for a short time. Then they called on Archangel Raphael to seal the cuts so they would not reconnect.

Raphael stood beside me. His was a gentle energy. He was

surrounded in a green-white light. I too was bathed in this beautiful light. I felt him gently massage my heart. Then he blew a flame of his green-white light into my heart, and I could breathe easily again.

Then they called on the Christ Jesus energy to cover me in His gold light to heal and protect me. I still wasn't too familiar with the Jesus energy but I felt strongly protected when He was called upon. I didn't feel instantly at peace; I found I had to come back to my sacred space and repeat the forgiveness ceremony again and again for several months before I had a sense of having let go of those men. It was difficult to cut the ties.

Some weeks later I was having dinner with Pauline and Rebecca and we were talking about life and the pain that often comes with it, why this happens and what we need to learn from all of our experiences. I found myself telling them everything about the journey I had just been on with Jack my Guide, and my Angels. They didn't blink an eye. They believed everything I told them and they confirmed how well I would feel from now on. Rebecca looked at me and asked, 'Now that you have forgiven those two men have they taught you anything?'

'Yes, in a way I consider them to be two important teachers in my life. You could say I am almost grateful to them, for it is through them that I learned so much about empathy, under-standing and how to forgive. The actions of these two men made me search for the real God, the God of understanding and unconditional love – the God that does not judge, the God of love, and the healing God. This God that lives in us: He is the inner peace that lies at the heart of every one of us,' I answered. I felt very strong and at that moment finally knew that I had let go of the past. I was standing tall and proud – and I was no longer a victim.

'Aidan, did you ever feel you were meant to do greater things with your life?' Rebecca enquired.

'Yes, I know now I need to do other things. It will all happen in Divine Order and Divine Timing,' I heard myself saying, as if the words had been put in my mouth.

That night as I gave thanks for the gift of an incredible day my two Guardian Angels and my beloved Jack stood beside me, smiling. They enfolded me in their beautiful healing energy.

'The mist has fully cleared from Sacred Mountain. You have learned your lesson very well. You are good at this,' Jack praised me.

'You are no longer a victim. You are now *Victorious*. In forgiveness you have allowed a new chapter of your life to begin and given yourself permission to move on,' Zechariah said while Hannah and Jack nodded their agreement.

Chapter Thirteen

I have decided to stick with love.
Hate is too great a burden to bear.

Martin Luther King, Jr

No more loud, nagging voices, niggling doubts and rampant guilt: enough was enough. It was the late 1990s and I was ready to live my life and live it to the full and let go of fear, pain and hurt; I was determined to finally put my past behind me. In my morning meditations I asked my beloved Jack and my Angels to guide me to be kinder, more patient and more tolerant with others and myself. I prayed for peace in my mind, in my heart and in my spirit.

To help others and myself I knew I had to find this peace within myself, which is the source of the Divine, the God within us. I also asked them to guide all the people I needed to meet, to bring me to this inner peace so that I, in return, could bring healing to others. I still had to get used to having Jack around. Sometimes I'd jump when I saw him, but gradually I got used to his comforting energy and felt an extra layer of protection knowing I had a Guide as well as my beloved Angels.

Some months later on a cold, bright winter's afternoon, Mam had gone for, as she put it, 'her forty winks'. My sister Rosaleen and I had a cup of tea and we got chatting about Angels. Rosaleen had known for some time that I was interested in them, but she didn't really know that I could see them. She too was curious about the spiritual world and had encouraged me to go on courses to learn as much as I could. She had just started an Angel course herself, and attended classes each week in the local school. Rosaleen was perceptive and had a good soul, and she found the classes both exciting and relaxing.

She told me of the Angels she was learning about, and described the lady who gave the classes. Everything she told me reaffirmed what my own Angels were telling me. So, when I told her about my experiences with them, and how I could see and talk with them, she was not at all surprised.

'You were always a little bit different, always helping people. And you're always there for the family,' she said.

I was delighted with her response because it put me at ease and it felt good to have a family member to talk these things over with.

I envied her having the chance to attend the classes, but as they were held in the mornings and I had to go to work, I didn't have the opportunity to go. The good news was that the lady running the classes was about to give a one-day workshop and Rosaleen had already booked me a place on it. She thought it would do me good and help me relax, as she felt I was a bit stressed out.

I was eager to do it. I felt that something about this workshop was going to change my life.

The workshop was called 'A Day with your Angels'. My Angels were pleased and their light shone bright. I knew they were excited for me. Hannah informed me it would be an important day, with many more to come. 'It will change your life and open doors for you,' she said.

When my sister went home I was very uneasy for some strange reason so I decided to go for a walk. My Angels were very quiet and Jack, who never stopped talking on a normal day, had few words. This rare silence bothered me and I asked had I done something wrong. But they assured me everything was OK.

We had walked for another few minutes when in the distance I heard a thud and a screech of what sounded like car brakes. Then I saw a blue van travelling at great speed about thirty metres ahead of me. It looked as if there was something trapped under it and being dragged at God knows what speed – was it an animal? The van was swerving all over the road and I felt afraid. The street seemed empty except for a car following the van.

I heard myself shouting 'Stop, stop!' but the driver didn't. A tiny bundle at last escaped from under the van and lay like a rag doll limp and lifeless on the side of the road. I was still a little distance away, but the couple driving behind stopped. As I ran along the road I saw a *multitude* of Angels gather around the spot. Finally I got to where lay the body of a small girl of about eight, with long blonde hair, still holding on tightly to her little bag of sweets.

The lady from the car held one hand while I bent down and held the other. All around the little child gathered the Angels, in great light, attending to her and holding her. Then from behind her came a vibrant purple light and from within that light came the most beautiful Angel shimmering in many colours. I stepped away from the child. I had never seen or witnessed this powerful energy before or experienced such great gentleness and strength.

He appeared in a mighty beam of light, tall, youthful,

bearded, and his radiant energy extended way beyond that of any other Angel I had come in contact with. All the Angels stepped aside for him as he made his way to the stricken child. He bent down, gently embraced the little girl and kissed her on both cheeks, first the right one and then the left. Then he held her in his energy for a couple of minutes. Her energy changed, the tension went from her and she became relaxed. The mighty Angel took her hand and the spirit of the child left her body and a shining white light radiated all around her. He took the child in his arms and stepped back into the beam of purple light and they slowly faded away.

'That's good, she felt no pain: she was smiling a little,' Jack said reassuringly.

'That Angel, who is he? I have never met his energy before,' I said, in shock and awe at the accident and all I had witnessed.

'This is the Divine-like energy you call Metatron. He is the one who protects and guides children in life and beyond. She is safe now,' Jack replied. 'The Archangel Metatron will take the body and soul of the child to a place of eternal love and light and of perfect peace. Here in the Crystal Temple this perfect and precious child will be loved and cradled by the Angels, and also by the soul family and relatives who have passed before her. Here all fear and pain is instantly removed. Then she is placed in the loving care and energy of God.'

'Why did she die so young? And she's so beautiful. It doesn't seem fair to me,' I said, still shaken to my core.

'It was her time. She had learned all she came to learn and her death was her last lesson. She will need time to adjust now, as indeed will her loved ones here,' Hannah replied gently.

Although Metatron had left with the spirit and the soul of the child the other Angels protected her body until the ambulance people arrived. They attended to the little girl very carefully and with the greatest respect as they took her body to the hospital.

I was in deep shock for a couple of days after that. It was a terrible experience on a human level but what an inspirational sight to see the Angels attend to her and stay with her, and then to witness the great gentleness and love of that powerful Angel, Metatron. This gave me great comfort in the days that followed. To see a young child die because of reckless driving caused me to question at a very deep level. All the while my Angels and Jack reassured me that there *is* a Divine Plan to all our lives and everything happens for a reason. But still it was very difficult to accept. Yet I knew that I had been very privileged to be allowed to witness a soul making the transition from this earthly dimension to the heavenly realms.

Having the workshop coming up kept me focused and I was really looking forward to it. Two weeks passed quickly and at last the Sunday arrived. The workshop was being held in a training college on the north side of Dublin, a very different venue from the first workshop I had attended in Navan. Mary Cullen, the lady giving the course, had a light energy and she was very friendly. She had many Angels around her, shimmering in a golden-blue light. Her two Guardian Angels stood very strong and firm and their energy was most protective.

She smiled and greeted everyone at the door as they arrived. In the centre of the floor were fresh flowers, crystals, candles, an Angel figure and Angel Cards spread out in a circle. Mary had incense burning, and calming music played in the background.

The atmosphere was peaceful and safe. About thirty

people were there at the workshop, all women, except for another man and myself. The room was full of Angels, and beams of Angel lights surrounded everyone. The energy in the room was animated and a little giddy before we started. Mary began with a short talk about Angels, then conducted a meditation as she felt everyone's energy needed grounding. It was a simple exercise but extremely effective and we all felt the benefits.

She asked us to close our eyes and take at least three deep breaths, loosening our muscles and at the same time position-ing our feet flat on the ground so they were making contact with Mother Earth.

Then she said, 'Exhale any negative energy you may have stored in your body, such as worry, anxiety, past hurts, grudges, or any mental or physical pain. Then, one by one, release them into the earth, watching them sink deep into the soil beneath you. Imagine that energy being soaked up and healed by Mother Earth's nurturing healing energies. Now imagine the healing energy of the earth rising up through the soles of your feet. Feel this energy and see it as the healing green light of the Archangel Raphael. Feel this energy rising up through your limbs, into your torso, arms, shoulders, neck and head, and then out through the crown of your head.

'Next, visualize the pure, healing white light of the Holy Spirit streaming down from Father Sky in through the crown of your head. Imagine this light flowing throughout your body, and sinking into the ground through the soles of your feet. See the two energies mixing within your body, harmonizing and balancing your energies. Allow both energies to run for a few minutes and relax and feel the calming peaceful energy ground you.'

After a couple of minutes she then asked us to gently bring ourselves back to the moment, feeling more relaxed and more at peace with ourselves and our Angels. I found myself feeling very relaxed and at ease after this calming meditation.

This set the tone for the day. Mary gave several short talks and opened up the group by asking questions and discussing what different things meant to us or what we got from them. I was keen to know what the Angel cards were all about that lay in the centre of the floor. They were colourful and I had already asked my sister about them but all she told me was that I would love them. The workshop was excellent but Mary kept staring at me and she was making me rather uneasy. I didn't say anything to my sister at first because I thought it might be all in my mind.

At last it was card time. 'Just pick one card,' Mary instructed.

Then one by one she explained each card. I picked *Harmony*. I can still remember it well. The cards were beautiful and on every one there was a word or a message. I knew I would have to get a pack as soon as possible. And as Rosaleen had predicted, I fell in love with them there and then. The energy was sacred and everyone was pleased with their message; we all agreed they were very accurate.

Mary explained my card to me. It was all about harmony and balance coming into my life. I was at the start of a very new and exciting time, she said, which would bring a lot of happiness my way. It was a really positive message and certainly meaningful for me. Later, we would have another chance to pick a card from a different pack. Over lunch my sister introduced me to a friend of hers from the Angel class. Her name was Michelle and she was from South Africa. She was a friendly girl and we hit it off at once. She was very into the Angel work and was psychic too.

On our way back to the workshop I mentioned to my sister that Mary had stared at me all the time and that it was making me feel a bit uneasy. She told me to relax and not to worry. When we got back Mary had changed the cards but the energy and the feeling in the room were still safe and quite high. The afternoon was much the same as the morning, light but interesting, and everything Mary told us seemed to verify everything the Angels had told me or were showing me.

Every now and then my Guide Jack would tap me on my elbow and nod his head as if to say, *We told you so.*

It was comforting and reassuring to hear all the other people's experiences of Angels, as well as Mary's. It came to card time again and I couldn't wait to pick one. These cards were a lot bigger. I picked *Love* this time. Mary asked us to tell her what we thought they meant for ourselves. I was slightly nervous but could relate to the cards instantly. Everyone went 'aah' when I showed them my card and then they all laughed and said love was coming my way and I had better watch out.

After a couple of minutes Mary wanted to know what I thought it meant. I told her it was not about falling in love, but it was about me loving me, and being good to myself. Mary smiled and agreed and called me a wise old soul. The end came too soon, when we made a circle and gave a group hug and then hugged each other. It had been a terrific workshop and one I enjoyed hugely. Mary's simplicity and her kind, powerful energy were wonderful.

Just before we left Rosaleen turned to me and agreed I was right, Mary *did* stare at me a lot during the afternoon. Michelle had noticed it too. When I turned around, Mary was making her way towards us. Her energy was high and her Angels were all around her. She looked as if she was floating, the nearer she got to us. Mary smiled and asked if I was aware of the number of powerful Angels and Spirits I had with me.

'Your energy lights up the whole room. Go work with it. Your eyes can see things not everyone can see,' she said. This is what she had been staring at all day; she couldn't help herself, she explained. Needless to say I was delighted that she could see all this: it affirmed all the messages the Angels were giving me. It is a day I remember with great joy.

As I drove home, the Angel cards filled my mind. I couldn't wait to buy a pack. I dropped Michelle to her house and agreed to meet up with her soon. I was like an excited child for the next few days; I couldn't stop talking about the workshop. Christmas was only a couple of weeks away and the year 2000 was just around the corner. At work nobody knew what to expect when the clock struck midnight. Was the world going to come to a standstill and would every computer system in the world crash? We were frantically copying and backing up discs morning, noon and night. Everyone was waiting with bated breath for midnight to strike on New Year's Eve.

The Angels had assured me no such thing was about to happen and not to let it cloud my mind. Everyone in the Mind Body Spirit field was talking about the dawning of the Age of Aquarius but the Angels told me it was the dawning of the age of AWARENESS, which made a lot more sense to me.

To be quite honest, all I was interested in was how I would get my hands on these Angel Cards. I couldn't find them anywhere – I was beginning to panic. (So much for my lessons in Divine Timing!) A couple of days before Christmas my sister informed me she had located Angel Cards and had bought them for me but I couldn't have them until Christmas morning and she was only telling me about them to put my mind at ease. I didn't care: Christmas was only a couple of days away.

The Angels are more visible than usual during the

Christmas season. It's the one time of year when they feel everyone remembers them and they are spoken of in church. I had noticed from a very young age that during the Christmas season the Angels glowed in a strong reddish gold light. They glowed rather than shimmered, and this Light made them look more solid, more human. This, Zechariah told me, was the powerful Child Jesus energy they stood in. This is the energy of pure love, rebirth, renewal and grounding. To step into this Red Gold Light is to transform your mind, body and soul. It is a light childlike energy that lifts your spirit and moves you forward with great calmness and trust.

That Christmas Eve I went to midnight Mass as I did every year. I entered the church and looked up to the altar. It looked like a golden sunset, a baptism of Red Gold White light. The Angels glowed in their splendour. It is an amazing sight to behold. Christmas morning came at last. I was like a big child waiting for Santa to arrive with my Angel Cards. At last my sister and her family arrived. The cards were *beautiful*. I connected with them as soon as I opened them and they felt sacred. I went through the entire deck and the book that accompanied them in about an hour, but then decided to put them away until everyone had gone home, when I could study them more closely.

In my room I wrapped them in a silk scarf I had never used before and put them in the top drawer of my dresser. At the time I didn't know why I wrapped them in a scarf, but it felt right. I did know these cards would change my life completely.

Chapter Fourteen

Every great work, every big accomplishment, has been
brought into manifestation through holding to the vision.

Florence Scovel Shinn

Later that night, when everyone had gone home, I returned
to my cards and again I did something which at the time I
didn't quite understand. I held the cards to my heart and
asked my Angels, and any other Angels who wished to assist
me, to work with me through these cards, bringing their love,
wisdom and healing.

Then I started asking questions and picking cards and going
to the book to look up the meaning. I was shocked at how
accurate they were. I can't remember the questions I asked but
I did ask many, and then asked again and was surprised how
often the same cards came up when I repeated a question.
I was dying to know what the Angels thought of the cards.
Surprisingly, they liked them very much and advised me that
once they are used in the right way, with the right intention,
and for direction, they can be a very useful aid. Cards, they
assured me, would not tell anyone their future and we must

never think they do. Angel Cards will give you direction and confirmation in an Angelic way, to help. They also told me I would use them in my healings and that through them I would bring healing and direction to many. The cards would confirm for me everything they'd show me that was trapped in the energy and aura of the people who would come to see me. From time to time I would combine them with my Hands-on Healing therapy.

'You will give card *healings*, not card readings,' Zechariah informed me.

Over the next few days I read and reread the Angel Card book and went through the cards one by one. However, I was having a small problem: I just couldn't remember what the book said about each card. There were forty or fifty cards in this deck and how would I ever remember all of them? I was a little down-hearted as I sat in bed not long after midnight.

'Stop worrying, Little Soul, I will help you,' Hannah said kindly.

'Thank you so much. I just can't remember anything in the book,' I said, very frustrated.

'Forget all about the book and look at the cards, deep into each picture – the colours, the flowers. Is it day or night? Are the Angels smiling or sad? Love them, don't be afraid of them. Each picture tells many stories. Be easy on yourself. You know you don't need the cards. You can already see the pain and trouble in the people that come to you. We show it to you in their energy or the aura. We, your Angels and Guides, will work with you and through you, to guide and help you give your client what is best for them. Either in the direction they need to take or the healing they need to receive. The cards are designed to help you see more clearly, to give you confidence and to verify what you will pick up from your clients when they sit in front of you. The cards are your sacred tools, a gift to you, a gift we want you to enjoy and love. They will enhance your blessed healing gift and guide you and help you bring healing to many,' Hannah said with her usual gentleness.

'Yes, I feel these Angel Cards will give me the confidence I need to get started. I already love them and with your help I know I can do it,' I answered with much more certainty, although for the first time the word 'client' had been used – and quite suddenly I realized how serious this all was. My Angels and my Guides were going to help me to become a professional spiritual practitioner!

The next day I had the house to myself and Hannah came and talked me through the cards. She showed me things in them I would never have seen. She told me about the colours, the bindings on the Angels' bodies, the rising sun, the sleeping moon, the clouds, and much more. It was all too much to take in, she agreed, and over the next couple of weeks I was tutored every day and made to study the cards.

'Feel the energy. Is it winter or spring? Feel the coldness. Feel the anger. Feel the love. What is this card saying to you? What are the Angel's eyes saying? Is the energy calm and grounded or is it a turbulent sea?' Hannah loved teaching.

The questions went on and on until I became comfortable with the cards and could see what each card was saying. I practised on my family during the time Hannah was teaching me and not only were my family impressed but I was also. The cards were very accurate. To this day Hannah still shows me messages in the cards to help my clients heal and move on. She is the Angel that sits beside my clients during the healing and gives me help.

It was all good and well doing it for my family but I needed someone I didn't know anything about. I didn't want to ask my close friends, yet I needed a few test runs before I began in earnest. Rosaleen suggested a lady from her class who was more than happy to have a card healing. She had been at the workshop and felt very drawn to me. She agreed to come the following night. I was really looking forward to it and not nervous at all.

Since Hannah had shown me how to look into the cards they didn't seem strange to me. It was as if I had worked with them all my life: they talked to me and they verified everything for me. Next morning I went to work and the day just dragged along. At last, five o'clock came and I rushed home.

After dinner I went into the sitting room to prepare. It was my first healing/reading and I didn't really know what to do. I had never been for any kind of reading so it was all very new to me. I covered the table with a sacred white tablecloth and then placed a picture of an Angel on it, lit a candle and burned some incense. I took out my cards, held them to my heart, closed my eyes and asked for the help of all the Angels and Guides and the protection of the Holy Spirit. I could feel the heat in the room rise.

When I opened my eyes I couldn't believe what I saw. The room was bright and high with energy. Each of the four Archangels, Michael, Gabriel, Raphael and Uriel, stood in a corner of the room smiling, while my two Guardian Angels stood beside me and the Angels of the Healing Green Light stood in different parts of the room. The energy was calm and relaxed and then my beloved Jack came in. He looked at me and laughed.

'Well, well, you have all the heavies here tonight. Nothing can go wrong,' he said with a smile on his face. Jack has a great sense of humour! It was time. The doorbell rang and I answered it.

There stood a tall girl in her early thirties with pale skin and shoulder-length black hair. She had lovely, kind eyes but they carried great sadness. I took her into the room and we sat facing each other. I then took both her hands and connected to her energy. Her Angels quickly gathered around her. As I held on to her I felt my energy change. First I could feel her fear and her pain and then a great sadness and then I saw a little child lost and alone. I disconnected from her and opened my eyes. Hannah looked at me and told me not to be afraid and to tell the lady everything.

So, I looked into her eyes and then all around her aura (the energy around the outer body). Grey energies in different areas around the aura were blocking the flow of her energy and preventing her from moving on.

Before using any cards my Angels guided me to tell her what I could see and said when I finished that then I could use the cards. So I took a deep breath and began. I told her I had picked up great sadness in her, a sadness that was robbing her of her energy and her life. 'You are carrying more than one kind of sadness, and you are also carrying blame,' I told her. I could see a small child trapped inside the energy around the stomach area. The child had her arms wrapped around her legs and had them pulled tight against her tummy. I knew at once it was abuse. I could feel her pain. I remember thinking *Please don't let me cry*. Then I saw a child, a little girl clinging to her side, a happy child of about three. The lady's heart was heavy and felt very low in her chest area. This had to do with love. A veil covered her heart. It was the veil of mourning.

She had lost her partner, the Angels informed me. I began to tell her what my Angels and Guide had shown and told me. First I talked about the huge grey area and how it sometimes gave her tummy upsets and this was going back to her child-hood. Someone had caused her great pain during this time. Shocked, she explained she had been abused and said she had just started therapy and had been dealing with it over the past couple of weeks. I explained about how I saw her sitting holding her legs pressed against her tummy.

The tears poured out, and I felt her intense pain. She gasped, amazed by what I had seen. This was the way she would sit for hours after the abuse, crying and rocking herself to sleep. I couldn't make out who the little girl was so Hannah told me to just tell her about her; it would make her happy. I told her I had picked up the spirit of a little girl around her, aged about three or four, and right away her eyes lit up and a big smile came to her face. It was a miscarriage she'd had three years ago and she was pleased I could see it was a little girl. She had always told herself it was a girl she lost and she had named her Angel.

Then we talked about her heart and how it was breaking. 'You lost someone very close to you, a partner, and you are still in mourning.' I repeated what the Angel told me. 'Mourning is very different for everyone. Some people mourn for a week, some a year and for many it can be longer. So stop beating yourself up and telling yourself you should be over it,' I explained. Relief spread across her face. Her partner had been killed four years previously in a boating accident and she missed him so much, she felt she just couldn't move on.

Out of nowhere the spirit of a handsome young man entered the room. A tall, dark-haired man with very tanned skin, small bright sparkling eyes and a big smile. He was wearing jeans and a white polo-neck jumper. I described him to the lady and she agreed it was her partner. He gave me a few basic messages for her and then he laughed and told me to tell her about the white polo-neck. He assured me she would laugh. Her face turned snow white and through the tears her eyes opened wide and she begun to laugh heartily. 'I always hated that bloody awful polo-neck and he knew I did. It was the only time we ever fought and he'd wear it just to annoy me.'

He bent down and kissed her on her forehead, then two Angels in pure white light stood on either side of him and guided him back to the spirit world. When he left she looked at me with her hand against her forehead and said, 'He kissed me, didn't he? Where did he kiss me?'

'On your forehead,' I replied. She shook her head and whispered, 'It was him, now I know it was him.' I described to her the beautiful Angels she had around her and said how much they loved her but that she needed to start asking them for more help and guidance. She had two Guardian Angels and at least another four around her helping her.

The helping Angels stood in the shimmering lights of blue, green and yellow. These colours, my Angels explained, were the healing colours. Blue for communication, which indicated her need to talk and stop holding things back. Green for complete healing of the mind, body and spirit and the yellow light was all about her having courage to face the future and heal the past without fear. These were the healing energies the Angels covered her in. She then picked some cards and they all related to what we had already spoken about. The direction they gave her was to be strong and to continue with her counselling, to be good to herself, go for healings and to ask her Angels for help and allow love to flow slowly back into her life and believe it would happen.

When I finished I looked at her: she was so relaxed and much brighter than when she arrived. She already had a little colour back in her cheeks. As I stood up to shake hands with her she gave me a big hug and thanked me again and again. 'Your hug is so special and so are you, you're incredible,' she said and hugged me again.

When she left I went back into the room. The Angels were

still there. I thanked them all and asked them to clear my house of any negative energy and to send it to the Light to be cleansed and healed. I also asked them to continue bringing healing, love and light to the lady over the coming months. They all left except for Jack and my Angels and they assured me I had done very well and said that this was only the start: soon I would be very busy. Jack knew I had a question.

'What is it you want to ask about?' he said.

'I want to ask about the spirits of her partner and child. How come they came in? I didn't invite them in, is that OK?'

'My beloved child, when Spirits of loved ones visit freely then you know they are coming in love and peace. When they come without restraint and without interference it means their period of transition and healing is complete and their energy has adjusted to the new vibration of God light. You should never call on or *demand* that Spirits come. This could disturb and prolong their healing period,' Zechariah explained and Jack nodded in agreement.

I was glad to know that. I looked at the time: it had taken two hours and fifteen minutes. It hadn't felt that long at all. I was feeling great. I had done my first healing with a stranger – something I would never have believed I could do and I had enjoyed it a lot.

As I gave thanks that night my heart was jumping with excitement and I begged my Angels to send more people to me. I had learned an enormous amount myself that evening and the Angels had shown me so much too. They had shown me anxiety in others: it was as if their energy was trapped and this had adversely affected them. I started to understand about the healing Angels and the healing colours and I was shown that you don't have to force loved ones who have crossed over to visit, they will visit when they need to or if they want to tell us something.

171

I slept well that night but still woke up around 4 a.m., which had been the norm for the past year or so. I was still only getting an average of about four hours' sleep a night yet I never felt tired. It was a dark February morning and I could feel the cold in the room. Despite this I felt warm in myself and my heart was happy. It was also Saturday and I had planned on meeting Michelle that evening.

We were going for an early dinner and then to a meditation evening a friend of hers had recommended highly. I couldn't wait to tell her how the healing went and how good I was feeling. We had met up a few times and enjoyed talking about the Angels and healing. We were coming from the same awareness.

It was the early afternoon when my phone rang. It was Michelle. She must be ringing to cancel our evening, I thought as I answered her call. She was so excited that I couldn't make out what she was saying at first. I asked her to slow down. She explained she had been to see a woman for a reading and she was amazing. I *had* to go and see her, she kept insisting. She was still with this lady and she could make the booking for me now. I decided to let her make the booking.

Michelle said she would phone back in a few minutes. Ten minutes later my phone rang.

'Take this down. Your appointment is with Jayne Fitzgerald at 4 p.m. next Saturday in the House of Astrology in Parliament Street. You won't regret it. See you soon – don't be late,' Michelle said, still excited. What had I let myself in for? But I trusted my friend's judgement and also felt instinctively that meeting this woman was an important step for me.

Chapter Fifteen

No man can reveal to you aught but that which already
lies half asleep in the dawning of your knowledge.

Kahlil Gibran, *The Prophet*

My workplace had become much quieter these days and I
missed Pauline's company. Just before Christmas 2000 she
had moved back to the country so it wasn't as easy to meet up
now. We still kept in touch by phone, but it wasn't quite the
same. I knew in time I would adjust and everything would
be fine again.

The corporate world was beginning to drain me and the
negative energy that surrounded me each day was taking its
toll no matter how much I protected myself. It was the start of
the Celtic Tiger years: the toxic energy of greed and ego had
begun to rule and take over everyone's life. People walked
on each other to get ahead and if you weren't in the 'Boys'
Club' in the workplace, well then nothing much was going to
change for you.

Yes, everyone's life did improve financially: the poor were
surviving and keeping their head just above water while the

rich grew even richer. Human life became cheap and money was the god. People were judged on the position they held in life, the money they earned, and how many homes they had. No one could see past material wealth. People accumulated vast sums of money, amounts they could not spend in many lifetimes, never mind this lifetime, and all just because they could, not because they needed to. The economy simply couldn't survive on this energy of greed and everyone knew it – but very few were willing to make any change.

'It's the greed of man and the lack of God that will bring your economy tumbling down as you have never witnessed before. These people can't see past themselves or their greed. What they don't understand and can't see is that they are stealing the future from their own children, the very people they say they are building for and protecting. They are not learning about the law of supply, which is, God is our supply and enough is our abundance. What God gives God can take back if it is not shared with love and gratitude and for the benefit of all God's children,' Zechariah said to me one day.

It was a time of great affluence. Ireland had a new buzz of confidence and power. If you weren't happy with your career choice or workplace, well then it seemed very easy to up and change career at any time. Opportunities were yours for the taking. I, however, just wasn't sure what it was *exactly* that I needed to do. No point in leaving my boring office job to go into another boring office; just as well to stick with the devil you know, as my Mam would put it.

So what was I to do? I was hoping this lady, Jayne, would help me sort myself out when I went to see her at the weekend. Michelle had raved so much about her.

Saturday came at last, and the day seemed to drag, as it always does when you are waiting to do something new and exciting. My sister Rosaleen decided she would come with me for company so we headed off early to walk into town. It was a balmy day and the exercise would do us both good. We took our time and chatted away. As we came close to the great Dublin Cathedral of Christ Church, in one of the oldest parts of the city, and walked along the cobblestones, my heart began to thump and I became nervous.

I could see Dublin Castle in the distance and within minutes we were winding our way down Parliament Street and approaching the astrology shop where Jayne held her clinics. On a gleaming nameplate in the window the words *Intuitive Healer and Reiki Master* were engraved below her name. The waiting area upstairs was dark and old but had a good energy, which made me relax and feel at ease. After about fifteen minutes we heard the sound of footsteps coming down the stairs. I looked at my sister and we smiled. A petite woman appeared at the door. She had short blonde hair and a very strong voice for someone so small. Around her many Angels shimmered in greatness, protecting her and her energy.

'Aidan, I presume?' she said with a smile, offering me her hand. She had a firm, warm handshake and she looked me straight in the eye. 'My room is upstairs, let's go and get started,' she invited me.

It was a wide staircase and Jayne walked in front of me. After every second or third step she'd look around, shake her head and then repeat the same thing until we were in her room.

The room was bright and filled with thick white smoke; it smelt of white sage. It felt very safe and sacred and Angels stood everywhere, in each corner and at every wall around the room. There were displays of ornaments and crystals, and Angel Cards spread on the desk in front of her. As she sat opposite me she looked all around me and then smiled again and said, 'Do you know how many Angels you have around you? Do you realize you came with an *army* of them? I have never seen anybody with so many. Are you aware of this?'

'Well, I do believe in my Angels and I do work with them,' I replied.

'I should think so. I do feel you know more than you pretend. Are you not able to see and communicate with them also?' she asked.

'Oh yes, I can. I do it all the time. So I'm not mad then, you can see them too?' I smiled back, relieved that she understood and could 'see'.

'No, you're not going mad. You know this. I feel you should be sitting where I am and I should be where you are,' Jayne declared.

She went on to tell me about how much my Angels loved me and how I needed to work with them. She also said I needed some healing to balance my energy. So she put on some relaxing music, burned more white sage and asked me to close my eyes and relax. She put her hands on my head and I could feel them burn into the crown of my head. It felt as if she lifted something from it and my head became light and clear: a river of light and colour came flooding in and I felt at peace.

She moved to my shoulders and instructed me to picture all the people in my life who had caused me pain and hurt and to see myself attached to them by a dark cord. She called in Archangel Michael to cut these cords and set me free. Michael stood in front of me in his powerful blue-white Light and cut the cords. I felt light and new again. His energy had become very familiar to me. It was that strong, gentle, wise old energy. The grandfather energy.

When the healing was finished Jayne sat with me again. She could see I had done a lot of clearing on myself and had gone through a lot of pain but she insisted I was on the other side now and would never have to go back to that place of darkness again. She told me I had a great deal of healing energy, which I needed to learn how to channel and bring to others. She would guide me if I felt comfortable with her, she offered.

I was delighted. I loved her energy and I trusted the deep connection to her that I'd felt from the moment I saw her. She got me to pick a card: it was *Friendship*. We both smiled as she explained, 'This card, and my Angels, are telling me you are on the cusp of great change in your life and God is placing all the right people in your path as we speak. You will have a wonderful circle of new friends in your life very soon.'

That sounded just what I needed. Jayne gave me a hug and walked me to the door. I'd made an appointment for another session and I felt great as I made my way home. The peace and calmness had energized me, and I was thrilled to have found another person I could learn from – another teacher who would help me to move forward along this new path of spiritual exploration.

Over the coming months I was to meet with Jayne every second week and she taught me a lot about myself and about healing. She was a strong individual and didn't let me get away with anything; often she would push an issue further than I would have liked or even wanted to. But it was all for my own good and it did make me stronger and increased my mental and spiritual awareness. I was never afraid to ask her anything. She was a wonderful teacher.

Jayne was one of the first people to show me how to administer Hands-on Healing. During her Hands-on Healing sessions with me a great sense of calmness and a feeling of God's immense healing power engulfed me every time. Afterwards we'd sit back and talk about what I had felt or seen. Time and time again she'd tell me I was a natural healer and I didn't need any training. 'You have the gift, you carry the Jesus Energy, and Jesus walks with you,' she said to me one day.

'The Jesus Energy? I carry the Jesus Energy? No, I don't,' I said, shocked.

'Yes, you have been told this before, Aidan, but you have chosen to ignore it. It's time for you to start doing Hands-on Healing work. This is very important for you and you must make sure you always work with your hands as well as with the cards,' Jayne said emphatically, looking straight into my eyes.

'I don't know how to do this. And anyway, what's the Jesus Energy?' I protested.

'The Jesus Energy is the highest healing energy you can carry. It's an exceptionally gentle and powerful energy,' she explained kindly. Then she informed me she had a course coming up in a few weeks which included Hands-on Healing. It would awaken my healing gifts and help me develop my psychic and intuitive abilities. So I agreed to attend, knowing it was for my spiritual good and development.

Jack and the Angels thought it was a wonderful idea. It would give me great confidence, they told me, and said I had *nothing* to worry about when every so often I was assailed by doubts as the days passed by.

'This course will enhance your life,' Hannah said.

'Can you please explain more about this Jesus Energy? I need to know more about it,' I asked, still rather confused.

'The Jesus Energy you carry is your healing energy. It's very high vibration energy. It is the energy that does not judge. It's a gentle yet powerful energy of stillness and warmth. It is the energy which touches the heart and soul and heals through empathy, understanding and selfless love. This is the healing energy you will bring to people,' Jack answered.

'This is such an honour and a sacred gift. Surely it should be given to someone more worthy,' I said, humbled by their words.

'Jesus chose you to walk with and to work through. You have learned many lessons during your soul journey and you have understood why this happened. You have also learned the greatest healing lesson of all. The lesson of forgiveness, the very essence of the love and healing power that is Jesus. This you carry and understand, Little Soul. This is the energy people are attracted to,' Jack said, giving me a big hug.

In the next couple of weeks I did a few more card healings for my sister's friends. They all went very well, and now I was looking forward to the new challenge of developing my skills and working with my hands.

The course was held in the room in Parliament Street. It was a bright, warm summer's weekend with clear blue skies. Michelle had decided to attend as well. When we arrived most of the people were already there. There were ten of us in total and we were all around the same age except for a young man and girl in their early twenties. All from different backgrounds. There was an air hostess, a trainee barrister, a student, some corporate people, a housewife and two holistic practitioners, all of us searching for the same thing: direction on our soul journey. The room felt clear and safe and it was full of Angels and Spirits of great light.

The course was one of the best, and most informative, I've been on. It was a mixture of Hands-on Healing, card reading, tuning in to each other and seeing what we could pick up. The whole course was designed to awaken and teach us to use our psychic abilities, and it sure did. When it came to the Hands-on Healing I was astounded at what unfolded.

Jayne paired us off and got us to place our hands on the crown of the head (crown chakra) and to see light passing through our hands into the person we were working on, to feel their energy and see what, if anything, they might need healing with. She got us to ask our Angels to work with us and to direct us to do only what was right and good. It was amazing; the first person I worked on was the young girl. Her energy was very cold and I couldn't get very much from her. Anything I asked her or felt I picked up she didn't agree with, so I felt deflated and feared I was no good at this at all. It really knocked my confidence until Zechariah told me the girl was very afraid and didn't trust anybody. She had a lot of work ahead of her and as a result she was blocking her energy flow and it would take a lot of healing sessions before she would open up. I explained this to Jayne and she told me not to give up. She reminded me that this was only my first time, and she felt the girl I was working on was resisting. After about half an hour we changed around and I was put with the only other guy on the course.

When I placed my hands on him I closed my eyes and breathed in gently, asking for help and guidance. I couldn't believe the energy and the power that came from this young man. I had to open my eyes to see what was going on around him. He was covered in a soft, pale green and white light that seemed to flow into the crown of his head. He had three beautiful Angels standing around him, also dressed in this beautiful light. They greeted me with a gentle bow. My Angels, the Angels of the Green Light, Jack, and for the first time I could see a most beautiful Gold Light which hadn't taken complete form just yet but appeared like the outline of a male figure who stood to the left of me.

This Gold Light almost embraced me. It was a good and safe energy. Closing my eyes again I could feel warm energy in my hands. The guy's chest and head felt heavy; the flow of energy wasn't very strong here and both areas felt very cool. I heard Jack say to me, 'Keep your hands here until you get the energy flowing again and you feel heat flowing gently and evenly at the same temperature as the rest of his body.' I then heard myself ask, 'When do I know it's time to take my hands away?' Jayne answered in exactly the same words that Jack had just spoken. 'When the energy flows gently and evenly.'

I was also picking up different images: for example, this guy was very happy when he was behind a desk but his head was heavy and I could pick up a headache. His chest was heavy and hollow but this didn't mean anything to me. When we finished and before he worked on me Jayne told us to discuss what we had picked up from each other. I explained about the chest and the head and told her about seeing him behind his desk. He said it made sense to him. He did suffer from headaches and very bad ones at that, and he loved his job. Then I put it to him that the hollow chest meant there was no love in his life and that he didn't make time for it because he was too caught up in work. Instinctively, I felt this and Jack gave me a gentle clap on my back, which told me I'd done very well. The young man admitted it was all true. I was pleased with myself and felt that maybe I could do Hands-on Healing in time and with practice.

Then it was my turn. I sat on the chair and this gentle giant stood behind me and placed his hands on my head. The energy flowed gently and I felt comfortable and safe. Becoming peaceful, I drifted away into a restful sleep. The thirty minutes passed by quickly, then I felt him disconnect like a plug from its socket. He came and sat opposite me, and was very nervous as he told me what he had felt. He felt a very uneasy tiredness around me, sensing I was uneasy in my workplace and needed to make change there.

My heart was heavy and I didn't trust easily, he said. He saw me walk out of a dark room and then enter a room of warm sunlight and this is where I was to stay. He looked at me, shrugged his shoulders and gave a nervous laugh. I then confirmed that it *did* make sense, I was unhappy in my workplace and I did want to make change there; the darkness was the past and that's where my trust was damaged and the brightness was me now. I thanked him, we shook hands, and he was now happier.

Jayne ended the course by giving us a short overview of each person and what she got from everyone. She told me I was to start making changes in my life and to walk the healing path I had agreed to walk before I entered this life. I had many great Angels and Spirits around me and with Jesus by my side I had nothing to fear. As she continued to pass from person to person I began to realize the Jesus I had always loved was indeed walking with me. This was the Gold Light I had seen standing with Gerry and with so many others over the past few years. This cool, strong, peaceful and caring energy that embraces your body and flows through you like a stream of love and stillness, this Golden energy that flows from you to everyone, to nurture and feed the soul. I felt safe, blessed and honoured knowing that the Jesus I loved also loved me and walked with me.

Jayne finished the day with a silent meditation and I gave thanks to my Angels, Spirit Guide and Jesus for this blessed and wonderful time. I knew I had made more lifelong friends. At last, I felt I belonged.

Chapter Sixteen

Lord, make me an Instrument of your Peace
Where there is Darkness, Light;
And where there is Sadness, Joy.

From *The Peace Prayer of St Francis*

It was 2002: time was moving quickly. The months were passing and during this time I had begun to meet more and more people in the healing field and was beginning to have clients every week. I loved doing my healing work and meeting people. My Angels were wonderful and gave me all the assistance I needed to help these people and give them direction.

The people who have become my clients over the years came to me with all sorts of issues and perhaps the only thing they have in common is the need for healing. One of my clients was Joanna, who was a very insecure, messed-up person when I first met her. She was in her late twenties but looked much older. Joanna had suffered sexual abuse at the hands of a relative from a very early age, and then went on to become addicted to drugs and alcohol. She was unmarried and had two children.

At the time she came to me she had been off drugs and drink for about six months. She was lost and very mixed up. She couldn't see any future for herself and was fearful that her children would be taken from her. After we had talked generally for a short while I connected with her, facing her and holding her hands. I called on the Angelic Realms and Spirit Guides to come to her assistance. Her Angels gathered quickly and they filled me in on how she had gone through a very hard time but said she was now making huge changes in her life. Although it was hard for her, I was told to tell her that everything would change for her in a very positive way and there was no going back to the past. Her past was an opportunity to learn a huge lesson and now she stood in a much stronger light and energy than ever before.

The Angels informed me that Joanna was a strong healer herself and that she needed to work with children who had suffered like her. They said that through her own past suffering she had gained much knowledge, understanding and empathy which she must pass on to other children to bring them hope and healing. Joanna couldn't believe what she had just heard. This was something she had been feeling for the past few months, but she didn't think she was worthy of doing such work.

Her energy lifted and the Angels told her to get in touch with some local groups first and to volunteer to help out on their drug rehabilitation programmes in any way she could. They had other messages about her family and private life but the main one was about her ability to work with, and help, troubled children. She was delighted with this news and told me that she would do this voluntary work if she could find someone to take her on. Her Angels assured her they would guide her to the right place.

I didn't hear or see Joanna again for about nine months. When she walked into my healing room again I didn't recognize her. She was radiant. Her eyes were bright and alive, her skin was clear and she walked holding her body firm and straight.

She was working on a voluntary basis with children who had come off drugs and was making great progress with them and loving every moment of it. She had also enrolled on a degree course in counselling and was enjoying her life again and spending lots of time with her own children. Joanna did fulfil her dream and became a counsellor and is still working with children who suffer from different kinds of abuse. She is happy, successful and at peace with herself again.

Vicky had a totally different background to Joanna. She ran her own very successful business in Dublin. She had started coming to see me a few years earlier, just before setting up her company, and everything the Angels predicted for her and her business came true. So twice a year, just like clockwork, Vicky came and had her cards read. She also came on a monthly basis for Reiki; she had great faith in the Angels and had followed everything they told her without question since her very first early visits.

Vicky was in her early forties and had been married to an equally successful businessman for the past ten years. They were happy together but neither of them wanted children. However, down through the years the Angels showed me the heartbeat of a child in her aura, which always indicates that a child will be born to that person. Any time I mentioned this to her she would reassure me it was impossible as she had something wrong with her womb which would prevent her from giving birth. But when the Angels show me this heart-beat they are very seldom wrong.

So it was with Vicky. She arrived on my doorstep unannounced with her husband, one dark winter night, in a panic, pleading with me to see her. It was an evening I wasn't working, so she came in. She had discovered she was pregnant and didn't know what to do. She wasn't sure she could cope and was thinking of having an abortion as she had just taken on a new contract which would mean she'd have to travel a couple of times a month and a baby would only hold her back. The husband sat there saying nothing and I could see in his eyes he didn't want her to have the abortion.

I made tea and calmed her down, then took out the cards and tuned in to her Angels. The Angels assured me that the baby was healthy and that she would have a very healthy pregnancy. This child had chosen both these people and wanted to grow and learn with them. The Angels informed her the abortion issue was just a knee-jerk reaction as she was fearful and nervous of the great change that was to come into her life. If she did go through with the abortion the long-term consequences would have a devastating effect on her and her mental health. It would be something she would regret doing and find very hard to live with for the rest of her life. This child would bring many blessings to their relationship, which needed a spark of romance put back in it. The child would not infringe in any way on her career: she would be just as successful with the baby in her life.

Vicky listened to what the angels had to say and later gave birth to a beautiful baby boy. Today she is still a very success-ful businesswoman – and a very happy and successful mum and wife.

I had started to try different kinds of healing. This was all still very new to me and if someone told me they had been to a certain healer and they were good, I would book myself in and have a healing. I felt energized, and ready to try new healing paths. The problem was, things didn't always work out exactly as I had imagined. Often I would come away feeling nothing and be disappointed and totally depleted. One day as I drove home after such a healing I asked my Angels why I hadn't experienced anything during the healing; nor did I feel uplifted or in any way good. In fact I was very annoyed that they had allowed me to go to yet another healer and be let down.

'My dear and precious soul, you do not listen to your heart – you listen to your head and then rush into something, afraid you might miss out. Your head is often the voice, the thoughts and the opinions of others. When you listen to your head you think, if it is good for someone else then it's got to be good for you. But if you listen and tune in to your body, your heart will tell you if you need such a healing,' Zechariah said.

'So I need to take my time and make sure I need this healing, and that I am doing it for the right reason and not just because a friend or client had a great experience?' I asked.

'Yes, that's right. Always remember not every healer is *your* healer. Just as you, my dear soul, are not everyone's healer. Healers work with different vibrations of God's energy to bring comfort and healing to people in different ways and with different ailments,' he said.

This time, my Angels were teaching me about discernment. It made so much sense to me and put my mind at rest. During this time I was also seeing a Reiki practitioner every other week. I felt very drawn to Reiki and wanted to be attuned. The man I was receiving Reiki from had been a Reiki Master for many years. He was in his mid-forties, tall, grey-haired and wore glasses. His energy was good but for some reason I never felt totally at ease with him.

After my healings he talked to me for about fifteen minutes and would always tell me how he had removed some black or heavy energy from me, which had been there either since I was very young or from some years back. I never felt that bad going, but often felt worse when I was leaving because of all the negative energy he had just told me he had taken off me, or that he still had to take from me the next time I came for a healing.

I had made some very good friends in the healing world at this stage and, because of my work, my name was beginning to be known and I was starting to get some recognition. It was around this time that I met a wonderful person called Susan Reddy.

Susan was a mine of information and someone you could trust implicitly and I loved her from the moment I met her. She had been on her spiritual journey for years and it was good to talk to her when you felt lost or confused. She had worked as an air hostess with Aer Lingus for many years, and more recently at management level in the corporate world. She had been to numerous workshops, had read a huge amount of books and was very aware and connected to her Angels and Spirit Guide. We talked for hours on the phone and well into the night when we'd meet in our homes or on a night out. We became each other's teacher and healer and we laughed a lot.

Learning with Susan, and from her, was very interesting and always fun. We never felt we took from each other but we did learn and share what we knew or thought. Susan was the first golden link in my chain of soul friends and what an amazing and gifted friend she is. When my Reiki session had come around again, I was feeling a little tentative about it. Finally I gave myself a talking-to. What the heck, I decided, I would go along, and I'd try to relax a little. Susan had felt the healer wasn't the Reiki person for me because he dwelled too much on the negative. He should be helping me move forward, she said, and I should manifest a more positive future.

On this particular day, after the session ended, he told me I had healed all there was to heal in my present life and I was in good shape. He had worked hard to get me to this point, but in order to stay clear and in good energy I would now have to heal all that had to be healed in my past life. My karma needed to be healed, and we should start as soon as possible, he informed me.

I was shocked. Just how long was this whole healing going to take and how much negative karma did I have? I really needed some help because I was very disturbed and anxious about all this. Would I ever be clear and would I ever be healed? I needed to ask my Angels. So I called them in.

'What do I have to clear from my past life?' I asked. 'I don't feel connected to any negative energy or fears taking me back there.'

'O my dear little soul, what are people doing? Listen to what we tell you. Time and time again, we tell you to put the past of this lifetime behind you, to leave the past where it belongs . . . in the past. You can't change anything from the past, only learn from it.

'Again I say to you: ask *What have I learned?* Not *Why did it happen?* If you choose to keep looking to the past, then you stay there and you won't move on. Now if we ask and tell you to FORGET the PAST of THIS LIFETIME why would we ask you to trouble yourself trying to recall and deal with something in *another* lifetime? In that lifetime you learned what it was you needed to learn and if you missed out learning something back then, well, you will always have another chance in another lifetime to learn that lesson. Stop worrying needlessly about such things and remember, God is a God of unconditional

189

love and you are here to learn about your imperfections. You choose to carry karma if you wish to and it can make your life difficult. Each lifetime is about learning different lessons and moving your soul to a different vibration of God's love, understanding and awareness,' Zechariah replied with immense authority in his voice.

'Thank you, this makes great sense to me and I can understand,' I replied.

Zechariah looked at me and smiled and said, 'Yes, Little Soul, you are beginning to understand very clearly now and you are stepping into your own power. Soon your path will become very clear.'

Happy with the answer Zechariah gave me, I decided not to continue with my Reiki treatment. I had decided this man was not my Reiki Master and I would not be learning or receiving my sacred Reiki attunements from him. I had always felt my Reiki Master would be a woman.

I was drawn to another Reiki Master whom I had got to know through Jayne, so I started to go to her for Reiki Healing once a month. Her healings were very gentle and I felt much more at ease with her. I felt good after each healing. It became clear to me during these quiet times of healing that life was about balance, finding peace within myself while interacting with those closest to me.

One thing I had learned on my journey to date was that my parents were, in fact, my master teachers. It was in 2002 that I decided to take my Mam on a holiday to Italy. She had always wanted to return to Rome and visit St Rita's shrine in Cascia. My mother was now in her mid-eighties and it had been over twenty years since her last visit.

The trip was to take us to the Vatican, where we were to have an audience with the Pope; we'd also visit the shrine of the Mother of Good Council and the shrine of St Rita of Cascia and then spend a week by the sea to enjoy the sunshine and the sea air. Rosaleen and my aunt were to come with us. There was a feeling of great anticipation prior to our trip. I knew that something magical was about to take place. Soon the day of departure arrived. It was a wet, dark morning in Dublin. The rain was persistent and heavy and it felt humid and sticky. It had been like this most of the summer and if nothing else we all thought it would be good to get some sunshine and clear dry weather to uplift our energy.

The flight was delayed for about four hours, which meant it was dark when we arrived at our hotel. It was a small, busy hotel in the middle of Rome, and it was located very near the Colosseum. This magnificent structure looked so impressive bathed in a ray of light against the darkness of the night. Rome is one of the oldest cities in the world, but noisy, polluted and fast-moving. Despite this, the people had a friendly and warm energy about them.

The heat was unbearable. Thank God for air conditioning! In fact, if the buses hadn't been air conditioned, we might never have seen any of Rome. Our audience with Pope John Paul II took place on our first morning, at his summer residence Castel Gandolfo, a little town perched high above Lake Albano.

When we arrived at the gates of his summer palace we were shown to our places. We had front-row seats, which my Mam and aunt were very excited about. Eventually, the frail body of John Paul II appeared on a balcony above us. This was not the man that stood in Phoenix Park over twenty years earlier. In 1979 he was a man of great energy, with a sharp mind and a warm heart. The years had not been good to him. Here was this once great world leader standing above us, old and frail and struggling with his words. He didn't stay long, nor did he come to meet anyone personally, he just said a few words of welcome, blessed us and retired.

Over the next couple of days we went to all the tourist places we could fit in and enjoyed every second. On our last day in Rome, when we were to visit the Vatican, I was one of the first on the bus. St Peter's Square was of course alive with tourists, which made it feel more like a marketplace, with everyone pushing and shoving to try to get ahead of you. Despite the name, it is a circle rather than a square, with rows and rows of pillars and statues.

The heat was stifling and there didn't appear to be any shade. The area seemed grey and dull and I felt uneasy and a little troubled by the energy that infused the square. The friendly, sacred relaxing energy I had hoped to find was missing. Maybe when I got inside St Peter's Basilica I would find and connect with a more sacred and peaceful atmosphere.

Entry to the Basilica was another nightmare; the security guards wouldn't allow me to enter because I was wearing a pair of knee-length shorts when full-length trousers were required as a mark of respect. I had no problem with that – until I noticed they were allowing women in with very short shorts and low-cut tops and bare arms. I got very annoyed and asked why they were allowing this to happen. They pushed me away and told me to go and get long trousers or go home. They were very aggressive and unfriendly.

I had seen shops selling paper trousers in the square but hadn't connected them with the Basilica. So I went down to one of the shops and bought a pair of ridiculous-looking black paper trousers with wide legs which pulled in at the end with elastic. I was now allowed into St Peter's Basilica, looking and feeling like a clown! In some weird way this was more suitable and more acceptable to the Vatican security guards. The Basilica itself, although beautiful, felt cold and empty. The energy felt more like the hustle and bustle of energy you'd find in a shopping mall rather than a holy and sacred place.

Everyone was walking around taking photos and talking loudly, while tour guides led groups of people from altar to altar. Little reverence was paid and it made me sad to see the lack of respect people showed while visiting a house of God. This was supposed to be a place of stillness, silence, meditation and prayer, a sacred place where you could connect and find peace with yourself and God.

I had to get out of there, to breathe some fresh air again as the energy was heavy. I could feel my own energy draining away, as if a panic attack was coming on. I needed to communicate with my Angels to have their reassurance that all was well, so I made my way outside.

My Angels told me that the Church was going through a deep cleansing and I was picking up on the heavy, sad energy which was being released and cleared. They explained that the Church was experiencing a major shift in energy as it let go of all the people who had caused so much pain and sorrow. They said that all this pain would be healed and be replaced in time with a new energy, new people and a new way of doing things. This was, of course, the time when the Catholic Church was under great scrutiny because of the stories of abuse and brutality that were emerging.

Feeling a little better, I went to rejoin my family on their tour. We didn't queue for the Sistine Chapel, as the queues were long and the weather too hot for my Mam and aunt.

It has been said to me that when expectation does not meet reality this can cause great disappointment, as it did for me on this day in the Vatican. However, when faced with situations like this it is always good to look for the simple explanation that our Angels are trying to show us.

On our trip I met a nice lady from our group, called Sadie. She was a down-to-earth Dubliner with a heart of gold and a strong faith and belief in God. Although she smiled all the time her eyes remained sad and lonely. I was unsure what part she was to play in my life but I could tell we had a strong connection and was willing to allow this to develop at its own pace. We were coming near the end of our stay in Rome and I have to be honest and say I was relieved to be leaving the sticky heat and crowded streets of this great city behind us.

On the way to Cascia, we stopped off at the shrine of the Mother of Good Counsel in a little town called Genazzano. It is a place of pilgrimage to Mother Mary where many healings have occurred and are still recorded. According to legend, in 1467 the image of the Madonna was miraculously transported there from Scutari in Albania. It came to rest precariously on a narrow stone ledge in the wall inside the church, the legend continues, and has remained there to the present day.

The first thing that struck me is how simple everything has remained. It is still a small church with an old, safe energy and a smell of candle wax and incense. Sacredness fills this hallowed place as you sit there in silent meditation. Looking at the fresco of Mother Mary and the Child Jesus I felt the nurturing energy of Mary embrace me and the love of the Child Jesus renew my energy and my spirit. A childlike energy filled my heart. People who were with me felt the same. There was love and healing for everyone. Even now, many years later, I still feel that joy and peace in my heart when I think of it.

On leaving Genazzano we travelled through Umbria, well known for its vineyards, olive groves, hilltop villages and medieval towns. Here St Rita of Cascia was born and her remains lie in the Basilica beside the monastery where she lived for the last forty years of her life.

At the age of twelve Rita was married to Paolo Mancini. Her parents arranged the marriage, despite the fact that she repeatedly begged them to allow her to enter a convent. Mancini was a rich, quick-tempered, immoral man, who made many enemies in the region. St Rita endured his insults, abuse and infidelities for eighteen years, and bore two sons for him, Giangiacomo Antonio and Paolo Maria. Although she tried to raise them with Christian values, her sons grew to be like their father.

Towards the end of her husband's life, St Rita helped convert him to live in a more pious manner. Although Mancini became more congenial, his allies betrayed him, and he was stabbed to death. Before his death, he repented and St Rita forgave him for his transgressions against her.

After her husband's murder, St Rita's sons wished to revenge their father's death. Knowing murder was wrong, she tried to persuade them from retaliating, but to no avail. She prayed earnestly to God for Him to take away the lives of her sons instead of seeing them commit such a terrible sin. God heard St Rita's words and her sons died of natural causes a year later. After the deaths of her husband and sons, St Rita desired to enter the monastery of St Mary Magdalene at Cascia but was spurned, for only virgins were allowed to enter the convent.

However, she persisted in her cause and the convent gave her a difficult task before they agreed to accept her. She had to reconcile her family with her husband's murderers. She was able to resolve the conflicts. When, after an eventful life, she was at last permitted to enter the monastery, how she actually did so has been described as a miracle. During the night, when the doors to the monastery were locked and the sisters were asleep, Rita was miraculously transported into the convent by her patron saints John the Baptist, Augustine and Nicholas of Tolentino. When she was found inside the convent in the morning and the sisters learned of how she entered, they could not turn her away. She remained there until her death. Many miracles and healings have been granted through her intercession and so she has become known as the Saint of the impossible, or lost causes.

Cascia is a picturesque hillside town with narrow roads and winding lanes and very little traffic. You can smell and taste the freshness of the air and the flow and energy are quiet and relaxed. The whole area is full of Angels and healing energy. Umbria carries a special energy you don't find in many places; it is a portal to a Spiritual Dimension, a holy place worthy of respect. A portal is a gateway or entrance that links us to other planes of existence like Heaven. It is where Heaven and earth energy connect and become one, and a powerful place to connect with all the Spirits of Light and healing. Umbria is famous not only for it scenic beauty but also for its powerful Saints such as Benedict, Francis of Assisi, and Saint Clare, to name but a few. In total we would spend four days in Cascia.

The hotel was basic, as indeed was the food. We had a choice of pasta with green sauce, red sauce or white sauce – the same food every time! But we just laughed as the staff were so friendly and the surroundings were beautiful.

The first couple of nights I started to have vivid dreams of a young man swimming against the tide, trying to make his way to a small boat in the distance. Every time he made it to the boat the tide would come along and pull him away and he'd have to start again. He was exhausted. The dream played on my mind all day but I couldn't see the face of the young man and couldn't make out what it was all about.

The next night I had the same dream but this time I could hear him calling out, 'Tell Sadie to let me go, I am all right. I need to rest.' At breakfast I told my sister about my dreams and she agreed I had to tell Sadie, who was the friendly lady I had talked to in Rome.

Unbeknown to me, the previous day Sadie had told my sister that she had recently lost her son in tragic circumstances. I met her that afternoon in the hotel foyer and we sat at a small table and I told her of my dreams. She was shocked but listened and was overjoyed and yet sad at the message. Since her beloved son had died the year before she just hadn't been able to let go of him; her heart was broken but she knew God would help her to live with her loss and pain.

She gave me a hug and thanked me and we parted. The dream made sense to me: because Sadie and the rest of the family kept pulling him back this was making things difficult for him on the other side. His soul longed to rest in the great Temple of Light where the soul heals the pain of earth life and becomes steadily attuned to the lighter God Energy of the new world it inhabits. Here in this beautiful place you also meet up with your loved ones who have crossed over before you and they help you to adjust to this new, pure light energy. The young man's spirit struggled to be back with his loved ones to comfort and console them. He was now tired and upset and in need of rest and healing himself, which was why he'd asked his mother to let him go.

That evening at dinner the tour rep announced she was running a day trip to Assisi the next day. She warned that it was a very hilly village and it wouldn't be suitable for old people.

St Francis of Assisi wasn't a Saint I had known much about while growing up, nor was he a Saint I had ever prayed to, though I probably did call on him when my cats or dogs were sick when I was very young. I felt great resistance to going on this tour but Mam insisted that Rosaleen and I go together.

She and my aunt would stay behind to give us both a day off from minding them. So on another beautiful day we boarded the bus and made our way to Assisi where St Francis grew up.

St Francis was the son of a wealthy merchant, and was a wild young man. He loved to sing and he loved fine clothes. But when the town of Assisi fought Perugia when Francis was twenty, he was captured and spent a year in prison. Once free, he completely changed his life: he gave all he owned to the poor, he tended lepers, and preached a message of poverty, humility, joy and simplicity. He began a life of meditation, prayer and penance. Four years later he publicly renounced his father's wealth and started to lead a life of poverty and penance.

Many soon followed his example, including Saint Clare, who founded the Poor Clares order of nuns. St Francis laid down a series of principles by which his community was expected to live. Poverty, chastity and obedience. He founded the Franciscan order that still abides by these principles today. He died in Assisi in 1230 and his body has rested there since.

St Francis loved and respected all living things, from the birds of the air, animals and the fish of land and sea to the plants of nature, and communicated daily with all of God's creations.

He was aware that respecting animals was a way to respect the environment. After all, it is the animals and plants that make the earth a healthy place for humans to live in. His wisdom was inspired by his love for God and his belief that every living thing was created from the love of God. In his compassion for the animals Francis wanted to see them happy and spiritually in their rightful habitats and homes.

We took a short taxi ride to the caves on the slope of Monte

Subasio just outside the walls of Assisi. Here St Francis often came to pray, contemplate and do penance. I could see why. The pure air, the stillness and silence fall peacefully around you and you become aware only of the beauty of nature. The only noise is the sound of singing birds.

As I looked down over Assisi I began to cry and my legs became shaky. The beauty of what was in front of me took me back to Sacred Mountain. It was just like my sacred place my Angels had taken me to so many years ago and where I had travelled so many times with my beloved Jack. I felt a deep presence within my heart.

As I turned to tell my sister what I was feeling I found I was on my own in this place, which had been full of people only a couple of minutes earlier. Standing beside me were my two beautiful Angels shimmering brighter than I had ever seen them before and Jack with his big smile and his arm draped around my shoulder.

'Yes, this is a very special place: it is the sacred place of our beloved Francis. It's his God space and his energy space. This is the space that many people are given as their sacred place where they find healing and peace. It carries a very high vibration of God's loving, healing energy and it is here Francis takes many to be awakened to the love, understanding and healing of God. You, my Little Soul, will hear the voice of gentle Francis in your heart this day and you will be afraid no longer,' Zechariah said.

Just as I was about to reply they disappeared and I saw my sister in the distance with some of our group calling me and telling me to hurry or we would miss Mass. We made our way back down the hill to Assisi by foot along the narrow pathways and through open fields where sheep roam freely and often jump out in front of you and frighten the life out of you.

In Assisi the group dispersed and my sister and I were alone again. The peaceful energy hadn't left me and I felt strangely at home in Assisi. Although the small streets were crowded and everyone was busy there was an almost uncanny yet sublime stillness and quietness in this very sacred town. Everything seemed to move at a much calmer pace.

We had made good time and had half an hour to spare and we decided to have a coffee and sit outside in the balmy heat. Just as I was about to sit down I noticed Sadie across the road. I waved and she came over. She was apologetic and said she didn't want to disturb me but she needed to talk with me. Then she saw my sister and was about to leave, but I insisted she stay.

We talked about the dream and her son and she told me the whole sad story. The Angels told me to tell her that her son was all right and in the Light and didn't feel any pain. He had been aware of her by his bedside before he crossed over. He didn't want her to be upset and he was very sorry for what had happened. He told her she was a great mother and that he'd always look after her. The Angels then gave me personal messages for her life.

As we sat there talking a peculiar out-of-body feeling took hold of us and we lost all sense of time and space. A protective white mist surrounded us. Suddenly the church bells rang out. We believed they were the bells ringing to remind us Mass was about to start so we jumped up. But when we checked the time, almost two hours had passed and the bells were ringing to tell us Mass had finished. We couldn't believe what had happened but decided God and St Francis had wanted it to happen this way.

We made our way towards the Basilica, and to the tomb of St Francis to pay our respects. On the way, Sadie stopped me, gave me a big hug and told me I was wasting my gifts working in my job. She told me that I should be using my spiritual gifts and doing this work to help people in need.

I thanked her and gave her a big hug back – just happy that I'd been able to help her a little.

Then she looked at me, smiled and said, 'That hug should be bottled, it makes you feel so safe and loved.'

We finally made it to the Basilica. A wonderful energy engulfs you as soon as you walk in. The church was packed, with people coming in and out but, unlike St Peter's in the Vatican, here no one made any noise. The sacred, peaceful, loving energy was not disturbed and we knew we were in a place of great healing and the true God energy. We then went to the lower church and into the crypt where St Francis is buried.

Here before the sacred tomb of this spiritual man whom I had honestly only welcomed into my life that day, I felt a strong connection. As I stood before his tomb my heart beat fast and then it returned to normal and a great calmness came over me. Again I felt a deep presence within; then I felt my heart open and in my mind's eye I saw a bright light flowing into it. I felt at peace and a oneness with the gentle Francis and I could hear him speak these words:

'Don't be afraid. Allow the light and love of God and his blessed Angels to flow freely. The love of God is simple. Keep everything simple as I did, dear child in God.'

From that moment my heart and energy lifted and I knew what I had to do when I got home. I realized that the resistance I felt at the beginning of this tour was the fear of walking on my true path. Now that I had stepped into the energy I felt focused and empowered.

The remainder of the holiday was to be spent by the sea, relaxing. However, the priest on the trip, who was our Spiritual Director, had decided he was on holiday that week so wasn't around to give guidance or direction. For some unknown reason the group came to me for advice and guidance. My sister and I laughed at this turn of events but I was really enjoying the whole experience and we agreed it was yet another clear sign that I needed to get more involved in my healing work when I returned home.

On the last night of the holiday many people thanked me for my help and told me how good they felt knowing that I was there during the week. I myself had found inner peace, strength and direction in the sacred energy of Umbria. As Florence Scovel Shinn, the author of a powerful metaphysical book called *The Game of Life and How to Play It*, says, 'Everyone is a golden link in the chain of our journey', and this for me was true. Sadie and all the people in that group are part of the golden chain of my life and it was thanks to them that I gained the courage to take a great leap of faith and move on.

Chapter Seventeen

For everyone who asks receives, and he who seeks finds,
and to him who knocks it will be opened.

Matthew 7: 7–8

The peace and inner strength I had felt on leaving Italy remained with me during the closing months of that year and into 2003. The loving, strong energy of Francis of Assisi was still with me and I could hear him speak to me in moments of meditation. He'd speak of my journey and my need to let go. To live in true trust and allow the energy of the soul to be my driving force. To do just as he did, and know that God was my support; He and His Blessed Angels would refuse me nothing if it was for the higher good of myself and all concerned.

Fear of the unknown still pulled at me. I longed to do my healing work and leave the day job that had sapped my energy and my confidence for so long. I also felt it robbed me of my creativity and was destroying my true soul purpose.

The energy in the company was becoming even more toxic and I dreaded going into work every day. One of the managers had retired due to ill health and a new, much younger man had taken his place. I felt I had gone from the frying pan into the fire. With the old manager what you saw was what you got. He was never the easiest man to work for, but if you ignored his frequent outbursts of temper and didn't answer him during these explosions he'd back away and leave you alone.

The new man was a very different kind of person. He started out being very pleasant and most grateful for any help you gave him. But once he found his feet and learned all he needed he backed away. He was the kind that ran with the hare and hunted with the hounds, saying one thing to one person and something else to others and never admitting that he had said these things at all. So you were left not knowing whether he told the truth or not.

It was very difficult to work under this kind of management or, rather, lack of management, as I saw it. Never before did I feel so strongly the need to leave and start doing what I enjoyed most: my healings. I didn't know where to start nor had I the finances to set up a practice of my own. I was still only doing my readings and healings on a part-time basis and I wasn't charging the clients that came to see me in the evenings, after work. My Angels kept telling me I needed to do it full time and not to be afraid. It was what I was here to do, they reiterated.

I still wasn't comfortable doing Hands-on Healing and felt the need to have some kind of qualification or certificate to say that it was safe for me to give healings and to lay my hands on people. Although I was still going for healings I had backed away from Reiki and wasn't drawn to it any more. To be honest, I was terrified of it.

During the previous summer I had attended a Reiki course where I was attuned to the first degree of Reiki. During the workshop I hadn't felt anything and was a little disappointed. I found the two days long and boring. The attunement was a total let-down too. There was nothing sacred or personal in it for me. The teacher explained we would go through a three-week cleanse and we might feel sick and out of sorts. I had experienced the most terrible after-effects, which put me off the whole Reiki healing idea. As I drove home from the workshop I asked Jack what was it all about. Why was I feeling as I did?

He told me it would all become clear for me and that it was about learning, and not to give up.

My whole body was drained of energy and I felt like a rag doll. Throughout the night I drifted in and out of sleep, dreaming that I was falling and sinking. More than once, I woke up in a cold sweat; my heart was pounding fast and I couldn't breathe properly. Panic set in and I longed for daylight to break through.

But when morning came I felt so unwell I couldn't seem to lift my head off the pillow. I felt sick and shivered uncontrollably. The Reiki Master had never said the clearing would be this severe. I couldn't stand up and I felt totally out of control. Scared and depressed, I begged my Angels not to send me down that road again. I just couldn't take it!

It wasn't until about three days later that I started to feel a little brighter. I decided to check with friends who had also been attuned to Reiki to see if they too had felt this way, but not one of them had gone through this bad a clearing.

I rang my Reiki Master and she assured me this was all very normal. I had just gone through a really deep energy cleanse and not to worry or be afraid. It was all good and very positive, she told me. I wasn't so sure of that and asked my Angels to help me to recover.

A short while later I was sitting in my bedroom when the green light of the loving Archangel Raphael entered the room and covered me in a pale, almost white green mist. The mist felt cool and I could feel it sink into every muscle in my body. As I absorbed this soothing healing gel I felt myself become more relaxed and the thumping headache I'd had for the past three days lifted.

My heart stopped beating so fast and it was as if the sun shone again as that dark, depressed energy that had taken hold of me lifted. I felt connected to my mind, body and spirit, and I was at peace again.

I thanked Raphael. He always came to my healings with his powerful gentle healing energy, accompanied by an abundance of Angelic green healing light.

'Do not be afraid: all is well with you again, this feeling will leave you now. Once again you have gone with your head. You allowed yourself to be talked into doing something you didn't want to do. You must choose your teachers wisely. This is a lesson of patience and trust. The right teacher will come and you will familiarize yourself with this ancient sacred healing,' Raphael said.

Since my visit to Italy I had learned to trust myself and my Angels and Guides. I decided I would try to sit back and observe more; I'd also try to hold back and not jump into doing things just because I'd heard someone else had tried something new.

My Angels and Jack were pushing me to leave work more and more. I kept telling them I would but that I just needed some more time to get things sorted out financially and then I would leave.

I felt I needed to get out and start doing things beyond the safety of my own house. I had been asked to do some charity nights, reading cards, and also to do some holistic fairs. I took up the offers and started doing these and found I really enjoyed the experience.

The holistic fairs were usually held on Sundays in hotels around the country. Here many therapists offered their therapies to the general public. The fairs were excellent places to get to know like-minded people and to find out about other therapies and what was happening in the healing world. My sister agreed to come and help me and we had a great time. I loved the buzz and the energy at these events.

At that time the fairs were very busy and people wanted to know and learn more about their Angels so I got a lot of enquiries. In the early days although I appeared busy and there were always people around my stand, most of the time it was enquiries, with just a very small number of readings and healings.

People would come to my stand and ask for a hug then go away happy and come back later and tell me how good they felt after my hug. I'd come home after a long day feeling worn out, but always contented and uplifted. No words can explain how you feel when someone thanks you and tells you you have made a really positive difference to their life, or that they feel you have uplifted them, or how much better they feel about themselves.

It is the best feeling you can ever get and no amount of money could ever buy that. The Angels were very good and I always made enough to cover the cost of the day, which included my travel, the cost of the stand and lunch for my sister and myself, and that was fine. However, I did realize even then that if I were ever to leave my full-time career, I would have to start earning enough to cover my living costs. To be truthful, it was a relief that I wasn't making money at healing. It meant I didn't have to make any decisions about leaving work. As bad as work was, at least I had a monthly salary and I didn't have to worry about my bills and that was a comfortable situation to be in.

I could do my healing work with a clear head and didn't have to worry about my bills – what could be better? Maybe this was the way I was supposed to operate, I reasoned.

Like many people, I was afraid of change and didn't like all the upheaval it could bring. The feedback from other practitioners at these fairs was sometimes very negative and this didn't do much to encourage me to set up as a full-time practitioner either. Very few of them could afford to give up their career and survive on what they made doing their holistic work. There was a lot of competition and it seemed to me that you had to work hard and long hours to survive in the holistic healing field.

I had become friendly with a girl called Suzanne Horgan, a physiotherapist who works with eating disorders and whom I met at the first ever holistic fair in Ireland. She was to become another very good friend and an important link in the chain of events in my life during this time. She had come to me for a reading and was more than satisfied with what the Angels told her. She took my card and phoned me a couple of weeks later and invited me to give a talk in Wexford to some of her clients and their families. The talk was to be on Angels, Angelic Energy and how to work with it.

Suzanne, like myself, believed you had to work on the mind, body and spiritual side of things to bring complete healing, understanding and acceptance. She has a huge, light-hearted energy of love and trust, she fills the room and uplifts your spirit. She is loud, direct and has an air of complete confidence. Like most therapists, myself included, she had gone through a painful past but had come out the other side determined to help others and to show them that although recovery may be painful and often slow it is possible to find happiness and peace again.

I was thrilled she had given me this opportunity but still scared, as it was my very first time to stand in front of people and talk about the Angels. I went over and over what I was going to tell them. I wrote pages of material and I rehearsed again and again everything I was going to say until I was word perfect. My Guardian Angels and Jack were very happy.

In accepting the invitation to do the talk, they assured me, I had nothing to fear. They told me all would go well and I was not to get into a panic.

The day arrived and I set out on my journey to meet Suzanne, who lived in Wexford. We'd arranged to meet for tea first so that we could get to know each other a little. Later that evening, we'd head off for the hotel where the talk was being held.

When we arrived at the hotel I went straight up to the room and lit the candles and incense and then did my Calling In. The room instantly filled with Angels and, as always, the four Archangels stood in each corner, hands outstretched sending healing energy in laser-like beams of coloured light. I thanked them all for coming and asked them to help me this night and to help me remember everything I had rehearsed over the past few days.

Michael, standing in the nearest corner to my right, spoke to me in his deep but warm voice and told me to fear not, and they would put the words in my mouth if I needed their assistance. He then breathed out blue light and covered my neck and lower part of my chest with this light that felt like a soft warm breeze around me and I felt very much at ease. Gabriel spoke to me and told me someone in the group was coming to test me but that I would pick this person out very quickly and they would admit this. I was glad I had been warned about this and, even though I knew it, I wasn't afraid or put off in any way.

The people started to arrive and I introduced myself to each person as they came in. It was a good mix of young and middle-aged and so far everyone seemed friendly. A great air of excitement filled the room. There were about twenty to twenty-five people in attendance and their Guardian Angels stood beside each and every one of the group, filling the room with a rainbow of shimmering colour and the most amazing energy of love and calmness. We started with a very short meditation. Then I introduced myself and gave a brief talk about the Angels. Before I knew it, the questions began.

Everyone had something to ask and they were more than willing to accept the loving messages the Angels gave me for them. That is, except for one woman who sat with her coat closed and her arms folded with little expression on her face. Behind her stood the most beautiful Angels dressed in deep shimmering pink with their heads slightly tilted as in prayer. When she did finally speak she was negative in her views and more or less told me I was away with the fairies if I believed in all that Angel stuff. She repeatedly questioned everything I said and tried hard to get me to change what I had told people. I felt exhausted but asked her did she want a message from her Angels. The Angels told me to tell her she knew all about them and had worked with their energy for a long time and to stop testing me.

There was a gasp of surprise and shock in the crowd. The blood drained from the woman's face and she admitted that yes, she had come to test me. She then apologized to the group and to me. The Angels asked that she apologize to them and step out of her ego and back into the Angelic light of love and direction. Ego had taken over and she believed no one knew as much as she did about the Angels. She did apologize and was embarrassed and ashamed by the whole incident. Before she left she did come to me and thank me for what I did, and apologized once again.

The night finished and everyone was pleased with the way the event had been such a success. The Angels were also happy and they provided me with all the answers I needed, as they always did. It was only when I had finished that I realized I hadn't referred to my notes once during the evening and what I had prepared to discuss never came up during that talk as the evening took on an energy of its own and everyone received what he or she needed for that time. I was buzzing. I'd really enjoyed delivering the talk. Little did I know that it was the first of many such talks I would deliver over the coming years – and not only in Ireland.

Suzanne was the first physiotherapist to send me clients and she sent me many over the following months and still does to this day.

I was to meet yet another very interesting person during this period, who would be an important link for me at that time. Suzanne had told me about a shop in Dun Laoghaire called The Angel Shop which she felt I should visit. I was eager to go there so I arranged to meet a friend, Mark, for coffee and afterwards have a look around the shop. It was a warm sunny day in late May, Mark had already arrived and was sitting outside having a coffee and a massive cream cake. I ordered my coffee and we chatted and caught up on each other's news. Dun Laoghaire was crowded with people out in their summer clothes and no one seemed to have a worry in the world that day.

The energy was fresh and light. Even the Angels appeared to be brighter and their energy was giddy: they jumped from side to side as people laughed and interacted with each other.

The reflection of the sun danced on the ocean waves. We talked for about an hour and then Mark had to leave and I made my way into Dun Laoghaire Shopping Centre and up the escalator to The Angel Shop.

What struck me first was the beautiful, serene energy that fell upon you as you entered. It was a small space but the Angels stood proud and strong everywhere around the shop. Angels were guiding people to what they needed and also protecting the shop from harm. To me it was an Aladdin's cave. It had everything you could ever want that related to Angels. I was like a child in a toyshop; I wanted one of everything. It had books on Angels, cards, figurines, incense, crystals and much more. I didn't know where to start. Then from behind me came a soft, kind voice. 'Can I help you in any way?'

When I turned around I saw a petite woman, well dressed and with a beaming bright smile and eyes like crystals. Her whole body oozed with joy and happiness. I felt an instant connection and wanted to give her a hug but I did resist, thinking she might think me a bit strange. She introduced herself. Her name was Mairead Conlon and she was the proud owner of this beautiful shop, a little piece of Heaven in this busy and fast-moving world. I spent a long time there and got talking to Mairead and we instantly hit it off and became good friends over the coming months and years.

This shop was to change my life and make me feel even more comfortable in my own body. It showed me I was normal and that many people believed in Angels; not only believed, but could also see, feel and communicate with these wonderful Beings of love and light as I could. To this day every time I see Mairead I thank her for her marvellous shop – but I also thank her for bringing the Angels back to Ireland and for the huge contribution she has made to Angelic awareness in this country. Here was yet another link in my chain; and to this day Mairead promotes my work and sends me clients.

The year was passing quickly and I was becoming steadily busier. I was enjoying my clients and was working almost every night. It is always so good to know you have helped people – though with some clients it may take a while before they realize that the healing really has made a difference. For example, one of my clients, Linda, on the outside appeared to be a very confident, bright girl. Full of fun, she was in her late twenties and her light-hearted energy filled the room when she walked in. As I greeted her I wondered why someone like Linda was coming to see me. When I shook hands with her I felt a very different energy. Her palms were hot and wet and a great sense of fear surrounded her. Her aura was tired and deflated and her crown chakra was pulsing and beating very fast.

We talked generally at first, as I always do just to let the person settle and gel with my energy before we start the healing. I had decided to give Linda Hands-on Healing as her energy needed to be lifted and her head needed to be cleared. The healing took about forty-five minutes, and during the healing I received some messages for her.

The Angels told me that Linda was extremely ambitious and loved her work. She had worked hard for the last six years for the same company. It hadn't been without its rewards and she had moved up the ranks rapidly. However, she had been overlooked for promotion a few weeks previously when the position was given to a guy who had been in the company for only a short time. She was very annoyed and angry about this.

When I related this back to her she was a bit taken aback but agreed with everything the Angels had said. What she wanted to know was where she should go from there. She didn't feel she could stay in the company, yet the Angels told her she must not leave. The guy who got the promotion would not be able to do the work and would resign within the next few months: then it would be hers. They felt she had a lot to offer this company, and if she were to move on she would have to start from scratch again, proving herself and her abilities, and this would take a couple of years.

Linda looked at me and laughed. She didn't believe that what I told her would happen as she felt the guy was very confident and would never resign. When she was leaving I asked her to let me know how things turned out, and I begged her not to move at least for a few months. She said that if what the Angels said was true, well, she would send me the biggest bunch of flowers she could find. I knew she didn't believe me or the Angels and I knew she was no happier after she had seen me. I prayed she would listen to what the Angels had told her.

I didn't have to wait a few months to hear from her. Six weeks later a beautiful bunch of flowers arrived at my door with a message 'THE ANGELS WERE RIGHT, ME WRONG X Linda'. That evening Linda phoned to thank me and to make another appointment to see me. The job had become too much for the poor guy and he resigned, and as the Angels had said, the position was offered to Linda. She gladly accepted it.

When I first saw Linda I'd been puzzled because she seemed so carefree and bright. Marcus was quite different. He came to me very upset and heart-broken after his wife of ten years left him because, as she put it, she was no longer in love with him. The marriage, as far as he could see, was good, despite the usual ups and downs. He was still very much in love with her and couldn't understand why all this was happening now as they had just moved into their new dream home and financially everything was going well.

As I tuned in to Marcus his Angels gathered around very quickly. I was told the marriage had gone through a rough patch a few years ago when Marcus had been unfaithful to his wife. At first he had refused to go for marriage counselling but finally gave in and now thought everything was fine again. He was sorry for what he'd done. Marcus seemed a little surprised when I told him this, but agreed that was what had happened.

Then the Angels told me his wife just needed a break from him for a short while to find herself again and when she did they would get back together. But they warned him he wasn't to rush things and he wasn't to take her back too quickly. First he needed to wine and dine her and start dating her again. They insisted again and again that he and his wife would be back together but that it had to be done slowly and they needed to get to know each other and fall in love all over again. 'Please warn him not to rush anything as to do so will have terrible effects on the relationship and he won't solve his issues in this way,' I was told.

I passed on the message. Marcus went away that night feeling confident and happy with all he had been told by the Angels. He agreed with everything they had said.

To my great surprise a week later Marcus rang in high spirits, saying he had met up with his wife at the weekend. They had agreed they needed to be with each other, they were back living together and everything was going very well. Alarm bells went in my head and I could hear my Angels saying, 'It will never last – tell him.' I told him he had done exactly what the Angels had advised him not to do and I wasn't sure how everything would work out for him now. He kept assuring me that it was going to be great and that he had over-reacted to everything his wife had said before she left him.

I heard no more from him again for about ten months but when I did it was to hear she had walked out on him again and this time wasn't coming back, she just didn't love him any more and she had had enough: she needed her own life back. Marcus was devastated and agreed he should have followed the directions the Angels had so clearly placed before him all those months previously.

I still wasn't sure about leaving my job, but I wasn't ruling it out either. I continued to do the holistic fairs and was getting bookings from these events too. That September at a fair Suzanne introduced me to Mary K. Hayden, a Reiki Master Teacher, among other things, and to Dolores O'Reilly, another Reiki Master, who was to become one of my best friends.

I was instantly drawn to Mary's bright and very friendly energy. She had many Angels around her and had a remarkably strong presence. She was immaculately dressed, had blonde hair and the clearest skin I have ever seen. She invited me to her house to do readings for her friends and clients whenever I could fit the time in. I knew at once she would be my Reiki teacher. Don't ask me why, I just knew it. (I guess I was now learning to trust my intuition!) Shortly after this I fell ill with exhaustion and was out of work for a few weeks and during this time the Angels were constantly at me to leave work and to do the healing work full time.

'You need to leave that toxic energy and set yourself free from that place: it is not for you any more. Your work is finished there and it is time to move on. This is why you are sick and tired. The energy is far too heavy in that world,' Zechariah coaxed.

'I'm not sure. If you can guarantee me the same standard of living I have now, well then I will give it up, no problem,' I responded.

'We have always told you to ask for what it is you want and if it is for your higher good then you shall have it. So what is it you feel you need in order to let go of the corporate world?' he asked.

'I would like a constant flow of clients. If I had to worry about money and paying bills then I would be unable to carry out my work with a clear mind,' I answered.

Zechariah nodded, asking that I leave it in their hands. In truth, I was very afraid to leave my pensionable job. My Mam and the rest of the family didn't exactly encourage me to do so either. My friends on the other hand were very supportive and encouraged me every step of the way. It was too near Christmas, I would decide in the New Year.

On my return to work I found things had changed with my job. But it wasn't until about two weeks later that I discovered they'd decided to take part of my work from me and, with no consultation, had given it to a couple of other people to do.

I requested a meeting so that the situation could be explained to me; after all I'd decided some time ago that no one was going to walk on me again. They couldn't have the meeting with me until after Christmas. That was it, my decision was made: I was leaving that place. Enough was enough. I had come to the edge and was now ready to fly.

Chapter Eighteen

What is a friend?
A single soul dwelling in two bodies.

Aristotle

Christmas 2003 hadn't been a great time for me. My mother had been sick during the holiday period, which was a big worry for me as she was now in her late eighties and becoming a little frail. Also, the whole work thing was getting me down. I'd felt hurt and let down by the managers. After all, I had almost twenty-six years' service with the company and to be treated with such a lack of respect was hurtful and degrading.

I had decided to leave in the New Year but I needed to put some things straight before I handed in my notice. I had let people at work bully and abuse me in the past, but not this time. My Angels and Jack assured me things would work out for me in a blessed and successful way and I was not to worry. It was not the old Aidan they were dealing with now. I had learned to love and respect myself.

But when the day appointed for the meeting arrived,

it didn't happen. I didn't want to finish my day with more uncertainty so I went to the Financial Controller, as he was my direct manager and someone for whom I had great respect, as he was a true gentleman.

I asked him why the meeting wasn't called and he didn't know either, nor could he understand the delay. He too had been waiting all day for the call. He assured me he would find out what the situation was before I went home that evening.

The meeting was rearranged for the next day, but I received no apology or explanation. The next morning the Financial Controller came to my office and walked with me to the General Manager's office. He told me not to be nervous and to be honest with them and tell them everything. All along the corridor Angels lined the way and again assured me I would be fine and that the outcome would be far different than the management were expecting.

Around the table in the office sat the General Manager and the new manager. All the way through the meeting they made no eye contact with me. I won't go into all the ins and outs of the whole meeting, but we reached a deadlock where I wouldn't take on any more new boring work and they wouldn't give me back my old work. The General Manager then asked me in a rather exasperated voice, 'Well then, what *do* you want?'

I knew they wanted me to leave, and before I had time to think I heard myself say, 'What do I want? I'll tell you what I want. I want that redundancy package you paid out a couple of years ago. That's what I want.'

'You can't have that – we are not doing redundancy packages at the moment,' he snapped back.

'Well then, I am going nowhere,' I replied, feeling glad that I had stood up for myself.

I walked out of the office, relieved and happy. My Angels

told me I had done very well. Within twenty-four hours I was offered redundancy. I was asked to stay on a few months, which suited me as it gave me the time to prepare myself and to build up my client list. I had the opportunity to take appointments in advance and to set myself up in business in the appropriate manner. It was a relief to have the work issue out of the way.

At this stage I was asking my Angels on a daily basis to send me more clients and to fill my diary a couple of months in advance. To my great surprise and with much gratitude I found this was exactly what they did.

It's strange to find that sometimes, when people do you an injustice and wrong you in a hurtful way, it can unexpectedly turn out to be one of the greatest gifts you've ever received. This is what happened to me. My Angels made it come about in this way and in doing so provided me with the financial support I needed. This made me make a decision by giving me a very gentle push in the right direction. It was proof to me that when one door closes another one always opens.

My mother was still very ill and I feared she was getting worse as the days went on. She had taken to her bed and remained there for the next couple of weeks. She was sleeping a great deal and able to eat only a little. The doctor had been to see her twice or three times and kept prescribing her antibiotics. They did not appear to be doing much good at all and she was becoming more frail as the days went on. She wasn't in pain but she was exhausted.

Her room was filled with the most radiant Angels all during this time and they promised me she was going to be OK. I sat with her and gave her healing and also asked the Angels to surround her with their love and healing energy. She always felt some relief after the healings and her beautiful eyes would sparkle again for a couple of hours.

The Angels explained that her earth body had become tired and restless and she was moving to the final stage of her journey where her body and soul would move to a vibration of inner peace and acceptance. Despite this, I was finding it difficult to give her healing due to my emotional attachment to her. I found myself becoming extremely upset after every session and the Angels assured me this was common.

I have since found that most healers can't work on their family for the same reason. I knew my mother needed healing so I phoned a colleague at the time, my friend Dolores O'Reilly. After meeting Dolores at the holistic fair she had come to me as a client for healings. We had met for a coffee and had formed a strong friendship even though we had only known each other a few weeks. Dolores had also given me a healing and it had been a wonderful experience, powerful yet gentle at the same time. She is a no-nonsense healer, very easy to talk to, and only does what she is instructed to do by her Guides and Angels. She keeps everything simple and explains in a language you can understand and gel with. She is a joy to know and it is an honour to call her a friend.

It was now late January 2004 and Mam had been sick for at least a month, so Dolores agreed to come up from Wicklow that evening and give my mother some Reiki. I was delighted, but Mam wasn't too thrilled and was nervous about the whole thing. I reassured her that it would be fine and the Angels would look after her. She agreed to the healing but insisted she would only let Dolores work on her for fifteen minutes or so.

The weather was terrible that night and Mam felt very guilty about having Dolores travel all the way from Wicklow for just fifteen minutes of healing. She asked me to rub the top of her back as her lungs were sore and as I gently rubbed her upper back I called on Jesus and the Angels to lay their healing hands on her and to bring her comfort and peace.

As I sat with her, a beautiful Golden mist filled the room and the energy of peace, calm and stillness fell upon us. The room became silent and the sound of passing traffic outside faded away. Mam had fallen into a restful deep sleep. The Golden light that surrounded her weak body was like an electric current and she began to breathe with ease.

The doorbell rang. It was Dolores. She had arrived earlier than I had expected and I was delighted to see her. While Mam was asleep we took the opportunity to chat about healing and Reiki over a cup of tea. I spoke to her about my earlier experience with my Reiki and said I didn't want to repeat it.

She explained that she had been taught differently and felt I should go and be attuned again as it would help protect, strengthen and empower my healing. I agreed to read up more about it in the coming weeks. I took Dolores up to my Mam's room. The energy was still peaceful and she gently came out of her sleep and greeted Dolores. I left the two of them together and went back downstairs. I felt relaxed and relieved that Dolores was with my Mam and prayed the healing would help.

I fell asleep and woke up about an hour later as I heard Dolores come down the stairs and into the room. She was smiling and assured me Mam was fine. She was, however, quite ill but her energy was very strong. She was sleeping again. Dolores said that Mam wasn't going anywhere yet – she meant passing over – for she still had a lot of life in her.

We had something to eat and I then went up to see Mam. She was lying in the bed awake, looking much brighter and breathing much more easily.

'Do you know what? I'm starving. I'd love some toast and an egg. And could you beat the egg up in a cup for me with plenty of butter?' she asked as she sat up in the bed. I couldn't believe it: my old Mam was back, her beautiful blue eyes alive again with that little spark of devilment in them and her face glowing in the twilight of the room.

'I sure will,' I agreed eagerly. I was so pleased. She had taken hardly any food since Christmas; nor had she longed for anything until now.

She ate the toast and egg heartily and enjoyed every last piece. 'That was gorgeous, I enjoyed that. I think I'm better. That Rachel' – meaning Reiki – 'is great. I will have to get Dolores to come again, she's very good,' she said. I couldn't believe it and was gobsmacked. It was a miracle. Dolores had brought my mother back to life! Mam could never remember the word Reiki, so she would always referred to it as 'Rachel' and it has become a standard joke between Dolores and myself. Even now we always book in with each other for a Rachel session. Dolores continued to give my Mam healings over the coming months and years until her death. She became another daughter to her and a much-loved member of our family. Mam would often say Dolores was better than any doctor or priest and you could tell her anything.

So that was it for me. I now wanted to learn Reiki and Dolores advised me to go to Mary K. Hayden, her own Reiki Master/Teacher. From the moment I met Mary K. I felt a powerful connection with her and I knew in my gut that she would be my Reiki Master/Teacher.

Every day after that, Mam became stronger and felt good within herself. I rang Mary K. and booked into her next Reiki Level One class, which was to take place some months later, in March. I was keen to make some form of connection with her prior to that and as luck would have it she very kindly invited me to her next Angel Course which she was having that coming Sunday in Enniscorthy, County Wexford.

The Sunday came around quickly and my sister Breda agreed to stay with Mam for the day to take care of her, as she was still weak. During her illness the family came and helped with Mam, making sure that she was never left on her own. I was still working full time so my sisters took it in turn to come and sit with Mam during the day and I took over in the evenings with the help of my brothers and sisters-in-law. With a large and extended family you always have someone to call on. It was quite normal in our family to care for sick relatives. Both my Mam and Dad's family had taken care of, and nursed, their parents up to their time of death. So caring for Mam was carried out without any question or fuss. We always felt it was a pleasure and a privilege to care for her.

It was a sunny late January Sunday morning as I drove down to Wexford knowing Mam was being well cared for and improving daily. The workshop was well attended and very enjoyable. Suzanne and Dolores were there and a few other people I knew from previous workshops.

One person stood out from the crowd that I had an instant connection with. Her name was Rina Beechey. A small, thin lady with blonde hair, she was very neatly dressed and rather shy. She had a beautiful soft energy and her infectious giggle lit up her face, lifted our spirits and made us all laugh. She had a health store in Gorey called Mrs Bees and she asked me to come and do a day of Angel readings and healings in the store. I was delighted and arranged to come down a few weeks later. It is one of the places I hold most dear to my heart and I love working from the premises, even to this day.

Angels flood Mrs Bees with wonderful healing energy of laughter and friendliness. An old Celtic energy that you don't find in many stores or shops these days. Over the years, Rina, her husband Brian and their children have become part of my family and I can't remember a time I didn't know them, or imagine my life without them.

Having stood up for myself in work and taken my leap of faith, doors began to open for me and Rina's was the first of many such doors. Shortly after the workshop I got a call from Nuala Ronan, owner of Evolv Health Store in Enniscorthy, who also invited me to come and do readings and healings from her store.

It's another beautiful store with magical energies and it's a place of healing. Nuala, a strong healer herself, had stopped giving healings and was hesitant about starting again. I christened her 'the reluctant healer' and suggested she write a book with this title. A short time later I received yet another call, this time from a lady called Catherine Fox, inviting me to work in her Dawn of Hope Therapy Centre in Kells. It is a very small centre, which carries a huge, solid grounding Druid energy.

This Druid energy radiates from Catherine, an unassuming lady with a big heart and enormous motherly love for everyone. She's a wonderful mother, wife and a special and dear friend. She lives a simple spiritual life, and has walked her walk and talked her talk – a powerful healer and teacher. These and many more people came into my life around this time offering places to work from and clients to work with.

I was so happy. I knew I had made the right choice. I was still working in the corporate world, but the Angels were making my future secure and safe. These people I met became part of my soul family and have remained in my life. During this time I was also to meet one of the most important people in my life and someone who was to become my best friend. Her name is Patricia Scanlan, the best-selling author of many great books and a person with the biggest and most loving heart I have ever encountered.

I had seen Patricia on television a couple of times down through the years and was drawn to her energy even back then. With her great sense of fun and ability to make me laugh she appeared to be a very down-to-earth lady with no airs or graces who never took herself too seriously. My Mam and sisters had read her books and were big fans. I just knew even then our paths would cross some day.

Patricia had got my number from a mutual acquaintance and had left a message on my phone asking for an appointment. When I phoned her back I connected with her voice there and then. I had just given her my address when my Angel Hannah whispered in my ear. 'No, Aidan, you will have to go to her: she is not able to drive at the moment.' I related this to Patricia and she was surprised but delighted as she was waiting to have a major operation on her back and was finding driving very difficult.

She was more than happy for me to go to her house so we made the arrangement for the following night at seven. I was dying to meet her.

That night Patricia opened the door and I knew immediately there was a huge connection between us. We hugged each other and it was just like meeting up with an old friend. We talked for an hour or so and then I conducted the healing – and then we talked for another couple of hours! And from that night we became best friends.

Patricia is the most caring friend anyone could ask for. She never tires of helping or advising and is at the other end of the phone any time of the day or night with her helping hand and her words of comfort. When you meet Patricia she embraces you with pure love and the warmth that is the healing Jesus Energy, and the gift of unconditional love.

Like Rina, Patricia is a soul friend and someone I have known in many lifetimes. I can't remember a time I didn't know her and I dread to think of a time when she is not in my life. She has taught me many things since we met and she is the teacher that gave me back my confidence and taught me about self-belief. My life has been deeply enriched by her love, support and friendship.

These were the links that quickly came together to form a solid golden chain of binding and everlasting friendships of unconditional love.

Chapter Nineteen

Just for today do not worry.
Just for today do not anger.
Just for today honour your parents, teachers, and elders.
Just for today do an honest day's work.
Just for today give gratitude to every living thing.
Dr Mikao Usui, The Five Reiki Principles

The long-awaited Reiki weekend had arrived and I was driving to Newtownmountkennedy, County Wicklow, to receive my first attunement to Reiki Level One with Mary K.

It was a bright March morning and peace and excitement filled my heart as I drove through the magnificent countryside that is called the Garden of Ireland. Yellow daffodils danced in the cold spring breeze, while the pale blue cloudless sky and the early spring sun held the promise of a beautiful day.

The azure sky was the backdrop to a sea of deep yellow gorse bushes covering each side of the road. In waves of golden light came the scent of spring and once again I was reminded that this was the season of rebirth that reflects the gentle energy of the Risen Christ Jesus.

The Angels of nature had sprinkled their magic of spring colours over the earth. Primrose yellow and fresh green hues of healing energy fell over the fields and gardens, spreading healing on Mother Earth and waking her from her winter sleep. What a perfect time it was to learn something new. I felt honoured and privileged knowing I was to be attuned to an ancient sacred energy on this lovely day.

Over the past couple of weeks I had read up on Reiki. There were many books and websites at hand to help me explore the history of this healing art and my research gave me a better understanding of its roots.

In the nineteenth century a Japanese scholar, Dr Mikao Usui, rediscovered the ancient lost art of healing; the type of healing he believed was used by Tibetan monks centuries ago. He was guided, through meditation, to go to the holy mountain north of Kyoto called Mount Kurama and here he fasted for twenty-one days. As a result, he became enlightened and received healing abilities.

On the twenty-first day he awoke to complete darkness around him and in the distance saw a very bright light coming towards him. He accepted this Divine Light and it entered him through his third eye (located in the centre of the forehead). Here he received the symbols that are used today in Reiki Healing.

On his way back from the mountain he stubbed his toe and, when he held it, the pain and bleeding stopped and he realized that his hands had become hot with energy. He experienced another few incidents where healing occurred almost instantaneously. He passed on his knowledge, and Reiki has now spread around the world. This tradition heals by the laying on of hands. The word 'Reiki' is made of two

Japanese words – *Rei*, which means 'Universal' or 'the Higher Power', and *Ki*, which is 'life force energy'. So Reiki is actually 'Universal Life Force Energy'.

It is a safe, relaxing non-manipulative energy, which is highly effective in the area of personal growth. The energy adjusts itself to the needs of the recipient, which helps to achieve a state of health and wholeness. It treats the whole person – mind, body and spirit – and its many beneficial effects include relaxation, the feelings of peace, security and well-being. Reiki clears energy blockages and overall increases the energy in the body, restoring balance and speeding up the healing process. It helps the body support its natural ability to heal itself. It is a complementary therapy, and not alternative. Reiki is non-religious and many people of different faiths and religions use it successfully.

I arrived at Mary K.'s about ten minutes before the class began. Everyone seemed as keen as I was. Mary made me very welcome, as always, and it was good to be in her energy again. I had been to her home a couple of times since meeting her at the holistic fair, but the energy in her training room that day was powerful.

It was a large bright room and the décor was simple and elegant. There was a delicate scent of incense burning, which created an ambience that was perfect. I immediately felt calm and peaceful. A group of ten people were taking the course and every one of us seemed to click right from the moment we met. A sense of knowing and a deep spiritual connection bound us as a group.

First Mary told us about herself and her journey. She explained clearly and simply the healing art of Reiki and about our attunement, which was the first thing she intended to do after the tea break. Mary explained that during the attunement she would stand behind us and place her hands on our shoulders and breathe in the required Reiki Colours.

She would focus on the main four chakras: the Crown, the Third Eye, the Throat and the Heart. Then she would place the Sacred Golden Symbols handed down from Dr Usui into these areas. She went on to explain that she would move around us as we sat in our chairs and blow these symbols into our Heart Chakra, sealing the symbols as she went. Mary requested that we keep our eyes closed during the process as everyone was being individually attuned and we needed no outside distractions. During the attunement we might or might not experience different feelings or emotions, she said.

Some might see colours or forms, or symbols. Some might hear sounds or have physical sensations, while others might feel no unusual sensations at all. It's a different but wonderful experience for each and every one, she explained, but whatever we felt would be natural and normal.

When we returned to the training room after our tea break I noticed that the energy had changed. It now felt fresh and light. A scent of white sage filled the room and all around the Angels and Spirit Guides stood. They held their heads back and raised their faces to the heavens. Their eyes were closed and their hands outstretched; a pure white light was flowing from them. In the centre of the room Mary had placed the chairs in a circle. My Spirit Guide, Jack, was standing by one of the chairs, which my Guardian Angels gently guided me to.

We were all seated with our backs to each other and once we were settled Mary took us through a meditation to relax and prepare us for our attunement. When it was finished she came into the centre of the circle and announced she would attune each of us, one by one, and during this time we should listen to the music and relax and not open our eyes until everyone had been attuned.

When she had completed the attunement, she would gently bring our energies back into the room and ask us to open our eyes. It all felt so right and in Divine Order.

My Angels and Guides had filled me with so much confidence prior to the course, by reassuring me that I was doing the right thing, that now I had a real sense of walking my true path. After some time Mary stood behind me and placed her hands on my shoulders. A peace and stillness filled my entire body and I was transported back in time to another lifetime, another place where I sat among a large circle of people.

The men and women were dressed in blue robes and a white light radiated around their outer bodies. Their eyes were wide open and they held their hands pointing to the skies in deep meditation. A great sense of peace and fulfilment surrounded them and they were at one with God. Here I sat with them in full view of a vast army of soldiers and we showed no fear or signs of surrender.

Outside the group immense fires burned and people ran, screaming, for cover into the surrounding hills and forests. Simultaneously this circle of people stood up and willingly and silently walked into the blazing flames. Their energy was powerful and victorious and they showed no emotion or fear. I was to discover later that this was a time that I shared as a Cathar in France.

Suddenly I was back in the present moment and aware of Mary standing behind me. This attunement wasn't new to me and the energy felt familiar as she placed her hands on the crown of my head. I could feel the Crown Chakra point open and in my mind's eye I saw a beam of white light enter my body and a great feeling of joy filled my entire being. She then moved to my Third Eye and my throat and began to work on these areas. I felt the gentle healing heat come from her hands, which gave me great comfort. Finally she placed the symbols in my heart, and my body fell back against the chair as if I had received an electric shock.

It felt to me as if someone had pulled my ribs apart. My heart felt open and a great waterfall of tears and sadness poured from it, leaving me feeling empty and hollow. This was followed quickly by a bolt of dazzling Gold light, which filled the empty space and embraced my heart in a feeling of warmth, love and total peace. Zechariah whispered in a low and loving voice, 'Receive the loving, healing light of Jesus and Buddha and in doing so know you are protected and loved. Now share this love and healing with others. Little Soul, you are safe and much loved.'

As Mary finished and left me I could feel the tears running down my cheeks, but they were tears of joy and happiness, not sadness. The attunement had opened me up and aligned me with much greater things to come. A feeling of rebirth and reconnection with my soul gave it a mystical and sacred touch. I experienced that familiar feeling of Zechariah, Hannah and Jack embracing me in a gentle hug and I knew then all was well. Some time later Mary quietly asked us to open our eyes and bring ourselves back to the present moment.

How beautiful it was to look around the room and see that everyone's aura looked brighter and clearer. All in the circle were beaming and their energy seemed to have lifted. The most wonderful sense of inner peace had fallen on us. My hands felt warm: a gentle, light sensation of flowing energy came from them which replaced the burning feeling I'd had in them before. It was a beautiful safe feeling.

We all just wanted to sit back and relax and everyone's Angels and Guides seemed to be glowing in a Golden light. I noticed that even Mary looked different. She was radiant and her energy had lifted even higher than it had been that morning. Around her stood many Angels and Guides and her face shone in love and delight.

She went around the room asking how each of us had felt during the attunement and reassured us that the Sacred Golden Symbols had fallen on each of us. It was now lunchtime and a few of us needed to ground ourselves by going out into the open air and connecting with the earth and nature.

After lunch we went back into the training room and found that Mary had set up plinths around the room. The energy had changed yet again. The Angels and Spirit Guides were still very much present but their energy was now a lot lighter. Mary selected one of the students to lie on the plinth and she talked us through the seven chakras in great detail. She explained what each one related to within our bodies and explained how they worked. She was also going to give us a practical demonstration of how to position our hand on the client during the healings.

A brief introduction to the chakras is given at the end of this book, for those who are not familiar with them.

When Mary had finished her demonstration she paired us off with each other to practise. I was teamed with a very nice girl called Siobhan. We had already connected during the lunch break and were both happy and comfortable to work on each other. I was first to receive the treatment. Siobhan's energy was flowing and very Angelic. It felt comforting and nurturing and made me feel safe and loved. I was in heaven – I didn't want this session to end. I gave Siobhan feedback about how her energy felt to me, explaining that it felt soft and gentle and that I was totally relaxed during the session.

Then it was her turn to get on the plinth. At the base of the plinth stood an Angel of the Healing Green Light and at the top the Archangel Raphael. My Guardian Angels were by my side and Jack stood straight and firm at the end of the plinth, watching me like a proud father at his son's first football match. They all sent beams of radiant Golden white light to Siobhan as she lay, eyes closed and deeply relaxed. I started on her crown and I couldn't believe the difference in my energy. It flowed more gently and was much more controlled; almost like a laser effect. My hands seemed to be directed to the different parts of the body that needed healing and it was as if there were spirits gently guiding them.

To my amazement I could also see her chakras and aura very clearly. My understanding was becoming clearer now as the Angels showed me the blocks or darker shading in the colours of her chakras and aura while showing me in picture forms why a certain chakra was blocked.

I found my energy didn't tire as easily and I felt good when the treatment was finished. Siobhan felt the energy very clearly too, and enjoyed her treatment very much. Her feedback was that my energy was gentle but firm and very powerful. We practised on different people over the course of the two days and every healing I gave and received felt different.

During the entire weekend Mary spent time with each of us, one on one, always making sure we understood everything and did everything correctly. We carried out each healing practice in a sacred and loving way and Mary was kind and patient. We were all sad when the course came to an end, but our spirits were lifted when we received our certificates. Mary told us we would go through a twenty-one-day clearing, as we would with each Reiki attunement we received.

The reason it takes this length of time, she explained, is that the energy spends twenty-four hours on each chakra, so it takes seven days to go through all the chakras, and just to be absolutely certain the energy goes around three times (the Divine Number), thus creating the twenty-one-day period.

The symptoms of this clearing for some people might only be a headache or the sensation of a head cold, yet for others it materializes as a huge shift in their energy. Regardless of the lesson or challenge we might or might not face during this process, she went on, our reaction depended totally on us and we should rest assured that we were always given the means to deal with whatever situation came up; we should not be afraid or feel alone.

As our Reiki Master, Mary was always at the other end of the phone for us during this clearing and I felt totally safe, as my energy was being uplifted and renewed. During the following twenty-one days I had very few symptoms in the way of cleansing except for a slight migraine for a couple of days. I felt great and had much more energy than I'd had prior to my attunement.

My friends and family noticed a difference in me and in my healing technique. I was able to see and feel things much more clearly and I just couldn't believe the difference Level One Reiki was making to my healings and to my inner confidence. I had decided to go back to Mary K. over the coming year and finish my Reiki studies to take me to Mastership Level.

During this time I learned the first of the Sacred Reiki Symbols and received my second attunement, which took me to Reiki Practitioner. Later in the year I received the additional attunement and learned how to teach Reiki to others and I then became a Reiki Master/Teacher.

No attunement was as exciting or powerful as my first but each was sacred and meaningful to me in other ways. And each level gave me more confidence and a deeper understanding of healing as well as increasing my healing energy.

Once I had finished my Reiki training I had no fear when doing healings or teaching this ancient healing practice. It had changed my life in a positive, uplifting way and I felt I could do anything. Everyone was commenting on how great I looked and I felt fantastic. My cousin and great friend Bernadette had recently come home from Canada. I hadn't seen her for over a year and when we met up the first thing she did was stand back, look me up and down, then give a big smile and say, 'Wow! I will have one of whatever you're on, Aidan.'

I was at last comfortable in my own body and I felt good and at peace with myself and in myself. Watch out, world, I'm back! I am very grateful to my Reiki Master, Mary K. Hayden, an excellent teacher. She inspired me to continue my studies and follow my path of healing and I found her classes immensely enjoyable and a pleasure to attend. I will always hold her dear to my heart and wish her a hundred thousand blessings each day.

Chapter Twenty

To every thing there is a season,
And a time to every purpose under the heaven:

Ecclesiastes 3: 1

It was April 2004 and the weeks were passing by quickly. I was looking forward to working for myself and everything was just about to fall into place for me. It was coming up to my final couple of months in the corporate world and I had never been so ready to let go of anything before in my life as I was right now. I was counting every minute until my final release with absolute joy.

I had discovered that holding a grudge against any of my work colleagues or management was stupid and completely useless. It was a waste of my precious time. As far as I was concerned I had finished working there mentally over the past few months and I was now just winding down.

I didn't allow the toxic heavy energy of greed and power to bother me, I felt safe and protected. I just didn't care any more, I was on the final run home and it felt fantastic. I was still doing healing during this period, but since my Reiki attunement I felt I needed more time for myself. So I made the decision to cut down these hours and free up some space for 'me' time.

In late April of that year, I had agreed to give a friend a reading. I had been feeling groggy all day in work and my stomach was swollen. I felt slightly sick but put it down to something I had eaten. I can remember coming home that evening and not being able to eat my dinner. I really was in no mood to do a reading but I had promised so I felt that I had to do it. My mother told me I was looking very pale and that I needed to go to bed but I assured her I was OK.

A short time later my sister called in and when she saw me she agreed that I looked very pale and tired. It was too late to cancel as my friend was on her way. When she arrived she told me I looked great, so I naturally thought Mam and my sister were over-reacting. I got on with the task in hand and all was going well until suddenly I felt the need to throw up. I excused myself for a couple of minutes and thankfully the feeling passed and I continued with the reading. As the session went on I began to feel light-headed and nauseous again. I finished the reading as quickly as I could and was relieved I hadn't been sick.

Unfortunately I hadn't made my friend aware of my discomfort and since she wasn't in any hurry to go home she continued chatting for about another half an hour. At this point I felt I could take no more so I had to ask her to leave, explaining that I wasn't feeling very well. She apologized for delaying and left immediately. No sooner had she gone than I had to run to the bathroom.

I got a terrible shock as I was vomiting up blood and it tasted foul. I panicked and called for my sister to come to my aid. She remained calm and made me go to bed. She suggested calling an ambulance but I asked her to wait for a while to see how things settled. Poor Mam went numb with worry. She was terrified; I think she genuinely thought I was dying and decided to take herself off into the sitting room to pray for me.

I lay in my room on my own and called in my Angel Hannah to help. She reassured me that I would recover but that it would be best for everyone if I went to hospital right away. In my stubbornness and fear I resisted for a couple of hours until just at midnight I became violently ill again, this time losing large amounts of blood.

My brother Jim was called and when he arrived he and the rest of the family decided to go ahead and call the ambulance. The Angels and Jack continually told me I was going to be OK but fear had taken such a grip of me that their soothing words were falling on deaf ears.

The ambulance took me to the hospital and my brother followed in his car. It was a cold, wet, dirty April night. A&E was packed with people. I was taken to a grubby little cubicle and a nurse came to take down all my details. She was very detached and didn't make any general conversation, nor did she tell me when I would see a doctor.

For about thirty minutes all I could hear was the sound of a drunk cursing and swearing at the staff and the cries of a very young child further down the corridor. There was a very strange, heavy energy around the A&E department.

My brother was waiting outside, so I got up and went out to him and told him to go home, as it was around 2 a.m. and he had an early start later that morning. He would only leave once I assured him that I would phone him if I needed him for anything. I went back into the cubicle and lay down. Shortly afterwards a doctor came to see me. He conducted a quick examination. He explained that they had no public or private beds available at that moment but that I could stay in the cubicle until a bed became free. He arranged for me to have an X-ray but they were very busy and I had to wait a long time before being seen.

How great was this? I'd been paying for both public and private hospital every month for the last twenty-six years and I couldn't get a bed! Terrific. So this is what the Celtic Tiger had to offer, I thought: a beautiful new hospital with no bed space and doctors and nurses who were overworked and exhausted. I lay fuming and feeling weak and frustrated. I was hooked up to a drip, which meant I could only lie on my back, and as the trolley bed was extremely uncomfortable it just added to the misery of the situation. Eventually, I drifted off into an uneasy sleep feeling disgruntled and dejected.

I awoke some time later to find Archangel Raphael standing at the end of my bed. He glowed in a fantastic brilliant white light and all around the outer part of this light shone a beautiful pale green light. He bowed his head gently and, putting his finger to his mouth, shook his head from side to side as if to say, *Don't say a word*.

He made his way over to me and lifted my right hand. He drew a winding circle on my hand with golden light, then covered it with both his hands and lifted his beautiful pale blue eyes to the heavens. He then repeated the same strange exercise with my left hand. When he finished, my hands had a tingling and warm sensation flowing through them.

'Receive the Angelic Seal of Healing, Love, Light, and use it lovingly and wisely. Allow it to now heal your own body and restore it to full health,' Raphael said.

I couldn't find my voice to answer him, nor did I fully understand his request, so I just nodded to show my acceptance. He raised his hands gently up over his head and a great rainbow of colour fell around him and each colour became a solid energy that formed an Angel.

Around my bed stood seven powerful Angels dressed in the individual colours of the rainbow. They were shimmering in power and light.

I was amazed. I rubbed my eyes to see if I were dreaming and when I was convinced that I was truly awake I reached out and felt their soft cool light energy. My heart began to race and fear took a grip of me once again.

I was dying! That had to be it! Why else would they all come at the one time and gather around my bed? Mentally I began to scream, *Oh God, please do not let me die in this horrible place and without my family around me*. My head began to pound and I got myself into a terrible state.

I asked, 'Have you come to take me home? Am I dying?'

Raphael smiled, as did all the other six of them. 'No, my beloved soul, you are not dying. These are the Angels of the Healing Rainbow Light, the Angels of the Divine Light. These great Angels and I will walk with you and assist you in your daily healings from this day on. Over the coming weeks these healing Angels will visit you to explain about their energies and how you can work with them. Do not be afraid: we are here to help and protect you. We will assist you with your healings and protect you from negative energy at all times.'

'I am very happy and will gladly receive you and accept all you have to tell me,' I replied, still shocked.

'We will remove ourselves from your sight for now but we will remain by your side. Rest assured that you won't be long in this place, as they will find nothing seriously wrong with your health. You are to enjoy good health for many years to come,' Raphael declared.

Before leaving they all placed their gentle, warm hands on me and bowed their heads as if in prayer. Then they blew gentle breath upon me and a warm, relaxed energy filled my entire body. I felt so uplifted and good. Slowly they began to leave and in their departure stillness and silence filled my cubicle. I felt safe and content and drifted back into a deep, restful sleep.

It was about 5 a.m. when I awoke and I was still waiting for a bed. I hadn't seen anyone to ask about this, and it was some time before an attendant arrived – a jolly man, extremely chatty and upbeat. He informed me that he was here to move me to another waiting area. The 'waiting area' was the corridor of the A&E department, which was lined with beds. I felt that I was one of the lucky people that day as I got a bed, even if it was in the corridor.

The bed was comfortable compared to the hard narrow trolley in the cubicle. The sheets were crisp and clean and I sank into the bed and just wanted to sleep. I was taken back to the X-ray department shortly after that and then returned to bed. I wasn't allowed food or water for the next two days but I did feel a great deal better. My visitors came and went but none of the medical staff could throw any light on my condition until after I had a gastroscopy.

I couldn't have this procedure done until I had a bed on the ward, and I couldn't have it done while I was still in A&E. How strange was that? So I stayed in the corridor for the next three days, fasting. In the late evening of day three they found me a bed and I was taken to the ward.

The doctor informed me that I would have my gastroscopy done next morning under general anaesthetic and I would have to stay in the hospital for at least twenty-four hours after that. If they didn't find anything serious, he went on to say, they would discharge me and I could go home.

I was happy that at last there was some positive movement in relation to my condition. Frankly, it was a mighty relief to be off that corridor. The noise and the constant movement of people toing and froing twenty-four hours a day was enough to make anyone ill.

The next morning came and I waited and waited and then at 1 p.m. I was brought to theatre and put to sleep. All I can remember after that was a nurse calling my name and gently shaking me to wake up. I was taken back to the ward feeling very groggy and tired. I drifted off into a deep sleep and the next thing I recall is a nurse waking me up and saying, 'You can get dressed and go home now: they found nothing seriously wrong. We'll send you out a letter and you can see the doctor in Outpatients in a week or ten days. Have you someone I can phone to take you home?'

I was confused and didn't know what day or time it was. All I could see was this nurse standing over me, her voice loud and booming.

'What time is it? Did I sleep all night?' I slurred.

'No, not at all. It's 4 p.m. and you've been back from theatre for about two hours,' she responded.

'I was told I'd need at least twenty-four hours for the anaesthetic to wear off before being allowed home,' I snapped back, just wanting to be left alone to sleep.

'No, no, not at all, you're fine. They found nothing wrong with you and we need the bed.'

So, there it was. Anaesthetic or no anaesthetic, I was being turfed out!

I gave her Rosaleen's number and she came and collected me. I still don't fully remember leaving the hospital that day. Three days in the corridor and less than twenty-four hours on the ward – and I was still none the wiser as to why I was ill.

Ten days later I went back to the hospital for a check-up and the doctor confirmed that they could find nothing wrong with me, but he felt it might be a small tear or rip on the lining of my stomach that had caused internal bleeding.

I was relieved. As always, the Angels were right again. The doctor advised that I should remain off work for a couple of weeks, which I did. I took this opportunity to do a lot of meditation and went for long walks which helped me to relax, unwind and sleep more soundly.

It was about two weeks after I left hospital when I was awoken from my sleep and found Zechariah and Hannah standing by my bed with Jack. The room was covered in mist and I knew I was about to be paid a visit or be taken somewhere.

'The Healing Angels are on their way, Aidan. Sit up and be still,' Zechariah instructed.

With that, the room filled with a great rainbow of coloured light and the Angels appeared and introduced themselves to me.

First to step forward was Uriel with a Swirling Red Flaming Light around him.

'I am the energy the earth people have named Uriel, the holder of the secrets of the earth, nature and the universe. I bring serenity, peace and knowing to each and every one of you earth children. My gift to the Universe is that of Director of the Soul, and Keeper of Records. I, Uriel of the flaming red light, bring you guidance when you are lost and tired, understanding when you're fearful, wisdom when confused, and information and knowledge to guide you along your life path. I will strengthen and deepen your connection with Mother Earth and ground you in times of unease. I will bring people ease and direction in their healing. I am the carrier of the Healing Red Light and protector of the Root Chakra,' he declared.

Next to step forward was Cassiel with a soft Orange Light flowing around him.

'I am the energy the earth people have named Cassiel. I bring you the sacred power to manifest and create quickly. I preside over the streams, rivers, lakes and oceans and I am the protector of everything that lives within the great waters of your Universe. I help and empower you to clear your negativity, leaving you clarity available to heal, feel and reveal the positive you. Call upon me when you're unable to solve issues that are concerning you. I will enhance your understanding of the situation and strengthen your ability to do what is right. I will open up your true gifts and awaken your creativity.

'Allow my energy that flows like a cool stream to flow with your energy into your body to bring healing and joy to those who come to you, dear soul, for healing. I will bring people happiness and positivity in their healing. I am the carrier of the Healing Orange Light and protector of the Sacral Chakra.'

The very gentle Gabriel stepped forward and a Golden Yellow Light radiated all around her.

'I am the energy the earth people have named Gabriel. I bring you the gentle, golden, yellow light of sun and in this God light I bring goodness and fortune. I will assist and guide you when you are making changes in your lives. I shall always walk ahead of you and open the doors of opportunity, so that your path can be made easier.

'I am the energy of protection and birth and the protector of expectant mothers. When you feel lost and cannot understand, ask for my guidance to bring you the information you need to resolve issues, concerns and problems. Allow my energy that flows like the warmth of the sun to flow with your energy to bring healing and laughter to those who come to you, dear soul, for healing. My mission is to bring hope and direction during a healing. I am the carrier of the Yellow Light and the protector of the Solar Plexus Chakra,' she said.

Then Raphael stepped forward with a light, breezy Green Light around him.

'I am the energy the earth people have named Raphael. I bring the great gift of healing to the Universe. I am the healer and protector of all healers and bring healing to the sick. Close your eyes when you are ill or weak, my dear earth souls, and ask me, Raphael, to send healing through your body. See a green light cover the place of discomfort and stay in prayer until the pain lifts and repeat the process if it should recur. I will also assist you in changing your eating habits and I can help you to achieve a healthier lifestyle.

'I am also the guardian of love, lovers and travellers. Call upon me for healing, support and love. I am the master of healing and I shall show you how to heal from your heart, the place of unconditional love and the powerhouse of the soul. Only from this place can you truly heal. This is the God love. Only God can bring complete healing and love. Allow my clear healing energy to flow with you to bring healing and unconditional love to those who come to you, dear soul, for healing. I will bring people love and peace during a healing. I am the carrier of the Divine Green Light and the protector of the Heart Chakra,' he announced.

Michael stepped forward with a mighty force in a bolt of electric Blue Light, which sparked from him like an electrical current.

'I am the energy the earth people have named Michael. I bring protection to the Universe and all its inhabitants. I will strengthen and help you speak your truth, keep your word, understand yourself and others and have faith. With my golden sword I will cut away all emotional ties with places and people that hold you back in your life.

'I provide you with a solid iron shield of protection when you are feeling vulnerable and in need of protection from others' energies. Call upon me when times become difficult and confusing. I will do everything to help and protect you. I am the Spirit Warrior and will come to your rescue and bring you calmness, fairness and wise judgement in any situation. Allow my energy that flows like the electrical storm to flow with yours to bring confidence and strength to those who come to your powerful soul for healing. I will bring protection and balance to a healing. I am the carrier of the Healing Blue Light and the protector of the Throat Chakra.' He smiled.

Then Camael stepped forward with an easy and gentle flowing Indigo Light around him.

'I am the energy the earth people have named Camael. I bring calmness to my earth children with gratitude and love. I help you connect with what is fair and just and direct you to bring this energy into your daily life. I always protect those who cannot protect themselves and walk with the bullied and abused.

'My gift to mankind is to give you courage to carry on when you are tired or depressed. Share your worries with me and I will, in return, send healing love beyond your belief. I will enhance your understanding of the situation and help you do what is correct. I help you plan for the future. Please allow my energy that flows like the calm summer sea to flow with yours to bring calmness back to those who come to you, precious soul, for healing. I will bring wisdom and foresight to their healing. I am the bringer of the Indigo Light and the protector of the Third Eye Chakra,' he said.

Last to step forward was the powerful and gentle Metatron surrounded in a gentle flowing Violet and White Light.

'I am the energy the earth people call Metatron. I am the holder of all that is spiritual. I watch over your thoughts and deeds. I will assist you in clearing your mind of clutter and bring you peace. I am your help and connection to the higher self. I show you the love of God and direct you on your spiritual journey. I comfort the dying and am the collector of souls.

'I am the healer and protector of children. I walk with them and bring them wisdom and understanding. Ask for my help and love when you need inspiration or motivation. I will assist you in understanding issues that are worrying you and that you are unable to solve. I am here to help you understand and to inspire you and show you the way forward. Allow my peaceful energy to flow with yours to bring stillness and peace to those who come to you for healing, my Little Soul. I will bring understanding and wholeness to a healing. I am the carrier of the Healing Violet White Light and the protector of the Crown Chakra,' he proclaimed.

*   *   *

It had been a long time since I had had such an intense visit. These seven Serene Beings of Perfect Light and Love stood around my bed, their hands outstretched with amazing rays of rainbow colour light shining from them.

That old familiar feeling of stillness, timelessness and peace filled the room and Zechariah indicated to them it was enough for the moment. They vanished, leaving me with just Zechariah, who told me to rest and sleep. These Angels would visit me again over the coming few nights and everything would become much clearer. Zechariah left my sight, the room became dark again and I fell into a most restful and peaceful sleep. I awoke early the next morning to a warm, sunny day with a clear blue sky. I felt energized and happy. The previous night's experience seemed like a dream to me but I knew it wasn't. I had learned not to doubt my Angels or my Angelic experiences.

The Angels didn't come that night but they did the following night. Again I was awoken from my sleep at about 2 a.m.

Zechariah and Hannah stood one at each side of me; they took my hand and instinctively I knew what was about to happen. I held on to their hands and slowly stepped out of my physical body: I was now looking down on my body lying in the bed below me and it was a surreal experience. Zechariah talked me through the procedure to keep me focused and calm. In each corner stood the Angels of the North, South, East and West: these are the directions that govern your flow of energy.

Then the Angels of Divine Light, the Angels of the Healing Rainbow Light, stood at each chakra and in an outer circle stood many more Angels and Higher Beings. Zechariah told me to pay attention and to watch and learn, as they would show me the healing techniques I would use and teach others to use. They began to do the healing on my body and they made my chakras visible. They laid their hands on me and they took energy from one chakra and placed it into another.

They blew colour into my chakras and did a very simple exercise to align all the chakras. Once this was done, the chakras would rotate in the correct way and at the correct speed. They kept it all very simple and sacred. Great white light covered my entire body as they worked on me. After what felt like an hour they gave thanks to God for the healing and they left my sight. I stepped back into my body that lay asleep and very much at peace.

The next day I felt disconnected and ungrounded as I always do after an out-of-body experience. Over the next two weeks these beautiful healing Angels came to me and taught me the secrets of Angelic healing and asked me to pass this method of healing on to others. On the last evening of training Raphael attuned me with the sacred Golden Symbol of Soul to awaken and enlighten me. This was to assist my soul journey and to strengthen and empower my soul purpose.

The sacred symbol he passed to me was to help attune others and help them also on their soul journey. I was instructed to use the new techniques in my healings from that moment onwards, which I readily agreed to do. However, it would take me a couple of years, he explained, before I could pass these techniques on to others and attune them to the Sacred Soul Symbol.

I returned to work and in a strange way I was glad to be back. I only had another two weeks before I resigned so it was very bearable. I set about tidying my desk as much as I could and tying up any loose ends in relation to the administration side. I also arranged to have lunch and dinner with my friends from work to say goodbye and thank them for their support and comradeship throughout my time in the company. I had made some very good and loyal friends over the years and we still keep in touch.

The last day of work finally arrived and my energy was buzzing. I can remember the day clearly because it was a gloriously sunny June day and the energy around had a happy feeling about it. The day went by quickly and at three o'clock I left my desk, and the company, for the last time. I had worked up twenty-six years' service with them and was feeling relieved to be putting an end to this chapter in my life. I truly had no sense of regret or sorrow. I got into my car, drove away and never looked back.

My healing work began full time from that day on and I have been blessed with clients and work ever since.

One of my clients was Tony. I met him in the summer of 2005 when he came for an Angel Card reading. At the time he was going through major life changes. He had many questions and was fearful of what lay ahead for him on the new spiritual journey he had started. Talking with him, I felt he understood exactly what it was he needed to do for the first time in his life. As a child Tony was bright in school and had been encouraged to follow an academic path which had proved very successful for him; but he didn't want this kind of lifestyle any more. He knew his real purpose was to help and heal people and to offer valuable advice, guidance and reassurance to them.

The Angels assured him his feelings were indeed right and they instructed him to follow the holistic and spiritual field of healing which he was already pursuing, as he had done many Angelic and healing courses over the past few years. The Angels were very clear with him that he needed to put himself out in the healing area as there were many people waiting for his healing and his direction. This he did, and today he is a happy and successful holistic practitioner.

'I thank you, Aidan, and the Angels for helping me find happiness and fulfilment in my life like I never experienced before' was the lovely affirmation I received from him.

It was also around this time that I met a woman of great strength and courage. She had booked herself in for a healing. Her name was Teresa – a mother and wife who had been through every parent's worst nightmare: the sudden and unexpected death of her child. Her beautiful teenage daughter had gone to bed happy and healthy early one night and was looking forward to everything life had to offer her. Sadly, this was not to be the way her story panned out. When Teresa went into her room the next morning to call her for school she found her daughter still and lifeless in her bed. She had passed peacefully into an eternal sleep during the night and no one to this day has been able to explain to her parents how or why this happened.

It wasn't long after her daughter's passing that this amazing woman set up a self-help group for other parents and grieving families that found themselves in the same sad circumstances.

During the healing her daughter did come to give her messages of love and to let her know she was now happy and at peace. She wanted to convey to her mum that no one was to question or blame themselves about the unfortunate event – they had done nothing wrong, she assured her.

She went on to explain that she had lived a wonderful life and felt blessed to be loved so much in her short life and now in her death. She also had personal and private messages for her mum that made her laugh and cry. Teresa was thankful that her daughter had made contact and she said that it made such a difference to the way she was feeling about her precious girl's early and unexpected death.

As we talked, Teresa told me about her other daughter,

six-year-old Zara, and how she had been sexually abused by her cousin. Teresa had discovered this shocking truth in and around the time of her other daughter's death. Zara was attending a counsellor following the terrible incident, but Teresa felt she wasn't doing so well with that. She felt that Zara had become very withdrawn and quiet and asked me if I would consider seeing her. I arranged to meet with her as soon as possible, which luckily enough turned out to be the following week.

We parted with a hug and I noted a considerable lift in Teresa's energy field. This lady's strength and love had an incredible effect on me in the coming week and I just couldn't get her out of my mind. Her courage and forgiveness were astonishing. I had agreed to meet her on the Sunday afternoon at a hotel where I was attending a holistic fair. I was very kindly given a private room for my meeting with Zara, and I felt nervous and restless for some reason about the whole event. The family arrived and I said I would meet Zara only if her mum or dad sat in on the session. Her mum agreed to come in and I could see immediately that Zara was very relaxed having her there. Zara is a beautiful child with fair hair, a nervous smile and the biggest hazel-coloured eyes I had ever seen.

She had a multitude of Angels around her, which was a blessing to see. She sat in front of me while her mother sat behind, just to my left side. We began to talk about things that were of interest to her like Christmas, Santa and school. Gently I approached the subject of her counsellor and asked if she liked her. She told me that she did and was relaxed in her response.

Then I asked her about the abuse and watched as her whole energy changed in the blink of an eye. Her eyes changed, becoming dull and lifeless. I noted that her whole body was rigid as she recalled the incident. She told me in a voice that was almost a whisper what the boy did to her, stating as firmly as she could that it wasn't nice and she didn't like it. Her little body was trembling and she was crying as she told me her story and I could see that she was very frightened and vulnerable.

I just wanted to take this precious child in my arms and hug her until I had squeezed all memory of her pain away. Inside my head I was screaming, *Please don't put this beautiful soul through my years of pain and guilt. Don't rob her of her soul and spirit. Please don't let anyone else hurt or harm her in any way.* How could anyone have harmed an innocent child like Zara? I asked myself.

With tears in my eyes I explained to Zara that we had something in common because the same thing had happened when I was young, and that in time everything would be OK again. I told her how brave she was to tell her mum about the boy and what he had done. I also told her how clever and brave she was, explaining to her that I was very old before I could tell anyone or get help. In her innocence she gave a little giggle when I told her this. Then I asked did she understand that it wasn't her fault what had happened?

'Yes, I know that,' she said.

'Good, so can you tell me why you won't talk with your mum and the counsellor about it, darling?' I enquired.

She looked at me, her beautiful eyes wide open with tears running from them, and said, 'It makes Mum sad when I talk about it. She cries and I don't want her to be sad any more.' She said this with so much love and concern for her mother that my heart ached. I looked around at her mother, who also had tears running down her cheeks. She promised her broken but brave little daughter that she wouldn't cry any more when she wanted to talk to her about it. I told her how lucky she was to have a counsellor and a mum who knew what had happened, that she could talk to.

I explained that she was safe now and very much loved by everyone and then asked if she knew who Merlin the Magician was. To my great surprise, she did. I took out a crystal and gave it to her to hold, explaining to her that it was a magic wand.

I told her I was going to call Merlin into the room and that when he came he would bring back fun and magic to her life. I asked her gently to hold on to the crystal magic wand and requested that we call him together. I often call on the energy of Merlin when I am working with children, as it is a light and fun energy to have around. It's also very powerful and I would associate it with the Archangel Metatron, the pro- tector of children, and with Mother Mary's nurturing, safe energy. So we both closed our eyes and called Merlin in and asked him to stay with Zara.

When I opened my eyes I could see the energy and the form it had taken. It was the energy of a very tall, old man wear- ing purple and with a big hat and a long white beard with a wand spreading magic dust as he danced around Zara. I laughed at the sight.

'Well, Zara, can you see Merlin?' I asked.

She looked at me with her big eyes as bright and shiny as two new buttons.

'Oh yes, I can see him. He has a long beard and is dressed in purple with a big hat. Look – he's there.' She pointed directly at Merlin, then giggled and said, 'What is all that silver stuff he is shaking all over us?'

'That's his power magic dust that will help you have fun again, and do you know what, Zara? He will be with you all the time from now on. So nothing bad will ever happen to you again,' I told her. She was very comfortable hearing this. I told her to keep the crystal with her at all times and explained that Merlin would always come to help her when she called him. Crystals find their way to us and stay with us for as long as we need them. They then either pass over to another or we find that they've disappeared – that we've lost them for some unknown reason. This is an indication that their work is complete.

Zara went away a lot happier and continued to make great progress in the coming months. She did open up and talk to her parents and counsellor much more, and the kind and gentle Merlin helped her through the whole experience.

Meeting that beautiful little girl helped me find perfect peace within myself and I finally knew for certain I'd had no part to play in my abuse. Just like Zara I too am innocent and free of all guilt. I thank God for sending me this pure and perfect soul called Zara to show me that those vile acts against me didn't tarnish or dull my soul, nor had they robbed me of my spirit. Zara had the most profound effect on my life and became my greatest teacher. I thank her from the bottom of my heart for the great gift of freedom she gave me that day.

I still hold that wonderful feeling of freedom within me today and I truly love my life and all the people that share it with me. My beloved Angels and Jack walk by my side daily and help me with all my needs.

I can now look back on my life of trials and challenges with gratitude for all that I have learned and for all that I can share with others. I no longer look back with regrets or blame, as it serves no purpose. Feelings of regret and anger will only make you bitter and twisted and leave you stuck in the pain and resentment of the past.

I am surrounded with love and give thanks for this wonderful gift daily. My life is blessed with a great circle of family and friends and my beloved, wise mother taught me at a very young age just what unconditional love really was.

She showed me daily that unconditional love never judges or looks for anything in return. She was, is, and always will be my greatest Guide.

Questions and Answers

I have asked the Angels many questions that I myself have been asked over the past few months and I would like to take this time now to share with you some of the answers that I received on: Love, the Global Economy, the Healing of the Planet, Death, Money, Abuse, Evil, Forgiveness, the Elderly, and how to work with Angels. It is my hope that by doing this exercise I can share with you some of the wisdom that these wonderful beings want us to understand.

Many people are afraid of death and of dying. This is what the Angels tell us.

'Dearest ones, please do not be afraid of death; we will prepare you for this great journey. For a period of time prior to your passing, your body and soul travel to the Crystal Temple of preparation. Here in this great Temple of Light you become reacquainted with your loved ones who have already passed over and you will become steadily attuned to the lighter God energy you have travelled to. You will become a child of both worlds for this blessed time and this is why so many people speak of loved ones, who have passed, before

they themselves journey to the land of eternal love and light. Be not afraid of death for beyond this earth awaits a beautiful place of perfect peace. This is a place of reunions. Here you are not judged by what you did or didn't do on earth but are asked what you have learned. Life is a path of learning and we all choose to learn certain lessons each lifetime. The God that creates you loves you with unconditional love. Unconditional love does not judge or condemn.'

What about miscarriages, stillborn and sudden infant death?

'Before a soul is born it gets together with its soul family and soul group on the great heavenly planes. Here they plan out their life together on earth. Within this soul family, the infant soul then chooses the parents they wish to be with and every soul within that group decides the part they will play on that journey.

'There can be a number of reasons why a child chooses to return to Heaven early. It could be that the young soul wants to experience a pregnancy or miscarriage. It could be that they themselves didn't feel they were ready to be born, that they felt they didn't have enough knowledge to carry out the lessons they agreed to learn. Perhaps they hadn't fully recovered from the trauma of their previous life. It could also be that they needed to bring the family closer together or to bring them to God/Spiritual awareness.

'Whatever the lesson is, it is never to bring guilt or unhappiness to the parents. Always remember this precious and wonderful soul chose you to be their soul parents, so in time this soul will always return to you. Mothers, never blame yourself for this event. Even if you were to cover yourself in cotton wool and stay in bed, this precious and perfect soul would still have chosen to leave and return when they were ready. This soul will always return to its soul family. It's important to remember it's the soul that returns – not the body.'

What is love? I asked.

'My beloved ones, you cannot touch love but you can be touched by an act of love. You cannot buy love but you can give it freely. Love is the light of God and God is love. God's love is unconditional and seeks only the good in man. Love is that smile you give a loved one or a stranger when they look tired or down and need a smile. It's a friendly greeting or a helping hand. Love is being trustworthy and truthful. It's about giving and not expecting anything in return. You can say no and set boundaries and be honest about what you have to say, but always say it with love. For to love is to allow the light and healing love of God to shine in your heart and soul. Be that light of love and healing that burns and illuminate the darkness of war and greed that has shadowed your world. You, my dear children, were created from love to be loved and to give love. Without love nothing will grow or flourish.'

Every day, people ask me about the planet. This is the answer the Angels gave me, when I asked.

'The blessed planet, Mother Earth, is being destroyed before your very eyes. You have raped and murdered this beautiful planet that God so lovingly created for you. You replaced God with ego as you cut down her forests, drained her flood lands, robbed her of almost all her resources, poisoned the seas and skies and then filled and choked the earth with concrete until it could breathe no more. This is what you humans carry out in the name of "progress" and for financial gain. Then you ask why Mother Earth is rebelling, why storms and disasters happen. When you and your leaders step back and see the pain and loss these terrible storms bring, you then ask why? Still not wanting to take responsibility, you ask: how could God let this happen? Again we tell you it is not the work of God but of man and his free will.

'Honour the land and its beauty, give thanks daily for everything

Mother Earth provides for you but do not over-use or dry up her resources. Allow her to rest, breathe and be replenished and then she will sustain you and all living things as God intended.

'You are all called to live in harmony with Mother Earth and respect all living things. Every day you use and abuse the resources she has provided for you without giving it a thought; you have become careless and wasteful. Be mindful of your actions, dearest children, and remember planet Earth is a sacred place. Be gentle, loving and respectful when you walk this precious ground. If you take responsibility for your own actions you too can play your part in healing Mother Earth. Invite the Angels of Nature to walk the earth and to bring with them their sacred healing essences so that it may grow and breathe again. Ask the Angels to bring love, light, healing and wisdom to Mother Earth and all of her inhabitants.'

Many times I have been asked what the Angels have to say about the global economy and the cause of this global unrest. So I put the question to them.

'My dear children, the cause of all this global upset and unrest is basic GREED. You have replaced moral values with career, property, selfishness and other material goods. You have turned your back on the poor, the elderly, the hungry, and on God. This is not due to God; it is due to the lack of God in your everyday life and in your dealings with one another. It's about the immoral values you choose to accept and teach to each other. The old way of doing things and the old systems don't work any more. You must learn to see and do things differently. You now need to learn from your mistakes and rise to a new vibration of awareness and understanding.'

People are afraid to ask for money so I ask the Angels: is it wrong to ask?

'Dear ones, no, it is not wrong to ask for money or to have money. Money is just an energy of exchange. It is the misuse of this energy and the immoral things that people do to gain more and more money that is wrong. Do not hoard money and do not let it rule your life or be ruled by it. When you live for money alone, you live in the coldness of want. In this energy you will always want and want and want and never have enough; nor will you find happiness. Money doesn't buy happiness. Unhappiness comes from something missing in your life. Happiness can only be found in your heart; it is God that is your real source, not money. God will provide money if you ask and understand your need for it. Money is a good energy and there is nothing wrong with having money. It can improve your life if you manage it wisely and treat it with respect and use it for your higher good. Call on the Angels of Finance when you have money problems and they will come on their golden ray of light to assist and guide you no matter how big or small your financial needs are. You see, my dear children, money is not necessarily the root of all evil. It is how you choose to use your money and how you view the energy of money that makes the difference.'

What are Guides?

'Your Spirit Guides, unlike Angels, have lived on earth, living many lives. They have learned all of life's lessons and so have become the perfect soul. They come as great teachers to guide and inspire you lovingly along life's path.'

What are Angels and where do they come from?

'God created the Angelic realm as he did mankind. Angels are Beings of positive energy and pure love and light.'

What do Angels do?

'*We assist in every aspect of your life. We are your direct link between Heaven and earth. We care for you during your life and in death. We are the guardians of your well-being and a light for all that is positive, good and true.*'

Do Angels know everything?

'*No, we don't. We too are a creation of God and subject to Divine Will. Only God holds all the answers.*'

How do we communicate with you?

'*When you wish to communicate with us, simply call on us and we will gently come to your assistance. Speak to us as you would to your beloved family or a dear friend.*'

When we ask you a question, how should we ask?

'*Ask clearly for what it is you desire and we will assist, direct and guide you to the best result, provided it is of positive energy and for your highest good and for the good of all concerned.*'

Why do you not interfere?

'*If we were to interfere we could prevent you from learning many life lessons and this in turn could alter your free will. Remember you chose to come to this planet to exercise your free will, so we can help you and guide you, but it is you who make the final choice.*'

Are there Angels for everything?

'*Yes, there are Angels for everything and every situation in your life and there are millions upon millions of us. There are Angels of Love,*

Romance, Finance, Career, Health, Fun, Protection, and we could go on and on.'

What about fallen angels? Is there such a thing?

'There are no such things as dark Angels. Darkness comes from human fear and human fear comes from lack of God, and from greed, dishonesty, cruelty and abuse. Angels are of light and do not know darkness. We come from pure God light and we radiate with the God light of love and healing every time you call on us or even think of us. Our protective loving energy is always by your side. Light will always outshine the darkness and love will always outshine fear, so think and feel the loving light of God at all times and know that you too are filled with the light and love of God.'

How do we call on Angels? Do you have names?

'No, we don't have names: it is mankind that gave us names. They put earth names on certain energies of Angels who constantly visit the earth planes like Michael, Gabriel and Raphael, to name but a few, and these Angels, as indeed all Angels, love and respect the energy of the name you place on them. So it is not necessary to have to know names: just call on the Angels of Love, or the Angels of Career, or the Angels of Healing, and a conclave of Angels will come and assist you in the situation you find yourself in.'

Do we all have a Guardian Angel?

'Yes, you all have at least two Guardian Angels. One Guardian Angel has been with you in every lifetime and a second and new Guardian Angel is assigned to you every time your soul is reborn.

'They come to help and guide you and to make your life path easier. Your Guardian Angel is always with you, never leaving your side, and walks with you during your entire lifetime on this planet.

We will help you in times of danger and comfort you in times of illness and mourning. We are that strength and support that comes from within during these hard times. These are the times we assist without asking because during these times you are often so lost you don't remember to ask. Remember also when you call on God and ask for His help, God will also send us to assist you and any other Angels you may need at that time. God and the Angels love you, and all mankind, without question. Before your soul is reborn to an earthly body, it meets on the higher planes with other souls that are part of your soul group. Your Guardian Angels and Guides are also there to decide the path and the lessons your soul needs to learn in this lifetime. Then God embraces your soul and fills it with the pure white light of life and the soul starts to journey to earth. It then moves through the different heavenly rays of light, wisdom and knowledge before it is placed in your mother's womb and here you start to adjust to the earth energy again. Your Guardian Angels and your mother's Guardian Angels stand side by side until the day you are born, watching over you and nurturing you.'

What about our parents – are they chosen for us?

'My blessed children, you choose your parents, your parents don't choose you. You choose your parents for all the positive things they give you in your life, not for the negative things they carry. Please don't dwell on the negative things they have passed on to you, choose to see them as the challenges that are set before you to draw on your strengths and weaknesses. The insecurities and behavioural traits that they exhibit, they sometimes don't know how to deal with, so they try to unload them on to you, their dear children. Always try to remember that your parents do the best they can with the knowledge that they have at that time and moment.'

What about adopted children – why do they choose two sets of parents?

'Adopted children choose both sets of parents also. They see the soul parents they wish to live and grow with. While understanding that these wonderful parents can't bring them to their earthly home themselves, they pick the perfect and willing parents to bring them body and soul to Mother Earth. This is one of the most precious gifts a person can give to another: the gift of a child, a perfect soul. You must thank, honour, love and nurture the birth mother for her great strength and selflessness. Adopted children are blessed beyond words to have two sets of parents who love and nurture them in different ways. Do not judge your parents: they always do what they think is best for you and with the knowledge and understanding they have at that particular time.'

What is a Soulmate?

'My dear children, you will have many Soulmates on your journey through life. These are your inner circle of immediate family, close friends, teachers, co-workers, employers or anyone who influences your life in any way. They will affect your life in a positive or negative way on a spiritual, physical or emotional level. There is not always a romantic connection between you but there is always a great bond of love and understanding. My dear children, you have spent many lifetimes together in past lives and will continue the relationship and enhance each other's soul journey in each lifetime.'

What is a Twin Flame?

'You only have one Twin Flame, so you will not have spent many lifetimes with each other. You are a complete mirror image of each other and your Twin Flame is the other half of your soul. Your Twin Flame is not always reborn into the same lifetime as you are, so it is very rare that you meet. These relationships at the start are

usually very intense and you are very aware of each other's thoughts, feelings, desires and needs, at a level that is hard to imagine. Twin Flames' level of love is so deep that to be apart even for a day is very difficult. Their hearts ache when they are separated from each other. This intensity can become very frightening for Twin Flames and can often lead to them walking away from each other because they have never felt like this about anyone before and are not really sure just what they are experiencing as the bond can become too intense. They will always find each other again as they are destined to be together. This reunion may only take days, although sometimes it can take decades, but the feeling between the two will always remain and somehow they will always find their way back to each other.'

How do you know when you're with the right partner?

'My dear, dear children, when your eyes never tire of seeing, when your heart beats in great joy at the thought of them and when your soul rests in peace, knowing that you are safe and happy in this blessed relationship. My beloved children, rest assured that when you are with the right soul partner you will never have to ask this question or ask for anyone's approval. You will never ask: is it right? Your great gift of knowing within your heart and the joy and relaxation within your soul will reassure you that this is the right soul for you and the God-given person.'

Why do people suffer illness?

'My beloved children, illness is not a punishment and it is wrong to believe God must be angry with you. It always has meaning and it is always about growth, and sometimes that growth may be incredibly difficult to detect and understand. You are not expected to understand illness and pain, and it is human and acceptable to feel angry with God during this time. In human terms there are no words to explain why illness occurs, it is between God and the

individual. *Only God holds the answer to this question and, like everything else in your life, you choose and accept to learn different lessons each time you begin your journey to earth. Remember God loves each one of us unconditionally and this love is constant and without limitations.'*

Can Angels change our life path?

'No, dear ones, we can't change your life path. This is something you chose before you came to earth and you are in control of your own life and how you might live it. It's only your free will and stubbornness that can change your life path. We hold the map and the direction of your great journey in every lifetime. However, we can help and guide you along your life path and make your journey easier and more fulfilling. So when you feel lost or confused on this great journey of life call on us and we will help clear away your confusion and lovingly guide you along your true path.'

Can we ask our Angels for something and get the opposite?

'My precious souls, we will always strive to give you what you ask for, if it's for your higher good and the good of all concerned. We would never send you the opposite if it meant it would bring you pain or upset. If we don't send what you ask for, we will always send you something equally good in its place. Your prayers and requests will never go unheard; trust us and follow our directions – we will never lead you astray.'

When we ask for Angels' help do they take this request to God or do they work alone?

'Always remember everything comes from God, therefore anything you ask of us comes through God and from God. We Angels act as a mediator between God and you, His beloved earth souls. We never

work alone; we always work with the Divine Will and love of God. Only God holds the power to grant your request.'

When asking the Angels for a favour, do we ask once or should we keep asking until we're sure that you receive our request?

'Ask as often as you wish, my dear children, but once is quite sufficient. When you ask, we will immediately take your request to the eternal love and light of God. Just have faith and leave it in our hands and don't worry, we will never forget anything you ask for in love. Just stand back and wait: we will give you guidance.'

When Angels answer our prayers how should we thank you?

'This, my dear soul, is so very simple. Just sit in stillness and silent prayer asking us to gather round you and then simply and clearly say "THANK YOU for your help, support and direction." In thanking us you are also thanking God. Two little words that mean so much to us and to so many earth people but these beautiful God-filled words are not used often enough. PLEASE use them more and fill the earth with the God energy that they carry. Make them a part of your everyday life, starting from today.'

What if I make a request and I do not get it?

'This is a case of God knows best. You often ask for things for selfish reasons or something that may not benefit you or your life in any way. So God in His greater wisdom may not grant it or send it to you on that occasion. Always accept the will and love of God as it is for your higher good and the good of all concerned in those particular circumstances.'

Many people don't want to know about their Angels and don't believe in them. What should we believers do?

'My dear earth children, that is their choice and don't allow it to affect your thoughts and knowing. If they choose not to work with us, we will still stand by them. In time, should they choose to call or look for us, we will be there to help and guide them on their way. Should they choose not to, their abilities will be limited.'

Are Angels male or female?

'Angels are androgynous. We were created before gender and before race were formed. So we carry the energy and the form of both male and female alike. Humans allow us to take on the energy that they feel most comfortable with. So if they need strength and protection they may choose to see or feel us as male energy and if they need gentleness and nurturing they may choose the female energy; it really is a matter of choice.'

Do Angels stand at your right-hand side only?

'O my dear precious children, where do you get such stories? We stand where we need to stand – in front of you, behind you and at either side of you. Wherever you may need us, we are there. Remember we are energy and therefore we can stand all around you at any one time. See us, feel us, hear us: we are everywhere always.'

How do I invite Angels into my life?

'This, my dear ones, is the easiest thing you will ever have to do. Sit in silent meditation and invite us in. We will lose no time in coming. Then simply speak to us, as you would do to your best friend. At first you may not feel our presence or hear our words, but in time you will become familiar with our energy and vibration. You may feel a change in the room temperature, the delicate smell of a scented

flower, the flicker of a light or a sense of knowing that someone is present. The energy will always be light and comforting. Please do not allow fear to block you from making this contact with us. Never be afraid: we won't reveal ourselves until you are truly ready and comfortable with us.'

Which religion is nearest to God?

'All religion is near God and all religion is far away from God also. Every religion believes it is the true follower of God and holds the true messages of God and within many religions there are man-made rules that are not of God but of power and control. Your place of birth and your culture usually determine which religion you are given or choose to take up. God is love and love is the key to growth, acceptance and understanding. Let all religions work on what they have in common and not what keeps them apart, and the love of God is what each and every religion has in common and ego is what keeps them apart.'

Why should we forgive?

'You can choose to forgive in order to grow spiritually and physically. Forgiveness is the greatest gift you can give yourself and your enemies. It holds the power and the energy of freedom and peace. Forgiveness is allowing a new chapter of your life to begin and it gives you permission to move on in love by letting go of pain and hurt.'

Will Angels make me happy?

'Happiness comes from within and only you can make yourself truly happy. Angels can lead you to happiness and bring joy and peace into your life . . . if you ask them to. It is your God-given right to be happy; no one ever truly wants to be unhappy. Open yourself

up to being happy and invite the magical energy of Merlin to bring laughter and fun back into your life. Do something every day that will create this happiness. It doesn't matter how small it is – just do it.'

What about abuse? Why does God let it happen?

'There are many forms and types of abuse: physical, emotional, sexual, political, employment and religious, to name but a few. They are all centred on having control, taking control and ultimately trying to overpower another person, race, country, etc. Abuse is ego driven and again is mainly due to a lack of God. The person or people creating the abuse have closed hearts and have shut themselves out from God's love and light.

'You blame God for allowing abuse but it is not our beloved God that creates or allows this. Remember you are living on a planet of free will so it is man's inhumanity to man and the need for power and control that cause abuse. God weeps to see such things happen. You must take responsibility for your own free will and actions and try to look for new ways to deal with these abusers and protect the weak and innocent.'

What is abundance?

'My dear children, most people think in terms of financial gain when they talk about abundance. However, it means different things to different people and it is far more than money and wealth. Abundance covers the areas of health, wealth, happiness, emotional and spiritual awareness and perfect self-expression. Having enough in your life is your abundance; you will never need any more than enough to live a happy, safe and balanced life. Abundance is not about storing and hoarding vast amounts of anything: that is just GREED and it shows a lack of TRUST in our Heavenly Father. Give thanks daily for all the wonderful things already in your life and this small blessing will

273

create more. Bring your awareness to all that is currently present in your life and you will understand that you are already abundant.'

What happens to people who commit suicide?

'Remember, my children, God doesn't judge our loved ones who have committed suicide. They are as welcome in Heaven as any other human that leaves your planet. We Angels come to their aid and take special care of these beautiful souls and guide them to the Light in loving care and understanding. Please do not fear for them or think they will be punished in any way. They are loved unconditionally and taken to the master house of healing. Here we enfold them lovingly in our wings and bring them complete healing and perfect peace. They rest in love, light and peace.'

Talk to us about the elderly.

'My beloved children, your once golden rule of caring for and respecting your old and infirm has sadly passed. You have cast your elderly aside, making them feel lonely, isolated and useless and a burden to their families and society. But these great people have made their mark on life. They have worked hard under very difficult and often very hard conditions. They have fought cruel and terrible wars to make your world a safe and better place to live in. They have a wealth of love, wisdom and information to share with you, so please don't turn your back on them. Listen and learn from these great masters of knowledge. They have earned your love and respect. Growing old is not a disease, it is part of the human cycle and a process that will come to you all one day. It is a part of the life cycle that you should honour and cherish. Embrace your elderly and care for them by giving them back their rightful place in society and allowing them to grow old with dignity and grace. Age is not a burden, age is honourable.'

Why can't all of us see Angels even though we ask and are very keen to meet our Guardian Angels?

'My dearest children, your fear is what keeps us from presenting ourselves to you, and our knowing that you are not yet ready for this joyous and powerful meeting. We will show ourselves to you when you grow and become more spiritually developed and have formed a personal and trusting relationship with your Angels. Always remember that the human way has always been "Seeing is believing" whereas the spiritual is "Believe and you will see".'

How do Angels send us messages?

'We send you messages in many ways that are comfortable and fitting for you, such as a small white feather, a gentle breeze on your cheek, finding a coin in an unusual place, a gentle voice in your head saying beautiful and encouraging things or what you humans describe as a "gut feeling". These are our most frequent methods of sending messages to you and this is to let you know that we are around you, protecting and loving you. We send messages to you all the time, messages of hope and inspiration.

'Sometimes we speak through other people – like friends, family or even that stranger you talk to at the bus stop who will inspire you and uplift your heart. It can at times be the message in that book that falls from the shelf and, when you read from it, it touches your heart in a special way or answers one of your most important questions. Perhaps at times it is the messages in the song you hear, the poem you have read, a photo or a gift that someone gives you. There are so many ways in which we try to communicate daily; sadly, however, because of your human conditioning you sometimes fail to see the simplicity in our way of speaking to you. Our messages will always be very positive and never make you feel uncomfortable or uneasy.'

How do we bring ourselves to a higher level of awareness?

'*Higher level of awareness is about becoming all that you are and fulfilling your life purpose and your potential by following your true path. It can be achieved through meditation, self-observation and prayer. It's about releasing your past/present from fear, greed, anger, selfishness and power. You need to find that place of stillness and silence in your heart and mind, allowing the reconnecting of your soul to God on a daily basis, and this daily practice will help you move forward into becoming more confident, fearless and compassionate. You will find peace with yourself, the universe and with God. It's about nurturing the body, mind and soul and connecting with your inner self, which is the God within. Follow a path that is right for you and be mindful and tolerant of others, whether you agree or disagree with them. Awareness is simply about achieving fulfilment and contentment in your life, being open to change and willing to face the unknown with truth and trust.*'

Why is there such anger towards women in religion?

'*It is not anger that religion expresses towards women, it is discrimination, fear and a total lack of respect for the feminine energy. Male and female energy are no greater or weaker than one another, they complement each other and are both powerful and equal in the sight of Mother Father God. Man will have to surrender his ego and power in order to listen more clearly to Mother Father God. This in turn will enable him to share all that is God with woman on a loving and more equal basis. Men and women must share peace, respect, co-operation, love and harmony, creating a space where neither male nor female will control or hold power over the other; this is Universal Law. My dear female children, please don't strive to be better than man, for then you make the same mistakes as man and you step into ego. Live to be equal and bring about this energy change in a loving, caring, nurturing and understanding way; that is the essence and power of the feminine Goddess energy.'*

How did Hitler, Pol Pot, Stalin, Idi Amin and others get to have such power that they could murder millions?

'Well, let me assure you this was nothing to do with God. He gave man dominion over the earth, and free will. This gives humans the right to love and respect their brothers and sisters or to abuse and murder them. It's up to you to turn your beautiful earth into a heaven or a hell. One man alone did not carry out these vile acts of murder and torture on so many human souls. It was very unaware and ego-driven individuals with no sense of God, love or self-love in their lives who brainwashed and threatened a lot of other lost, unaware and fearful individuals into carrying out these atrocities. It is easy to point the finger at one person and assign blame because then you don't have to take any responsibility or deal with the situation. So, you tell me: which is the worse? The people who carried out these acts against humanity or those who sat back and did nothing? Again I ask you, please don't ask WHY did it happen but ask what are you to LEARN from these terrible holocausts. Then when you learn the lessons of love and respect you will choose to turn your earth into a heaven instead of a hell.'

How does Robert Mugabe get away with what he is doing in Zimbabwe?

'My beloved children, like so many before him he has brainwashed, controlled and threatened his people for decades and is allowed to get away with it by the people of Zimbabwe. Why? Because his people are fearful, terrorized, beaten, raped and murdered, not only by him but also by their fellow countrymen and women who follow this godless man blindly and without question for their own selfish reasons. The Zimbabwean people are trapped by their own FEAR

and are rendering themselves powerless to do anything about their situation. In the meantime, the rest of the world stands back and allows these vile acts of man's inhumanity to man to continue to happen on a daily basis. They allow this man to attend international meetings, state functions, and hold state talks all the time knowing what terrible acts of cruelty he is enforcing on his own people. So you see, my dear children, nothing has changed. Even now in your world of great technology, when the eyes of the world and your media show you these injustices live on your TV screens, you and your leaders sit back and do nothing. So don't ask the question "Why does he get away with it?" Ask, "Why are YOU letting him get away with it and what are YOU doing to change this situation?" Again I say to you, God leaves it up to you to reform the world. This is not to say that God has stepped away from us; remember he loves you and will help you when you ask for help. Pain and suffering are always caused by the LACK of God in a situation, not BECAUSE of God.'

Why are so many marriages breaking up?

'My beloved children, the Universe is going through a massive energy transformation and many of the emotional issues that humans hold are being brought to the surface. This can cause great difficulty within relationships that were made in the name of LOVE initially, but that were really built on insecurity and neediness within the individual.'

If you marry the wrong person are you bound to stay with them because of the vows you took?

'My dear children, there is no such thing as marrying the wrong person. Nothing in your Universe happens without purpose. You are drawn to the perfect person in every situation to help teach you more about yourself. Relationships help you question more about who you are and to look at new ways to grow through your experiences. If *you did not know HATE how would you know LOVE? If you did not experience DARKNESS how would you know LIGHT? Life is all about learning; that is what your planet is about – the great school of learning – and this is what your soul chooses to experience. Relationships in whatever manner they present themselves are a great opportunity of learning through your emotions, and, remember, nothing is carved in stone. You must believe you have CHOICE in everything you do, so therefore you cannot BLAME "vows" for your unhappiness. You have to take responsibility for yourself and choose what is best for you.'*

Chakras

I hope this will give you a little understanding and insight into chakras and the technique of Hands-on Healing. It is taken from material that Dolores O'Reilly and I prepared for our 'Angels of the Rainbow Healing Light' course.

Chakra is a Sanskrit* word that means wheel or disc. And like all wheels chakras are meant to move, rotate and spin. You have seven main chakras in your body: Root, Sacral, Solar Plexus, Heart, Throat, Third Eye and Crown, and each one has a colour related to it. There are many more minor chakras but we will only deal with the main seven. Like air you cannot see them but you know they are there. Each chakra relates to physical organs of the body but they also relate to the emotional, the mental and the spiritual. When the chakras are awakened, they turn in a clockwise direction. Your chakras can also become dark and dull, which means that they are not working to their full potential.

*An ancient Vedic language of Hinduism and the Vedas and the classical literary language of India.

The Crown Chakra is located at the top of your head. It is generally believed to be your connection between yourself and your God. It is your Divine Energy. It is connected to the upper brain and right eye. It is violet in colour.

The Third Eye is located in the middle of the forehead, between the two eyebrows. This chakra is placed front and back and is connected to what we would call your intuition. It is connected to the lower brain, left eye, nervous system, ears and nose. It is indigo in colour.

The Throat Chakra is located in the throat, again front and back, and is about your freedom to express yourself and your communication skills. This chakra is connected to the bronchial and vocal apparatus, alimentary canal and joints. It is your communication, creative self-expression and speaking the truth. It is blue in colour.

The Heart Chakra is located in the centre of the chest, both front and back, and it relates to our emotions of joy, compassion, empathy, love, and how we love ourselves and love others. It relates to expressing the true love we are. This chakra is related to heart, lungs and circulatory system. It is green in colour.

The Solar Plexus Chakra is located just a hand above the navel; this is the seat of many emotions. We talk about 'gut feeling'. Again, this chakra is both front and back. It generally needs a lot of healing and is known as our 'Seat of Power'. It relates to stomach, liver, gall bladder and the spleen and to thoughts, opinions, confidence, self-worth and personal power. It is yellow in colour.

The Sacral Chakra is located just a hand below the navel, front and back, and deals with our views on sexuality: how we feel about others and ourselves sexually. It's the seat of creativity, which brings confidence, freedom and pleasure into our life. It is connected to the reproductive system, lymphatic system, body fluids and to our emotions, sexuality, pleasure and physical creativity. It is orange in colour.

The Root Chakra is located at the base of your spine and goes all the way down your legs, into your feet and into the ground. This chakra is generally linked with survival. It relates to how you feel about your life, whether you are happy in your relationships, where you live, where you work, etc. It relates to intestines, the spine and kidneys and also to your physical sensation, earth connections and security. It is red in colour.

Suggested Reading

Gibran, Kahlil, *The Prophet*, Pan Books, 1991

Hay, Louise, *Heal Your Body*, Hay House, 1994

Neylon, Margaret, *Angel Magic*, Thorsons, 2001

O'Donohue, John, *Anam Ċara*, Bantam Press, 1997

O'Donohue, John, *Benedictus*, Bantam Press, 2007

Scanlan, Patricia, *Winter Blessings*, Headline, 2005

Scovel Shinn, Florence, *The Game of Life and How to Play It* and *Your Word Is Your Wand*, DeVorss & Co., 1999

Sister Stan, *Gardening the Soul*, Transworld Ireland, 2009

Virtue, Doreen, *Angel Therapy*, Hay House, 2006

Walsch, Neale Donald, *Conversations with God*, Hodder Mobius, 1997

White Eagle, *Walking with Angels*, White Eagle Publishing Trust, 1998

AIDAN STOREY

Aidan offers a range of Angelic & Reiki Workshops as well as organized special events and retreats.

Connecting with your Angels

The Simplicity of the Angels

Angel Card Reading Workshop

The Healing Angels of the Rainbow Light

The Fear of Becoming You

Forgiveness Workshop

Reiki Level 1, 2 and 3

For further information log on to
www.angelicireland.com or
Email: aidanstorey@eircom.net

If You Like Happy Endings . . .

You have just come to the end of the book.

Before you put it aside, please take a moment to reflect on the 37 million people in the developing world who are blind.

90% of this blindness is TOTALLY PREVENTABLE. In our world, blindness is a disability. In the developing world, it's a death sentence.

Every minute, one child goes blind – needlessly. That's about the time it will take you to read this. It's also the amount of time it will take you to go to www.righttosight.com

And help this wonderful organisation achieve its goal of totally eradicating preventable global blindness. Now that *would* be a happy ending. And it will only take a minute.

Aidan Storey supports RIGHT TO SIGHT and would love it if you would too.